Made to Matter

White Fathers, Stolen Generations

Fiona Probyn-Rapsey

SYDNEY UNIVERSITY PRESS

First published in 2013 by Sydney University Press

Reproduction and Communication for other purposes

Sydney University Press
Fisher Library F03
University of Sydney NSW 2006 AUSTRALIA
Email: sup.info@sydney.edu.au

National Library of Australia Cataloguing-in-Publication Data entry

Author: Probyn-Rapsey, Fiona, author.

Title: Made to matter : white fathers. stolen generations / Fiona Probyn-Rapsey.

ISBN: 9781920899974 (pbk.)
9781920899981 (ebook : epub)
9781743323687 (ebook : kindle)

Notes: Includes bibliographical references and index.

Subjects: Stolen generations (Australia).
Race discrimination--Australia--History.
Aboriginal Australians--Mixed descent—History.
Racially mixed people--Australia--History.
Whites--Race identity--Australia--History.
Fathers--Australia.

Dewey Number: 179.3

Cover image by Brian Rapsey
Cover design by Dushan Mrva-Montoya

Contents

Acknowledgments

In writing this book over the last decade or so, I've come to understand that books are not so much finished as stopped. The time comes when you have to hand it in, stop fiddling with it, adding things and taking things out (no one warned me how long all that could take!). For putting up with me in the process of writing (and stopping) this book I have many, many people to thank. All my colleagues (past and present) in the Department of Gender and Cultural Studies at the University of Sydney, particularly the extraordinary Vicki Grieves, Linnell Secomb, Kane Race and Elspeth Probyn and also Sara Ahmed and Sarah Franklin who shared an underground bunker/office near me in the early days of this project, and whose intellectual generosity continues to be an inspiration. I was very lucky to be able to sit and talk with Stephen Kinnane about Shadow Lines, the book and the concept, and also talk with Kim Scott, Henry Reynolds and Pauline Mullett. Big thanks also to Gillian Cowlishaw for reading through some very early drafts of chapters. And to Vicki Grieves (again!), Alison Holland, Anne Brewster and Ann Curthoys for their advice and comments on earlier drafts of the introductory chapter, and Clive Probyn, who read through the whole manuscript. I also owe a big debt of gratitude to the research assistance provided by one time postgraduate students, and now fabulous scholars in their own right; Esther Berry, Ann Deslandes, Adam Gall, Jodi Frawley and Nikki Savvides. I also gratefully acknowledge the support of the Australian Research Council Discovery Scheme (DP0557139) between 2004 and 2011, and the Editors of the following journals where earlier versions of chapters have appeared: *Journal of Australian Studies*,

Australian Literary Studies, JASAL: Journal for the Study of Australian Literature, Antipodes, Postcolonial Studies, Australian Cultural History and *Australian Humanities Review.* Thanks also to the anonymous peer reviewers whose comments on previous incarnations of a few of these chapters have helped to shape the work that is here today. Thanks to Sydney University Press for their incredibly skilful copy-editing and their professionalism. It's been a real pleasure to work with the editors, particularly Agata Mrva-Montoya. Thanks also to friends and family here and far, human and more than human: Peter Donaldson, Meg Probyn, Clive Probyn, Netty Noble and Lucy Nias, and of course, last but never least, Brian, Sunday, Olive, Billy and Alice. Now I'll stop.

Guess who's not coming to dinner

In *Guess who's coming to dinner* (Kramer 1967), wealthy white American parents meet their prospective African-American son-in-law for the first time. The new family *comes to the table*, an act that signals fraternity, equality and, from 1965, the legality of mixed-race marriages across most, but not all, states of America. Australia, by contrast, does not have an equivalent textual or cinematic moment (however fraught and mythic it is) to mark the beginning of a new era for race relations. *Bran nue dae* (Chi 1991; Perkins 2010) comes close with its acknowledgment of already mixed families, with its 1960s reconciliation theme revolving around the acknowledgment of suppressed family connections. But whoever *comes to dinner* in Australian cultural texts is likely to enter the scene from the closet, rather than the front door. This is because Australian racial history is distinct[1] due to the embedded nature of two seemingly opposed colonial policies regarding Aboriginal people: segregation on the one hand and biological assimilation on the other. While segregation separates and denies, biological assimilation seeks a radical embrace and swallowing up of Aboriginality. Segregation might be challenged head-on at the dinner table, but biological assimilation confounds it, seemingly more at home in the closet, as it

---

1   Margaret D Jacobs makes the point that both the US and Australia 'proposed to "assimilate" American Indians and "absorb" Aborigines in the majority population' but that the US reformers and government officials 'believed Indians could be whitened through cultural assimilation; in Australia many authorities focused instead on the biological assimilation of Aboriginal people' (Jacob 2009, 66).

were. This is especially the case for white fathers of Aboriginal children during the early to mid-20th century, the focus of this book.

In 20th-century Australia, white paternity of Aboriginal children was positioned as key to the biological assimilation of Aboriginal people. For different and, I insist, still often unknown reasons, these white men would often not *come to dinner*, figuratively speaking, nor invite their unacknowledged children or lovers, nor tell their friends and relatives, nor allow Aboriginal people access to the dinner table, that 'kinship object' par excellence (Carsten qtd in Ahmed 2006, 80). White fathers who *did* recognise their Aboriginal children are also a part of this story of public secrecy; the bushmen who rejected the dinner table and all its white pretensions. I discuss these white men as critics of white culture, whose acknowledgment of their Aboriginal children and partner was often circumscribed by the threat of removal, of prosecution (for cohabitation), and whose positions lend textual flesh to the tensions played out in the broad scheme of settler colonialism and its desire to 'replace' indigenous people (Wolfe 2006, 389). Australian settler colonialism is, as Wolfe points out, marked by a 'logic of elimination' (1994) that includes conflicting aims: to eliminate but also to *be* the indigene. Wolfe argues that this desire to eliminate but be the indigene foregrounds settler colonialism's 'contradictory reappropriation of a foundationally disavowed Aboriginality' (2006 389). These contradictions are evident in the lives of, and discussions surrounding the white fathers, from autobiography to parliamentary debates, dinner tables to family trees. All are subject to the 'jangling nerves' (Byrne 2003) of Australian settler colonialism 'simultaneously predicated on incorporation and distancing' (Stoler 2002, 83). Such tensions manifest in intimate relations, and within individuals but also across broader cultural sites: the domestic, familial and national.

Those 'jangling nerves' (Byrne 2003) can be felt in Prime Minister John Howard's 'Motion for Reconciliation' (1999) presented to Australia's federal parliament in response to *Bringing them home* (1997), a report written by the Human Rights and Equal Opportunity Commission (HREOC) about the devastations wreaked upon Aboriginal people by the removal of children from their families under the policies of biological (and cultural) assimilation. John Howard rejected the call to apologise to the Stolen Generations on the basis that 'present generations cannot be held accountable ... for the errors and misdeeds of earlier generations' because 'for the overwhelming majority of the current generations of Australians, there was no personal involvement of them or their parents'. Many have commented on the absurd nature of his short view of history and accountability (Manne 2001; Schaffer 2001; Rose 2004; see also Thompson 2002). Mick Dodson's 'Corroboree speech' (2000) asks:

> Where or who is this generation of Australians Mr Howard blames for the removals and the assimilation policies. Are my sisters part of this generation? Are not John [Howard] and John [Herron] part of this generation? Indeed, am I not part of this generation? … Who was it that tried to take me from my kin in 1960? What generation do we look to if Mr Howard says it wasn't this generation? Where is this mythical group of Australians who made these laws, adopted these policies put them into practice. Who took the kids?

Moreover, how is it that the white father's 'personal involvement' is not known to current generations? They were one half of the biological assimilation policy that underwrote child removal and are frequently (if briefly) mentioned in *Bringing them home* and numerous Aboriginal life histories:

> Especially during the nineteenth and early twentieth centuries, relationships between European men and Aboriginal women were often abusive and exploitative. Many children were the products of rape. The European biological fathers denied their responsibility and the authorities regarded the children with embarrassment and shame. (HREOC 1997, 272)

The meaning of skin (colour) the white fathers left behind is frequently the reason given for removal. How do the white fathers fit in with Howard's unapologetic dissociation? Does their 'personal involvement' in the misdeeds of the past make them disappear in Howard's unaccountably good community? Or do they in fact appear as its unmentionable, dissociated bad blood? How might Howard's 'misdeeds of earlier generations' account for Mick Dodson's own white father who was 'jailed for 18 months for breaching the Native Administration Act

1905–1941 of Western Australia in that he was "co-habiting" with my mother' (2000)?

In fact, rather than disappearing, white fathers of Aboriginal children were made to matter in very specific and significant ways. They were made to matter by white authorities who saw white paternity of Aboriginal children (called 'half-castes' at the time) as an opportunity to 'breed out the colour', to eliminate the threat of being outnumbered by 'half-castes'. They were made to matter because they were envisaged as providing white Australia with a future 'aboriginal inheritance' (Cook 1935, 3) that would solve some aspects of white biological (and cultural) inferiority related to living, thriving and belonging to this country. The white men themselves were made to disappear within this biopolitical vision; made *into* matter by being disappeared into *white matter*, a 'thing' to be administered, manipulated, bred in and worried over.

Making whiteness matter

The whiteness of the fathers, whether in skin colour or in character (assessed in rudimentary terms of their proximity to middle-class norms) was seen as one of those ordinary subjects of broader public health concerns about racial hygiene that Warwick Anderson discusses in *The cultivation of whiteness: science, health and racial destiny in Australia* (2002).

In his book, Anderson accounts for the racial theories that were mobilised and transacted by 'colonial scientists and ordinary doctors' (2002, 3) and the period of time in which Anderson bases his study makes his observations (roughly from 1880s to mid-20th century) especially pertinent to my (more literary/cultural studies) reading of the white fathers. Anderson's historical analysis makes clear that it was not simply other races that were of concern or interest in relation to the cultivation of certain forms of whiteness; it was also the racial hygiene of the white population itself that was of interest, or, as Anderson puts it, 'the bad seeds, the diseased and degenerate elements, that were sprouting up inside white Australia' (2002, 165). This included the 'urban white child' between the wars, but also the white father of Aboriginal children. He was the subject of continuous policy debate between Protectors and public health officials during the same period, focusing on whether or not his relationships with Aboriginal women and the children he fathered (if only biologically) made him a white race traitor (a 'charred character' as Ann McGrath describes him, 1987, 70) or a key player in white expansion and adaptability to the continent of Australia.

Anderson points out that the transformation of 'Britons from sojourners to settlers' (2002, 13) has involved transformations in the meaning of being white, measured and analysed according to its adaptability within harsh Australian conditions. Securing possession of the north of Australia was dependent on testing whether whites could labour in, reproduce in and dominate the tropics, or whether something more than Anglo-Saxon-Celtic whiteness would be better suited. As such, whiteness, though a term that defied definition within a 'racial Ur-script' (2002, 2) was 'filled with flexible physical, cultural, and political significance' (2002, 3).

The Adelaide scientists (led by JB Cleland) who took up the policy of 'breeding out the colour' with enthusiasm had a particular view of whiteness which gave it the power to cannibalise others and to replenish itself, rather like a magic pudding. They 'maintained a commitment to a broader, less differentiated concept of whiteness, sometimes even calling it Caucasian and suggesting it might ingest and consume, without damage, anything on its margins' (Anderson 2002, 228). They subscribed to a view that Aboriginal people were 'dark Caucasians' and thus close enough to whites to enhance and extend the adaptability of whites in the colonisation of Australia. In the development of these scientific theories on race, the Adelaide group was able to provide the state with the scientific justification for a 'reproductive intervention' on a scale unseen before, and without comparison:

In effect, they were able to urge the state to intervene, on scientific grounds, to replace, or at least supplement, errant white males on the reproductive frontier. They were free to advocate, and to justify, a breeding program for half-castes – though not strictly 'eugenic' in the sense of being directed toward the improvement of a race, it was nonetheless a scale of reproductive intervention that would not usually be countenanced in even poor white Australian communities. (Anderson 2002, 228)

The policy of breeding out the colour was a cruel farce. It conflated skin colour with culture and assumed that Aboriginal women and their children would acquiesce to produce future whites. It also assumed that white men would comply as ready appendages, administering whiteness through marriage or, if not marriage, then simply biology. And so white sperm was ascribed enormous power: to elevate, uplift and *disperse* Aboriginality in whiteness, to blank out, to aid cultural forgetting. In the biopolitical imaginations of the so-called Protectors, the white 'cock was a displaced gun' (Rose 2004, 109–10), and the 'white phallus' was a 'powerful demolisher of tribes' (Kenneally 1972).

But the biopolitical and instrumentalist view articulated by the policy could not keep up with the sheer complexity of white men's lives, as they interacted (violently, illicitly, sympathetically, lovingly) with the Aboriginal women and children that they were imagined to 'breed out'. What AO Neville and Cecil Cook (Chief Protectors of Aborigines for Western Australia and the Northern Territory respectively, and the most vocal proponents of biological assimilation) forgot to mention in their submissions to the Canberra Conference (where the policy was endorsed by a majority of Protectors) was the trouble that they were having with white men; in getting them to marry Aboriginal women, to pay maintenance for their children, in their mistreatment and abuse of Aboriginal women and children, and in their contempt for and avoidance of white authorities. As the biopolitical other half of the policy to 'breed out the colour', they were highly unreliable and irregular servants of the grand plan to absorb Aboriginality into whiteness.

'Low types'

Biological assimilation was frequently presented as the best option for 'half-castes' because they were otherwise 'poor creatures', their white fathers 'wasters' (as Daisy Bates wrote in *The Observer*), and also 'low types' (Bates again, this time in the *West Australian*, 5 May 1927). Even WEH Stanner worried that 'half-caste's' fathers 'tend to be inferiors, and the *combo* (a white man who habitually keeps a native mistress) is thought to have degenerated' (2009 [1938], 140).

None of these beliefs went by uncontested at the time, from either Aboriginal people themselves, such as the delegation of 'full blooded

[A]borigines and half-castes [who] waited on the WA Premier [Mr Collier] to ventilate grievances in regard to the treatment of blacks' (18 May 1928, 7), or from the occasional white man. Daisy Bates' description of half-castes as 'poor creatures', shunned by their Aboriginal relatives and neglected by their white fathers (the 'wasters'), was met by a series of letters to the editor of the *Northern Territory Times* in the following year (1928).[2] They objected to her 'sweeping indictment' of white fathers and the qualities of their 'half-caste' sons and daughters. One letter, written by 'Trepanger', asks if Bates is aware of the 'share of the half caste in opening and developing the country, and the positions that some of them have held? … they are smart men all.' He boasts of excellent property managers triumphing where 'many whites would have failed', willing participants in the war 'for their country', and 'practically invincible' footballers, adding that their white fathers are

> men of various occupations including station owners and managers; men who have held important positions, and some of them long and honourable careers in the civil service. In some cases the offspring has been denied by the father, but in most cases they have been acknowledged and are a credit to their sire. (4 May, 8)

'Old Trepanger' agrees, adding that Bates 'only took notice of the bad ones both of the half castes and their fathers' (Old Trepanger, 11 May, 4). 'Old Timer' writes in a few days later to qualify the image they construct:

> To the white man who fathers and supports his half-caste children I 'tips me lid' in the language of the Sentimental Bloke. For the white man who deliberately discards and disowns the fruits of his promiscuous sowing, I have nothing but the most utter contempt. (15 May 1928)

Any kind of white father of 'half-caste' children was of great interest to white authorities because monitoring the white men was envisaged as a means of controlling the 'half-caste' population. In his treatise

---

2 I am grateful to Shino Kinoshi for pointing me in the direction of this exchange of letters.

Australia's coloured minority (1947), AO Neville complained that there was a problem when 'we began to breed white natives, because the grandchildren of the full-blood women were often nearly white and, in most cases, separated from their relations, could be taken as European' (1947, 75). Here 'taken as European' meant passing as white. But to be taken as European the children had to be taken *by* Europeans and separated from their Aboriginal relatives, or else they would be white natives. In Neville's view, white natives were effectively still Aboriginal people because their white fathers/grandfathers were 'doing nothing to ensure their children's future except as natives' (1947, 53). To be white, in Neville's view, one had to be not just white/fair in skin but white in attitude, training and community. The white natives that AO Neville worried about were an example of wayward whiteness, whiteness gone astray, lost to its connection with civilisation and dominant white social norms. On the other hand, native whites were whites (with Aboriginal 'blood') who identified with white culture and who would refuse their Aboriginal relatives, be required to ignore them if given an 'exemption' from Aboriginality, or, like the children taken from their mothers at the age of two in his statement to the Canberra Conference, they might not ever be told of their existence.

The waywardness of white men was not something that particularly bothered Neville if he was able to keep the children, as is clear from his chilling description of the situation of Aboriginal women and girls under his 'protection'. Neville told the Canberra Conference:

> Every administration has trouble with half-caste girls. I know of 200 or 300 girls, however, in Western Australia, who have gone into domestic service and the majority are doing very well. Our policy is to send them out into the white community, and if a girl comes back pregnant our rule is to keep her for two years. The child is then taken away from the mother and sometimes never sees her again. Thus these children grow up as whites. Knowing nothing of their own environment. At the expiration of the period of two years the mother goes back into service so *it really does not matter if she has half a dozen children.* (1937, 12, emphasis added)

Sixty years later, *Bringing them home*, with its accounts of over 534 members of the Stolen Generations, brings Neville's instrumentalist view into stark relief. He says it didn't matter if she had 'half a dozen children'. What mattered was that the children would 'grow up as whites'. The matter that he is speaking about here is both whiteness as matter, the breeding of white citizenry via Aboriginal women in service, and matter in the sense of what has value and also, to use Judith Butler's phrase, what is framed as a 'grievable life' (2004, 2010). Butler explains that in particular contexts (such as war), national sovereignty places the value of some lives over others:

> Some lives are grievable and others are not: the differential allocation of grievability that decides what kind of subject is and must be grieved, and which kind of subject must not, operates to produce and maintain certain exclusionary of who is normatively human. (2004, xiv–xv)

Neville's insistence that it 'really does not matter if she has half a dozen children' is a clear indication of his determination to situate an Aboriginal woman outside of the 'normatively human' and her children's connection to their mother as secondary to (white) national sovereignty. Neville also implied that the children's removal from their mother really did not matter to the white fathers either; thus articulating the relationship between the policy of biological assimilation and the cultivation of white paternal indifference, the focus of a later chapter of this book, 'Jim Crows'.

Neville's description highlights the significance of placing Aboriginal women in domestic work in white homes, reconfigured 'as a kind of apprenticeship to Australian citizenship', as Francesca Bartlett has put it (1999, 15). While Aboriginal women were in service and under the so-called protection of government-run institutions, many suffered sexual abuse, alongside the trauma of loss of family and cultural dislocation. These are the white lines through Indigenous kinship circles that Anna Haebich's work *Broken circles* accounts for (2000). In 'I hate working for white people', Jennifer Sabbioni describes the experience of Aboriginal women (including in her own family) in domestic service as exploitation 'emotionally, physically, sexually' (1993, 8). *Bringing them home* quotes Archbishop Donaldson, visiting Barambah (later Cherbourg) in Queensland, in 1915, as saying that of those Aboriginal girls sent to work as domestics 'over 90% come back pregnant to a white man' (HREOC 1997, 75).

Victoria Haskins argues that the NSW Aborigines Protection Board was aware that the girls it sent into domestic service in white homes would be sexually exploited and that it 'colluded in, condoned and indeed encouraged the systematic sexual abuse and impregnation of young Aboriginal women in domestic apprenticeships' with the ultimate aim of 'eradicating the Aboriginal population' (2003, 53). Vicki Grieves' analysis of her family history in colonial NSW also notes that authorities were well aware of the conditions under which mixed-race children were born, but that there was little intervention. She argues that, 'the lack of concern about the blatant abuse of Aboriginal women in the district indicates that they [the authorities] were anxious to preserve gender relationships that approximated slavery, in line with Aboriginal workers at the time' (Grieves 2011, 128).

How did the white fathers relate to the authorities? How did they negotiate, perform and situate their own whiteness in respect to the interest in them? The white men rarely speak for themselves and so a degree of secrecy surrounds them, though not their position within the policies of biological assimilation – that was not a secret. They are spoken about and written about by Aboriginal relatives, biographers, scholars and writers, by government officials, public health officials, parliamentarians, Protectors, white women activists; all of whom could benefit from their own book on the subject. In the cases of WE 'Bill' Harney, Daryl Tonkin and Bill Liddle, the meanings attached to the white men's border crossing depend on who is doing the telling, listening and writing; who is witnessing, as Kelly Oliver puts it, the subjectivity embedded in dialogue. Howden Drake-Brockman, who does not speak for himself, appears very differently in the narratives of his Aboriginal son and white daughter, Arthur Corunna and Judith Drake-Brockman, for instance. Daryl Tonkin's narrative, co-written with Carolyn Landon, is redirected by his Aboriginal daughters, Linda and Pauline Mullett, in vital ways. Bill Yidumduma Harney's narrative of his white father, Bill Harney, similarly contextualises the silences in his father's life stories, as well as highlighting, crucially, I believe, the benefits accorded to him by *not* being publicly recognised as Bill Harney's son and not being removed from his Aboriginal family.

Aboriginal kids without their white biological fathers appeared as rescuable orphans, 'nowhere people' (Reynolds 2005). But as Victoria Haskins points out, the Aborigines Protection Board were not 'rescuing fatherless daughters; it was creating them' (2003, 121). Part of Haskins' point here is to show that the taking away of children who were 'light skinned with a white father' was underscored by a conception of father-hood that was different to that found in Aboriginal kinship structures. The father of an Aboriginal child was the mother's husband. Very few children would have been fatherless (see also Kinoshi 2011). It was, is, a particular set of family values, including the emphasis on biolo-gical paternity prevalent in the West, that provided a key component in child removal. White paternity came to matter too much, providing an alibi for the 'state as father' (McGrath 1994) to intervene. Still today the white father's absence is too quickly interpreted as lack: 'we must ask why our culture allowed so many white men to feel they could leave their Aboriginal children like this' (Bolt 2001). The deficiency of white parenting, the deficiency of fatherly connection and responsibility, was also keenly noted last century. It reveals a consistent cultural view of biological fatherhood; that it ought to guarantee a degree of interest, protection: that biological fathering should count, should matter, and that in its absence something had to be done. In writing about the white fathers of Aboriginal children, I do not want to imply that putting him back in the context of his paternal responsibilities would make things better. Rather, I am interested in how the white fathers in the follow-ing chapters complicate the attempt to make the white father matter, to make his absence matter as deficiency and thereby provide the grounds for *good white father government* to step in for and over Indigenous kin-ship, belonging and identity.

Chapter outlines

The first chapter, 'Husbands', examines a series of letters dated to 1901–1914 between white men and the Protectors of Aborigines in Queensland. It shows that the interest in white men as securing the white futures of Aboriginal people started well before the 1937 policy of breeding out the colour. This exchange of letters (some seeking per-mission to marry Aboriginal women) shows that marriage and maintenance played a crucial role in the regulation of race, nation, ethnicity and sexuality. By entering into marriage, the white men were fostering a new partnership with the state, declaring a loyalty to its interests by tacitly agreeing to control the number and identities of mixed-race children and, it was believed, putting a stop to the violation of Aboriginal women. If this married state could convert white men from violators to 'protectors' of Aboriginal women, then it could also help to turn the white men themselves from the ungovernable to those in whom governability was entrusted (see also Kidd 1997; McGrath 1994; Lake 1998a, 2003). What is of particular interest in the letters that are discussed in this chapter is how the white men themselves articulated their allegiances to whiteness, and how they, in some cases, sought to represent themselves as the obedient servants of the state, partly, it seems, in order to gain some autonomy outside of the surveillance that they were under.

The second chapter, 'Breeders', examines the 'whitefella skin politics' of two white men in the Northern Territory who, in their proximity, articulate the tensions of the assimilationist project in Australia. I examine the stormy relationship between Dr Cecil Cook, Chief Medical Officer in the Northern Territory, who is credited with the invention of the phrase 'breed out the colour', and his one-time friend then foe, author Xavier Herbert, who promoted the idea that the best way he, as a white man, could imagine belonging in Australia, was if he was to father a 'half-caste' himself. He promoted a hybridisation of white Australia and started a rumour (that still circulates today) that Cook was an albino – the whitest white. Their disagreements, their different sense of what kind of whiteness would be best for Australian settlement, reveal the ways that white paternity and paternalism come together as a political vision for Australia's future. Their differences, however, show the very flexibility of whiteness that situates white fathers as at the centre of the plans to biologically assimilate Aboriginal people.

Chapter three, 'The combo', examines Bill Harney's writing, focusing on the silence-shaped gaps in his memoirs and his criticisms of the white men of the north. Harney's works are a rich and vibrant (though also shadowy and obscuring) testament to what could and could not be said about the white men of the frontier, especially if you happened to be one. Harney was one of those white fathers who sometimes did 'nothing to ensure their children's future except as natives' (Neville

1947, 53). Harney, himself a patrol officer at one stage, was critical of the policy of removal: '[f]ar better a hundred times that these children should be left with their mothers to grow up around the stations' (Harney 1946, 154). Harney's absence from his son's life could be read as tacit recognition that he already belonged, that he was not parentless, that his mother's culture was his rightful inheritance, something also explored by Katharine Susannah Prichard in her novel *Coonardoo* (1929) where Hugh Watt wonders if he 'could ... do for Winni what Warieda was doing, teaching him to handle horses, fit him for an independent life in his natural surroundings?' (138).

Chapter four, 'Black sheep', examines the stories of Matt Savage, Daryl Tonkin, Bill Liddle and Roger Jose. These men married or were in de facto relationships with Aboriginal women and were positioned (or position themselves), to different degrees, as white Australia's black sheep – strident critics of the pretenses of white Australia. Bill Harney writes of the 'transformation' that white men in relationships with Aboriginal women underwent, and this chapter seeks to highlight how these men did not uplift or make themselves useful to state paternalist interests at the time, but instead moved into (to various extents) Aboriginal kinship networks themselves. Moreover, Daryl Tonkin's narrative is significantly redirected by his Aboriginal daughters (Linda and Pauline Mullett).

While the previous chapter examines narratives of white bushmen who were open (but still guarded like Tonkin, or secluded like Jose) about their relationships with Aboriginal women, the final chapter, 'Jim Crows', focuses on white men who were not open about their relationships and who hid and denied, kept their tables and tea rooms for whites only. These were the men whose 'raw nerves' might have jangled, as they lived with the 'coexistence of aversion and attraction, desire and repulsion' as Denis Byrne indicates in his reading of racially segregating NSW towns (2003, 169). This chapter asks how the white men who enforced segregation by day and pursued Aboriginal women by night managed these jangling nerves, if indeed they did jangle. How did they manage to be seen and known and have their secrets kept for them, as much as by them? How did this contradiction of segregation and sexual intimacy, if indeed it is a contradiction, actually work? One thing is clear and that is the sheer effort that went into maintaining control over the public secret that Harney and others wished to 'out'. In his desire to expose what he called the 'Jim Crows' (1934, 94), Harney would find himself up against the cultivation of paternal indifference, brought to the fore, indeed already outed, by the policy of 'breeding out the colour'; a policy on paternity that instrumentalised white sperm while making social fathers largely incidental. The role of indifference, and in particular the cultivation of paternal indifference, is an important part of the story of Harney's Jim Crows. In this chapter I take up Harney's use of the term Jim Crow (once used as a perjorative against African Americans) because, for Harney, it was those white men who publicly espoused segregationist views but privately sought to possess Aboriginal women who were capable of the greatest cruelties.

The conclusion, 'Embracive reconciliation', returns to some of the major preoccupations of the book; how the cultivation of whiteness in Australia relied on harnessing white fathers, and what these white fathers (as individuals) did in response to and in avoidance (and often ignorance) of broader public policy interest in them. I examine what I call 'embracive reconciliation' (a 'we're all family!' response to Howard's severed family tree), to see how it dips into, genealogically, past arguments about white fathers, and how contemporary liberal articulations of reconciliation are still invested in an anxious race–reproduction nexus (Weinbaum 2004) that privileges white belonging in and through Aboriginality.

Husbands

Not being a man of the Laws of Q'Land
I got myself into a little trouble[1]

In August 1903, a white Australian stockman, Paul K (a pseudonym), wrote a letter from Dubbo Downs Station to the Northern Protector of Queensland, Archibald Meston, in which he claimed paternity over a 'half-caste' girl. Paul K wrote:

> I found out about two months that she is supposed to be my child so would like to her & send her to school if there is nothing in the ab-originals acts to prevents me from doing so [sic]. Please reply to this & let me know if I can take the girl & give my word to you I look after her as father and send her to school. I am waiting your reply, Yours ... Dubbo Downs Station, Queensland.[2]

It was unusual at this time for white fathers to actively claim their 'half-caste' children. Northern Protector of Aborigines Walter Roth (1898–1904, and then Chief Protector from 1904–1906) notes in his Annual Report for 1904 that fathers who registered the birth of their children, contributed financially and tried to 'give their half caste children even such a measure of their rights under the law' were excep-

---

1   Letter to Dr Walter E Roth, Northern Protector, Queensland State Archives, Colonial Secretary's Office, Miscellaneous Subject Batches, 1904, A/58764, (here-after referred to as QSA, A/58764).
2   Letter to Harold Meston, 22 August 1903, QSA, A/58764.

tional. Instead, the pursuit of white fathers for maintenance seems to have been the norm.

In his willingness to recognise his child, Paul K[3] appears to be the model white father that 'the aboriginals act' was aiming to support and foster. He also demonstrates a willingness to make use of the powers and duties ascribed to him under the Act, to 'look after her as father and send her to school', as well as, ominously, to 'take the girl' (from who?). The 'aboriginals act' to which Paul K refers is most probably the State of Queensland's *The Aboriginals Protection and Restriction of the Sale of Opium Act 1897*. The 1901 Amendments to that Act made naming and holding white fathers of 'half-caste' children accountable a central platform of its reforms. As such, it precipitated a flurry of letters between white men and Protectors on the subject of marriage, maintenance, paternity and prosecution. While the legislation was meant to 'bring to book' white men who had abused Aboriginal women and girls, reneged on their paternal responsibilities and shifted them onto the state, it also opened up a dialogue between white men about the culture of white paternity in the Australian colonial context.

An emphasis on the social importance of establishing paternity and maintenance was not exclusive to the colonial management of relationships between whites and Aboriginal people at this time. Susan Tiffin notes in her reading of paternity and maintenance issues in the period 1890–1920 that because of 'the emergence of the population debate and the publication of statistics on the incidence of illegitimacy, the high rate of mortality among children born out of wedlock and the proportion of such children surrendered to relief agencies, parental, particularly paternal support was raised as an area for increased state intervention' (1982, 132). Tiffin argues that 'desertion and non-support were seen by reformers of the period as serious threats to the social order' whereby 'today's destitute child was tomorrow's delinquent' (131). She notes that the legislation showed 'a desire to deter or punish reluctant parents' (133) and yet putative fathers were 'protected' from paternity claims by the following stipulation (also contained in the *Aborigines Protection Act 1909*) that 'no man shall be taken to be the father of any such child upon the oath of the mother only'.

---

3   This chapter uses pseudonyms for all non-officials.

The interest in the rising generation and the future of the race was not exclusively targeted at the management of Aboriginal people. It was advanced universally. But it was coded specifically along the lines of white 'uplift'. The effects of an interest in paternity and maintenance were therefore very different where Aboriginal and white relationships were concerned. The problem was that those white men who abused and exploited Aboriginal women and children were imperilling the legitimacy of the white nation in two interconnected ways. First, they were 'fathering' increasing numbers of illegitimate 'half-caste' children that were racially ambiguous and threatening to white hegemony. Second, the white men's cruel exploitation of Aboriginal women and children threatened the assumption that whiteness was itself an elevated and uplifting condition of being to which all should universally aspire, or be compelled to aspire. By examining letters from reluctant and, in the case of Paul K, enthusiastic white fathers, it is possible to discern some of those differences as primarily relating to the nature of white colonial paternalism rather than state paternalism (such as that described by Tiffin). Thus, in the first letter quoted above, Paul K was writing to the Protector of Aborigines because the Protector was the girl's legal guardian (acting *in loco parentis*), with greater control over her life and a specific interest in his. Were his claims legitimate? Was Paul K a good man in whom the state could entrust its charges? The Protector was to decide. The girl's Aboriginal kin were not mentioned.

Debating the Act: Queensland Parliament 1901

When Home Secretary Justin Fox Greenlaw Foxton introduced amendments to the Act into the Queensland Legislative Assembly in late 1901, he did so in a way that echoed national concerns with paternal responsibility (as Tiffin outlines), while minimising the differences between the ways in which Aboriginal children and white children became wards of the state and what they were being protected from. Foxton emphasised the need to support and regulate marriages between Aboriginal women and white men because forming legitimate families with legitimate children would be less of a burden on the state: 'it would make one more legitimate child in the colony and one less illegitimate, and the onus of maintaining that child or any other children that might be born to them would rest on the men' (613).[4] He quoted the situation of one woman with four children whose father did not support them:

> I believe it was the practice of the father of these children, who is, I understand, a well-known man in a certain district of this State, to send money for their support at one time, but he does not do so now, I am informed ... Those children are, therefore, to a large extent thrown on the resources of the State and of the people who assist in the maintenance of the institution. That is a condition of things which ought not to be allowed to exist, and it is with a view to bringing to book gentlemen of that kind that this provision is introduced (209).

Foxton presented the legislation as dealing with 'gentlemen of that kind' as well as non-white employers of Aboriginal labour, who very often bore the brunt of accusations of mistreating Aboriginal people. But the chief architect of the amendments to the Act, Northern Protector Walter E Roth, was concerned, as we will see, not just with maintenance issues, nor necessarily with promoting marriage between white men and Aboriginal women. What concerned him most was child sexual abuse, abuse of Aboriginal women and the 'trucking' or trafficking of Aboriginal children for unpaid, slave labour.

The legislation covering marriages between Aboriginal and non-Aboriginal women was a tacit recognition that such unions were an ongoing feature of colonisation. Paul K's case, for example, reflects a shift in policy to regulate and not separate (Kidd 1997, 48) non-Aboriginal and Aboriginal relations. Such recognition was not an explicit and uncontested sanction. In the Queensland Legislative Assembly (Lower House) David Bowman MP (Member for Warrego) stated that white men and Aboriginal women marrying would 'foster a piebald race' and that he did not 'believe in mixing the race at all' (1901, 613). Foxton replies that the permissions system was 'putting a restraint in that way, because those people could not marry without the permission of the

---

4   The following references to MPs Foxton, Browne, Hamilton, Bowman, Givens refer to the debate in Queensland Legislative Assembly, 1901, Aboriginal Protection and Restriction of Sale of Opium Bill, 1897. Parliamentary Debates, Queensland State Archives.

protector', placing inordinate faith in marriage as an institution that could contain sexuality.

Southern Protector Archibald Meston, whose reports on Aboriginal people had previously been instrumental in the soon to be amended Act (Taylor 2003, 121), told the Legislative Council that he 'was not consulted with regard to the present Bill' (1143). He added, 'I have a strong aversion to the intermixture of the black and the white races; and without express instruction from the Home Secretary, I would never sanction such a marriage of this kind' (1143). Northern Protector Walter E Roth, the instigator of the amendments to the legislation, reported that: 'In some cases I have considered them desirable, but in most cases not, and they should not, in my opinion, except under proper supervision, be allowed' (Roth 1901). For Roth, the recognition of white paternity and marriage to respectable white men could lend itself to the protection of Aboriginal women and children from ongoing abuse. For others, they risked being traitors and degenerates who would foster a 'piebald race'. By 1937, such racial purity arguments dominated, and thus it is not surprising that at the Canberra Conference, decades later, Queensland's Protector Bleakley refused to endorse the 'breeding out the colour' policy agreed to by the majority of Chief Protectors.

White men were named by Protectors as more likely than men of other races or ethnic groups to abuse Aboriginal women and children and this is probably why they were also less likely to 'own' their children. In 1903, Roth reported to parliament that 'it is my experience that they [Aboriginal women and girls] are invariably got into trouble by some unprincipled white man, who only laughs at the poor unfortunate whom he had seduced. It is almost impossible to prove paternity'.[5] Two years later, Chief Protector Richard B Howard noted that 'Each year we have cases reported of young half-caste girls being seduced by Europeans but no corroborative evidence forthcoming to warrant taking further action' (Howard 1905, 13).

The low rate of marriage between Europeans and Aboriginal women between 1901 and 1914 (but a high birth rate of 'half-castes') suggests unwillingness to form recognised unions. From the Annual Reports from Chief Protectors (1901–1913) the following statistics are

---

5   Walter E Roth, 'Annual Report of the Northern Protector of Aboriginal for 1903', 1904, 13.

noted. They include the number of marriages to whites or Europeans within the total of 'mixed race' marriages (all of which required permits) for each year: 1901 – four of 40, 1902 – two of 14, 1903 – four of 26, 1904 – six of 17, 1905 – four of 24, 1906 – eight of 25, 1907 – five of 15, 1908 – five of 41, 1909 – nine of 27, 1910 – 11 of 25, 1911 – four of 21, 1912 – three of 24, 1913 – ten of 29. The number of marriages between Aboriginal women and European men fluctuated but was never in a majority. Marriages to South Sea Islanders and Pacific Islanders were in far greater number, with Chief Protector Howard noting in 1910 that Pacific Islanders 'make really good husbands and treat their Aboriginal wives well' (Howard 1910, 17). Pity then that Pacific Islanders were targeted for deportation from 1906 onwards, unless they were exempt from the Act that was designed to protect white labour in the Queensland sugar industry.

The changes sought in the 1901 amendments involved trying to find ways to establish paternity in order to force white men to maintain their children. Members of the Queensland Parliament (themselves white men) believed that it would be unlikely for white men to admit paternity of their children because to do so would also involve admitting that they had had sex with an Aboriginal woman or girl outside of marriage. William Browne (Croydon) objected to clause 16, subsection 3 which he believed 'goes a little bit too far' in that it 'proposes to do what almost any man would protest against', making him 'compellable to answer whether he had or had not sexual intercourse with the mother of the child, and if so at what time or times' (Browne 1901, 211). Browne goes on to say that 'There is no man in the community worth calling a man who would answer such a question' (211). William Hamilton also objected to the clause, telling the House: 'I do not think it is necessary or proper ... he would be a pretty clever man who could find out the father of the half-caste.' The following views were then expressed:

The Home Secretary: That subsection 3 is one way of finding it out.
    Mr W Hamilton: How is it possible to make a man go into the box and admit that he is the father of a half-caste child? I do not think that is a nice, or proper, or fair thing to do.
    The Home Secretary: Anything is fair with a man of that sort.

Mr W Hamilton: A half-caste may belong to a syndicate, and it is hard to tell who the father is.

The Home Secretary: Then there is joint and several liability.

Mr W Hamilton: If you make every member of the syndicate contribute, of course, that would be right enough, but you are going to give the inspector a very big contract when you invite him to dis-cover the father of a half-caste child. (215)

Casual sex with Aboriginal women is positioned in this discussion as both endemic and organised (as in a 'syndicate') but also something that is not proper to discuss. Subject to silencing, shame, the phrase it is 'hard to *tell* who the father is' suggests both propriety as well as knowledge. On the one hand, it seems to recognise an organised, ende-mic use of Aboriginal women and links this to a structural (syndicate) nature of the relationship, one which is itself mirrored in the makeup of the parliamentary session itself: a syndicate of white men discussing the impossibility of determining individual paternity. The legislation made it especially hard for Aboriginal women 'to tell', and be heard. The mother's knowledge was discounted in advance, and could not be used to establish paternity. This discourse on paternity that discounts what the mother knows and pleads ignorance through white male syndica-tion highlights what Sedgwick has called 'ignorance effects' – the ways that opacity and ignorance can be 'harnassed, licensed, and regulated' (1990, 5) so as to be as 'potent and multiple a thing there as knowledge' (4). That is, what the white men claim not to know, and the very terms in which that claim not to know is made, can be as revealing of power dynamics as that which is acknowledged. Explicit in their denials (their 'ignorance effects') is a recognition of a systemic abuse of Aboriginal women and girls.

In relation to the passing of the amendments to the Aboriginal Protection and Restriction of Sale of Opium Bill, 1897, Roth was ques-tioned by the Legislative Council on 8 October 1901. Roth wanted changes to the guidelines relating to how to prosecute for sexual abuse of Aboriginal children when their ages could not be proven in the ab-sence of birth certificates. Roth wanted this changed so that the onus was on the accused to prove the age of the child. This was perceived to be 'un-British' and 'un-English'. Thomas Givens MP told the House: 'I think hon. members have been long enough in the colony to know that in this climate young ladies become fit for the married state long before they arrive at the age of 16. It is not an uncommon occurrence' (221). As Anna Haebich observes, the debate over this legislation demonstrates 'a mixture of voyeurism, preconceptions about Aboriginal female sexuality, acceptance of sexual abuse which would not be tolerated for young white girls, as well as anger, revulsion, and a determination to put a stop to the practice' (2000, 307). In his answers to the Legislative Council (reviewing the legislation), Roth remarked that:

> If hon. Gentlemen could suggest any better way of punishing those who commit such bestial offences upon little children I should be very glad. I am not particular about the wording as long as I have some means of taking steps to punish such outrages. (1141)

Roth was also disturbed by the event that men who were, for reasons of bad character, refused permission to employ Aboriginal people, married them instead, thereby creating a labour source in the form of family: 'There are many cases now where we know a white man to be a disgracefully bad character, but, if we try to prevent him employing a gin, he marries her, and thus defies the protector' (1140). It placed marriage, as an institution of civilised settlers, under further scrutiny. Meston had found that there were men who were 'willing at any moment to go through a marriage ceremony merely for the sake of evading The Act. To such men marriage has no other meaning. It implies no reverence or sacred obligations'.[6] One man who wished to renew his 'permit' to employ his housekeeper, whom he was teaching to read and write, was refused permission on the basis that he was not married. Three months later he married the housekeeper instead, the file reading: 'Marriage of ... to Aboriginal female: previously denied permission to employ her' (6). This illustrates the ways in which white men were able to navigate the legislative controls on their access to Aboriginal women by selecting either a license to employ or license to marry. If some men were using it to evade the law, the state and its Protectors were also using it to imagine and enforce civil standards, a sacred obligation of a different sort. Roth wanted to put an end to the evasion of

---

6   Archibald Meston to the Under Secretary, Department of Public Lands, 24 October 1903, QSA, A/58764.

the Act through marriage; marriage was not necessarily uplifting or legitimising anyone, and it was in some cases merely a cover for taking possession of, 'owning', Aboriginal girls and women.

At the same time that the state wished to ultimately shift the responsibility for maintaining Aboriginal life onto white families, the family was used as a means of avoiding state protection of Aboriginal people, particularly children, who from the time of the earliest Australian colonisation have been incorporated into white families, usually as servants and experiments in civilisation, where 'possession of the children indicated ownership of the future' (Haebich 2000, 130). Kidd notes that 'Roth had been horrified at the rush of applications from whites claiming Aboriginal girls had been "brought up as one of the family" and were therefore exempt from official controls. Many girls, he reports, were worked without wages and evicted "when they get into trouble" ' (50). These applications were exploiting a loophole in the legislation that made Aboriginal 'half-caste' girls in 'trustworthy families' exempt (Kidd 1997, 49).

Shirleene Robinson notes that Roth was aware of the 'evils and abuses' that these children were often subject to, but prior to the legislative changes there was no legal means by which he could regulate their employment, even forcing employers to pay them (2008, 11). This included men like the following: 'Dr F— is willing to keep this half caste in his employment but will not enter into an agreement to pay her any wages'.[7] 'Trucking' of children was also a problem. Roth writes in his Annual Report for 1902 that 'it is known that in past years a most obnoxious practice grew up of the police supplying their friends &c., with aboriginal children … This "trucking" in children is still going on' (11). In her study of the employment of Aboriginal children in Queensland between 1842 and 1902, Robinson finds that 'The largest proportion of female child workers …were aged between 10 and 12 years of age, with the youngest employed female child recorded being two years of age. The largest proportion of male child workers were aged between 12 and 14 years of age, with the youngest employed male child recorded as being five years of age'. She points out that 'Given that such a high proportion of indigenous child workers were kidnapped, the fact that

---

7   Rice to Breene, 21 November 1904, QSA, Director of Native Affairs Office, Correspondence Files, 1904, A/58749 and A/58750.

Europeans did not pay these children wages is hardly surprising' (2008, 20). Robinson describes these conditions as slavery (24).

'wishing to believe you a man of honour'

In 1904 Roth wrote a letter to one man who had admitted paternity:

> I understand that you are a single man, and wishing to believe you a man of honour, hope you will see your way to doing the right thing to the woman you have wronged. If … [she] has been living with you as your wife for the past eight years, surely there is nothing to prevent your marrying her, and then legitimating your little girl, over whose interest and welfare you profess such deep interest. How sincere this interest is I shall be able to judge when you communicate with us again as to what you propose doing in this matter.[8]

Roth's desire for the man to legitimate his child and his relationship was couched in terms of the man's honour, duty and sincerity and as such was aimed at fostering an ideal image of the white settler father and husband. If we recall that the legislation was aimed at 'bringing to book gentlemen of that kind', those who refused to pay maintenance, but also, in the words of Archibald Meston, those 'low Western whites who cohort with Aboriginal women' (1903), then we can see that at stake here was an image of an 'honourable' white man in whom the state could entrust its own, and his child's legitimacy. Protectors fostered an ideal white man (see also Lake 1998b, 2003); his uplift being the foundation upon which the uplift of the 'natives' could be realised. But, I suggest, taken together, the program to uplift white men and their families could also legitimise a form of white uprising in the guise of protection; a reaction to the fear of being outnumbered, outbred by 'blacks'. This became more critical in the decades that followed, as the fear of racial outnumbering (by 'half-castes') gained popular expression.

---

8   Letter from Roth, 13 July 1904, QSA, Director of Native Affairs Office, Correspondence Files, 1904, A/58749 and A/58750.

Despite the presumed improbability or impossibility of white fathers owning their children, the Act encouraged, under threat of prosecution, white men to provide for their children. In the case of Paul K, whether or not he had really 'just found out' that the girl was his daughter, or was responding pre-emptively to being held to account for her maintenance, is not clear. Marriage, maintenance or prosecution were the options available to men found to be fathers of 'half-castes' or partners to Aboriginal women, as this note from Roth shows: 'I would advise that the opportunity be afforded S ... of marrying her (for which I am prepared to give the necessary permission): if he refuses I would recommend that he be prosecuted for harbouring etc'.[9]

There are other men, like Paul K, who wrote to the Protectors of their paternity. One man who wrote to request marriage opposed it to desertion: 'She has one child and I do not want to desert either her or the child'.[10] A white man's lawyer wrote to the Inspector of Aborigines in 1903, 'As you are aware she is the mother of a half caste child, my client still asserts he is the father of this child',[11] and pressed his case to be allowed to marry. Another case comes with a letter of recommendation: 'There is no doubt M ... and she are infatuated with each other and it is just as well to let them marry'.[12] Another man wrote, 'Sir, I have the honor to inform you that I am the father of a ½ caste female child named ... '.[13] This father requested that his daughter be granted an exemption from the Aborigines Act, which required that she no longer associated with any of her Aboriginal relatives. There is also an example of a white stepfather requesting the return of his wife's eldest boy, a removal that he opposed: 'I would have objected the boy is neither an aboriginal nor a half caste, he has a mere dash of colour'.[14] Some white men agreed to maintenance, but not to marriage: 'He states

---

9   Roth to Sub-Inspector Martin Breene and the Under Secretary, Department of Public Lands, 11 January 1904, QSA, A/58764.

10   Letter to the Protector of Aborigines, Townsville, 15 May 1902, QSA, A/58764.

11   John FF Lockett to H.R.P. Durham, Esq., Inspector of Aborigines, 26 November 1903, QSA, A/58764.

12   Protector B Lowe to R Cane, Acting Chief Protector, 8 September 1904, QSA, A/58764.

13   Letter to J Bell Esq., Minister for Lands, Brisbane, 23 June 1904, QSA, Director of Native Affairs Office, Correspondence Files, 1904, A/58749 and A/58750.

that he is willing to contribute towards its support, but will not marry the mother.[15] In another case, an ex-police officer wrote: 'I am willing to make an affidavit that I am their father, but do not wish to further disgrace myself and relations by marrying the Gin, but should all fail rather than have my children taken will do so'.[16] He asked the Protector to 'allow me to keep the children without having to further disgrace myself', adding that 'I have the same feeling for them as if they were white'.[17] It seems that the government department did not press for marriage. Inspector Galbraith noted that 'Under the very peculiar circumstances Mr A— is situated in, also the age of the children, I strongly recommend that they be allowed to remain with him' (54). It is not clear whether this treatment is related to the white man being an ex-police officer.

'as if they were white'

The applications to keep children, to marry, to 'maintain' without marriage in the latter case, situate whiteness as a measure of love ('I have the same feeling for them as if they were white' [55]) and as a goal, guaranteed to appeal to aims to make white children. One white man reported that in regards to his daughter he wished to 'rescue her from camp influences'.[18] Another man, applying for a licence to marry his Aboriginal partner, intended to 'treat her like a white woman'.[19] However, in this case, when the Protectors learnt that he intended to keep living in a tent, his application was refused. Archibald Meston wrote that this man

---

14   Letter to the Officer in Charge, Aboriginal Protector's Department, 19 July 1904, QSA, Director of Native Affairs Office, Correspondence Files, 1904, A/58749 and A/58750.
15   Acting Sergeant John Rice to Breene, 15 August 1904, QSA, Director of Native Affairs Office, Correspondence Files, 1904, A/58749 and A/58750.
16   Letter to the Commissioner of Police, Brisbane, 30 October 1903, QSA, A/58749 and A/58750.
17   Letter to the Commissioner of Police, Brisbane, 30 October 1903, QSA, A/58749 and A/58750.
18   Inspector CB Marrett, Esq. to Roth, 15 June 1904, QSA, A/58764.
19   Constable L Bell to Sub-Inspector HRP Durham, 17 August 1903, QSA, A/58764.

was 'one of those low Western types who would go through the process of marriage merely to evade the law'. Written on this application is also the following: 'I am not satisfied that B— is anything more than a "nomad" and cannot consent to the marriage until he has provided a proper home and has some settled and permanent work'.[20] The whiteness of the men, their capacity to settle rather than be nomadic, was at issue here.

The letters also revealed a strategic use of whiteness and paternity itself in order to gain access to Aboriginal women. The men were not ignorant of the politics of whiteness (though perhaps ignorant of the extent of the network that could scrutinise them as well). They were not merely the instruments of the state, nor its 'obedient servants', but they could use the legislation for their own purposes. The privilege that was attached to whiteness becomes all the more clear when we consider how non-white men, who could not make the same statements of loyalty to whiteness, argued for permits to marry.

In 1917, the Chief Protector received a response from a Cairns lawyer acting on behalf of a Chinese man whose application to marry his Aboriginal partner was refused: 'The fact that [he] ... is a Chinese alien does not appear to us a very strong argument against his being permitted to marry'. They refute the allegations of him supplying liquor and point out that

> Here is a man in a business of his own, who is quite capable of supporting a wife and children, refused permission to marry, whereas, an indent[ur]ed Malay has been granted that permission, and as everybody knows the indent[ur]ed men are in a very much worse financial position than our client.[21]

Not able to make the argument for whiteness, his lawyers placed emphasis on his financial security, and his capacity to stay in Australia, as opposed to indentured labourers, who were, from 1906 onwards, under

---

20   Durham to the Commissioner of Police, Brisbane, 24 August 1903, QSA, A/58764.
21   A Murray and Marsland to the Under Secretary, Brisbane, 21 July 1917, QSA, Home Secretary's Office, General Correspondence, 1918, HOM/J259.

threat of deportation (see Regina Ganter 2006 for further discussion of mixed-race marriages).

Good character

Given that police inspections into paternity cases were based on hearsay, rumour and the opinions of good men (married, literate, educated white men in authority), it is not surprising that 'character' is one of the most frequently used words in the letters from men applying to 'own' their children or marry their child's mother. Having a good character was key to the success of applications. Requests to marry were answered with an 'inquiry and report as to [the white man's] ... age, occupation, earnings, character and habits'.[22]

Inquiries were also made into the character of the Aboriginal woman, including who she consorted with, previous relationships, children, employment history, but mostly just in terms of whether or not she was a willing party to the marriage. It is not clear how such information was collected, as few Aboriginal people are quoted or in the reports. Most of the information seems to have come either from the white men being investigated or their employers (if they had one). Letters of support were received from employers and also lawyers acting on behalf of the men: he is 'a hard working young white man ... his character is as good as the average bushman'.[23]

One man who applied to marry was refused on the basis of previous criminal convictions for 'unlawful possession of opium', 'harbouring [a] female half caste' and on the basis that 'His father ... [was] alleged to have been sentenced at Warwick some time previously to three years for incest'.[24] Another man did 'not bear a good character and ... [would] not contribute any money towards his aged father's support'.[25] Having a good father or being good to a father was an indicator of good character.

---

22 Durham to Acting Sergeant Daly, 10 November 1903, QSA, A/58764.
23 Lowe to Cane, 8 September 1904, QSA, A/58764.
24 Letter from Acting Sergeant Cleary, n.d., QSA, A/58764.
25 Constable JW Dawes to Breene, 17 November 1903, QSA, A/58764.

Character was necessarily a fluid thing, subject to rumour, and also class-coded. In the Queensland parliamentary debates in relation to the Act, the Member for Flinders, Peter Airey, complained about the Member for Bulimba's reference to certain men as 'scum': 'He did not precisely know what the Hon. Member meant by "scum", but he could assure him that offences of the kind he had mentioned [sexual abuse of children] were just as prevalent amongst the well-to-do' (1718). Walter Barnes (Member for Bulimba) explained that 'there were men who, judging by their clothes, occupied good positions, who were as much the scum of the State as the shearer, when he was a bad man, or anyone else who was bad' (1718). Class was clearly an important factor, and a 'critical class based logic' (Stoler 1989, 158) formed a plank in the management of white men. While the members struggled to (at times) downplay the prevalence of sexual violence against Aboriginal women and children as well as paternal indifference, they were also at pains to point out that it was occurring across all classes of white men, from the shearer to the best dressed amongst them: those in good positions could also be 'bad'.

The implications of being labelled a 'bad character' are revealed in the following exchange. A report written by a local constable who contradicted one man's statements about his good character argued that the man was in fact

> a drunkard, he is willing to marry the Halfcaste gin ... The 1/c Const has been informed on good authority that 'W—' has been in the habit of visiting her camp previous to Andy's death and that on several occasions he has supplied her with drink. In the attached letter he gives his address as Yandarlo Station which is not correct. He is living in a tent on the Nive River.[26]

Archibald Meston's rather bizarre response was to suggest that the woman be married to someone else entirely: 'Advise that this woman be sent to Tambo to marry the tracker provided she is willing'.[27] Roth intervened, advising that permission to marry be granted to the applic-

---

26 Constable James Hayes to the Inspector of Police, Longreach, 22 November 1903, QSA, A/58764.
27 Archibald Meston, 4 December 1903, QSA, A/58764.

ant, adding: 'It seems to me a pity, judging from the attached papers, that after "W—" had applied for permission to marry the gin on 31 October last, he was prosecuted for harbouring, when he again, according to his statement, offered to marry her'.[28]

Dubbo Downs, 1903

In 1903, the character of Paul K, who wished to take his daughter away to be educated, was about to be investigated. But before this happened, another letter was received from Dubbo Downs Station. On 24 October 1903, Harold Meston (Protector, Officer in Charge of Police at Bedourie) wrote:

> I have had several verbal complaints about a white man living at 'Dubbo Downs' with a half caste gin. I believe this man is cook on the station, that is, if he is there now. If this is correct, could not this man be prosecuted under 'Section 14' of the Aboriginals Protection Act of 1897. I should be pleased to hear from you on the subject. I am sir, Yours faithfully, Harold Meston, Protector.[29]

The verbal complaint did not make clear who these people were, only that one was a white man, the other a 'half-caste gin'. Constable Wilkinson was sent out to investigate. Wilkinson's curly, large handwriting squashed the last word of the line so that it fit on the page, but it made it look like each line was a kind of contracted disappointment, heading steadily downwards. Wilkinson replied, saying that the permits to employ Aboriginal workers were lodged in Birdsville, that the man in question (could it be Paul K?) was 'under medical treatment in Townsville Hospital'. As for prosecuting him under section 14: 'it would be necessary to find this man either sleeping with or living in a room [with her], or having her under his control … I may mention [that] a married couple are now residing on the Station building Dubbo Downs'.[30]

---

28   Roth to Durham, 24 January 1904, QSA, A/58764.
29   H Meston to the Officer in Charge, Bedourie, 24 October 1903, QSA, A/58764.
30   Constable A Wilkinson to H Meston, 3 November 1903, QSA, A/58764.

The white man referred to was a cook, not a stockman like Paul K Wilkinson appeared reluctant to prosecute due to the difficulty in procuring evidence. He ended on a 'positive note' with news that a 'married couple' were now residing on the station, indicating his belief that the presence of married couple would put a stop to whatever had been going on. As employers, single men were under much greater scrutiny than married men.

When Wilkinson heard that the cook had returned to the station, he made another visit to 'make further inquiries re half-caste gin there'. He talked with the manager of the station (one half of the married couple) who told him that 'the half caste gin in question was pregnant and it was rumoured that John H [the cook] had placed her in that state'.[31] Wilkinson informed the Protector that:

> The gin is now well protected and cared for under the hands of Mr & Mrs M—and she is not allowed to visit the blacks['] camp or associate with strangers or passers by. M— and wife state … that the girl appears to be between 16 or 17 years of age and will be cared for by them during their stay at Dubbo Downs unless she misconducts herself in which case they will promptly communicate with the police to have her removed.[32]

The married couple (managers of the station) enforced a strict moral code that focused on limiting the girl's contact with everyone ('blacks', 'strangers' and 'passers by'). If she transgressed any rules of the house, she would have been removed by police: the white domestic space was reinforced by white law enforcement; white law enforcement extended right into the white domestic sphere. The 'gin's' pregnancy placed her under strict surveillance from both the white managers and the state, represented by Wilkinson and his letters to the Protector.

Wilkinson talked with John H and reported that John H 'preferred to marry the gin rather than to pay for maintenance of child'.[33] But this was not exactly what John H had written, as is shown in this letter to the Protector:

---

31 Letter from Wilkinson, QSA, A/58764.
32 Letter from Wilkinson, QSA, A/58764.
33 Letter from Wilkinson, QSA, A/58764.

During my time cooking I took a half caste girl out of the camp and kept her at the kitchen. I took her for protection as she was getting abused in the camp. She is now pregnant and I have been informed that I will get in trouble about it. I have made a good girl of her while she was up at the station ... to read a little and keep her well supplied in clothes so if you will give me permission I will marry her I am able to keep her respectable. I am a good cook and can always get work and will keep her in a proper manner if you will agree to what I have mentioned. I will carry it out at once please to write to constable Wilkinson and let him know as it was him that advised me to write to you about the matter trusting a favourable answer. I remain, your obedient servant ... [John H].[34]

John H's promise to marry the girl was couched in terms of respectability, protection, education and clothing, much like Paul K's promise in relation to his daughter. The fact John H feared he would 'get in trouble about it' is present but not pressed. The phrase 'I took her' reflected the possessive nature of his interest in her and this expression is not uncommon in the letters: 'I had her two years up to the time she was taking [sic] from me' and 'I also would like to have her', 'let me know if I can have the girl' (Paul K).

In January 1904 John H's application to marry was accepted, although Roth added that because 'the girl ... [was] a minor, it ... [would] be necessary for John H to obtain consent from her father, or from a Magistrate empowered to give consent to the marriage of minors'. When he sought permission from her (white) father, Wilkinson found that the girl was the same one that Paul K was claiming paternity over. Wilkinson summarised: 'it is a case of who can lay claim to the half caste gin between these two men mentioned, one claims parentage the other protective and marriage rights'.[35]

Wilkinson was again sent in to investigate and in February Wilkinson advised the protector 'not [to] recognis[e] Paul K as the father of the gin' and presented the following reasons why:

---

34   Letter to H Meston, 12 December 1903, QSA, A/58764.
35   Wilkinson to the Inspector of Police, Longreach, 19 February 1904, QSA, A/58764.

Firstly, [a]s Paul K has been on the same station as the gin for 10 years it is strange that he did not recognise her as his child before.

Secondly, it is strange that he did not think about her education until he left the station or was on the point of leaving the station.

Thirdly, [i]t is strange he did not provide her with clothes or keep her from running wild in the blacks['] camp adjacent to the station house.

Fourthly, [i]t is generally believed in the district that Paul K is claiming parentage under the pretext that he will be allowed to take her away and by doing so will be able to live with her himself.

Fifthly, [u]nder those circumstances he would not be likely to give permission to John H.

Lastly, [t]he reputed father of the gin is said to be a man named L— who was last heard of years ago in Western Australia. I now ask for further instructions on the matter and will be pleased to be favoured with an early reply.

I have the honour to be Sir,

Your Obedient Servant, J Wilkinson, Const of Police.[36]

In response to this, Roth instructed the local protector that 'no notice be taken on Paul K['s] letter which is neither a claim nor proof of paternity: I suggest that the consent from a magistrate empowered to give it (as per my letter CD98/4) be obtained as soon as possible etc so that the child may be born legitimate'.[37]

Four months later, another constable reported that the marriage did not take place. John H had said that 'he would much sooner not marry the girl but would be quite agreeable to maintain the girl and that he has heard she is in the habit of cohabiting with Black fellows'.[38] Such a statement placed the child at risk of being removed, regardless of whether or not John H was willing to pay maintenance. It also situated John H as loyal to whiteness in his refusal to sanction her 'cohabiting with Black fellows'.[39] Where previously 'one claim[ed] parentage [and] the other protective and marriage rights',[40] now neither men claimed

---

36 Wilkinson to Roth, 19 February 1904, QSA, A/58764.
37 Roth, 24 March 1904, QSA, A/58764
38 Constable Kelly to the Inspector of Police, Longreach, 20 June 1904, QSA, A/58764.

her. However she was clearly still under the scrutiny of the state, as was her child.

The child and his or her mother were, in the terms of these letters, subjected to the tenuous nature of paternity claims and paternalist interest in securing them. In the records the mother was moved from her father to the cook, to a pregnant 'state', to virtual imprisonment by the married station managers, to a potential husband, to 'Black fellows' (and her kin?) and back again to Roth. The reporting of her movements, her state and her acquaintances occurred always at an arm's length on the basis of what 'he' had heard – 'he' being the white men who claimed her, the constable who reported on her to the Protector, who passes it on to the Chief Protector who, hearing them, also heard the demands of the legislation.

Maintenance, marriage and paternity functioned biopolitically to protect Aboriginal women and children. But the discourse of protection, as many have noted, is profoundly ambivalent (Haebich 2000; Young 2003; Brown 1995), invested and tangled up in the very thing (violation) that it seeks to ameliorate. That contest between protection and violation is intrinsic to colonial paternalism. The emphasis on white paternity here did more than bring gentlemen within the scope of their protective responsibilities. It introduced Western paternity models that emphasised biological paternity over social paternity. It undermined Aboriginal kinship practices, keeping Aboriginal women from their Aboriginal families, separating kin, country and culture.

'I know what her future will be'

Aboriginal women with children were under constant threat of being removed and/or having their children removed, particularly if they were not married to the father and unable to work to support their children. One man wrote to Roth about a woman who was 'kept by the late — who died some months ago leaving her and her children destitute'.

---

39   Constable Kelly to the Inspector of Police, Longreach, 20 June 1904, QSA, A/58764.
40   Wilkinson to the Inspector of Police, Longreach, 19 February 1904, QSA, A/58764.

The man informed Roth that the woman wished to return to where she had relatives but was 'afraid to move thinking her children might be taken from her. Is there any chance of that being done?'[41] He inquired whether or not she might get into trouble for doing casual work.

In red in the margin of this letter, one inspector wrote, 'Does — associate with blacks?'[42] and another wrote that as long as the locals agreed to her working casually, and as long as she 'behave[d] herself',[43] she was allowed to work. Neither of them replied to the question of whether or not she was in danger of having her children removed.

Roth replied, telling the man that he knew the woman's partner and saying that 'I regret I can do little on their behalf, in that they are quadroons to whom the Aboriginals Acts do not apply'. While the Act did not apply to them, the children, if 'neglected', came under the Reformations Act, on which the Aborigines Act was partly based. Roth went on to write that 'I am indeed sorry for [the daughter]... because having to "find herself" at 18 years of age on 3s per week, a miserable pittance, I know what her future will be.' Roth agreed that it was acceptable for her mother to work in the hotel on a casual basis on the proviso that she did 'not act ... as the intermediary for supplying liquor to the other blacks, is leading a regular life and looking after her children'.[44] Roth did not answer the question of whether or not she was at risk of having her children taken away, just provided reasons for why they might have been.

Removal to mission stations, to the cities or to reserves was described by Foxton in parliament as better than 'out West, where they are left to the mercies of unscrupulous whites' (1901, 226):

I believe it does an immense amount of good for a young girl to be brought down to Brisbane, or other large cities or towns, where she will be under the proper control of some official, or where she may get into the hands of some good family. Then there is nothing to pre-

---

41 Letter to Roth, 12 December 1904, QSA, Director of Native Affairs Office, Correspondence Files, 1904, A/58749 and A/58750.
42 Letter to Roth, 12 December 1904, A/58749 and A/58750.
43 Letter to Roth, 12 December 1904, A/58749 and A/58750.
44 Roth to Protector Driscoll, Maryborough, 9 June 1904, QSA, Director of Native Affairs Office, Correspondence Files, 1904, A/58749 and A/58750.

vent her from going to some mission station, marrying and settling down, and I am quite sure that the education and refinement she experiences during her period of service in such a family cannot but be of inestimable benefit to herself, her husband, and her progeny. (226)

'Refinement' in the 'hands of some good family' was contradicted by the evidence collected together in the *Bringing them home* report (1997). The Aboriginal women spoken of here were positioned in such rhetoric as belonging to the state, and, as such, it was up to the state to determine what their futures might be. The figure of the unscrupulous white man necessitated (in state terms) white intervention. Again, the class-based logic of white civility positioned white men from good families as being entirely non-threatening while the private sphere was deemed to be a space of protection, refuge and refinement. Tracing the involvement of white fathers depicted in these letters outlines the complex efforts that the state went to in order to uplift white men, and also what this fantasy encountered: the manoeuvres that white men were themselves using in order to evade, utilise and strategically engage with the state's paternalist interest in them.

After Roth had left his position as Queensland's Chief Protector (1904–1906), Richard Howard took office (1906–1914). In 1906, Howard explained how he saw the future:

all such infants taken from the camps should be brought up as white children, and not in the aboriginal mission reformatories as black ones. Legislation should be on the lines of raising, and not of lowering, their positions and especially so, with a view of preventing the interbreeding of half-castes with full bloods. What should be aimed at is the opportunity of getting half castes to marry either half-castes or Europeans. (1906, 13)

This statement came three decades earlier than the announced policy of 'breeding out the colour', proclaimed at the 1937 Canberra Conference. It was endorsed by a majority of Protectors, but not by Queenslanders, even though they had worked with the idea long before.

Queensland's JW Bleakley did not agree with the policy of biological assimiliation as it was announced in 1937, arguing that 'half-castes' had been fathered by a low type of white man. The result ... [was] that the half-breed, although he may not have the colour of the aboriginal, has his habits, and consequently cannot happily be absorbed into the white race.[45]

While Cook and AO Neville were the most vocal proponents of the policy to breed out the colour, other states followed suit. The work of this policy of breeding out the colour, though a failure, articulated a strategic investment in white paternity as a way of dealing with the fear of being outnumbered by 'half-castes'. It also worked to articulate and foster a further biopolitical interest that gained popularity over the course of the 20th century: a pressing desire for white indigeneity; a need to belong. Whiteness remade threat as opportunity and chose to swallow rather than be swallowed up. Just how this policy of breeding out the colour and *breeding in the Indigeneity* related to white paternity is the subject of the next chapter.

---

45   Commonwealth of Australia, *Aboriginal welfare: intitial conference of Commonwealth and State Aboriginal authorities.* Canberra: Government Printer, 1937.

Breeders

It is a striking paradox that the white man credited with inventing the phrase 'breed out the colour' was considered to be an albino. Dr Cecil Cook, Chief Medical Officer and Chief Protector of Aborigines from 1927 to 1939 in the Northern Territory, is described in *Xavier Herbert: a biography* as a 'tall albino, conspicuous for his ruddy face, snow-white hair and pale blue eyes (one of them glass)' (de Groen 1998, 59). Again, in an edition of Herbert's letters, Cook is presented as a 'striking and controversial figure (he was an albino with a glass eye)' (de Groen & Hergenhan 2002, 467).

When I first came across the idea that Cook was an albino, I thought it strange, funny even, that the man known for 'breed out the colour' had no colour himself. It sets in motion a series of painful and ridiculous puns such as: the man who invented the phrase 'breed out the colour' had a problem with whiteness; he lacked colour but professed the need to 'breed it out' of Aboriginal people; he was attempting to 'pass as white' by dyeing his hair; his skin epitomised the unsuitability of the Northern Territory for white Australians; he was the bearer of a genetic disorder (an excessive corporeal whiteness), while his role was to order (genetically, socially and by skin) the future 'stock' of the Territory as ideologically white.

But photographs of Cook from 1923 and 1928 do not show him with snow-white hair (Austin 1997, 111).[1] Ann McGrath, who interviewed Cook before he died, confirmed that he did not appear to be a person with albinism (2005, 2006). Tim Rowse, who wrote the entry on Cook for the *Australian dictionary of biography*, had not heard this idea before[2] and neither had Suzanne Saunders who has written about

Cook and Herbert's relationship (1990). Saunders had also interviewed Cook's daughter about his work and she did not mention it.[3] This leads me to conclude that Cook's albinism was most probably a rumour spread by Xavier Herbert, a friend and foe of Cecil Cook.[4] More interestingly, it might also have been built upon an image of extreme or excessive whiteness that inhabits Herbert's fiction, politics and letters.

So while the attribution of albinism to Cook's body is, I believe, a misreading, it is also instructive and revealing. It points to the lack of self-reflexity in Cook's own racial dreaming, or at least that to which he put his name as proponent of the policy of biological assimilation. Herbert's rumour drains Cook's body of colour, echoing Cook's plan for 'half-castes'. Herbert's rumour does something else as well. It capitalises on (or makes literal or corporeal) Herbert's interests in securing Australia for a certain kind of whiteness. Herbert's white Australia/n did not lack colour (as a person with albinism might be thought to), and did not have colour bred out. Rather, colour is reclaimed in Herbert's fiction to stand for indigeneity, a desirable state of belonging. This is ultimately what brings Cook and Herbert's race fantasies together: a fascination with skin and colour, belonging and strangeness inhabit both Cook's racial science and Herbert's fiction. Both expressed the view, in different genres and discourses, that white paternity of Aboriginal children was a vital source of white Australia's future. The parallel lines and divergences between Cook and Herbert's views represents a point from which to reflect on how the policy of breeding out the colour found its imaginary flock of white fathers spawning a cul-

---

1   See National Archives of Australia, photograph of Cecil Cook. Northern Territory Chief Protector of Aborigines, Dr Cecil Cook (right), with his Queensland counterpart, JW Bleakley, 1928, p 68b. NAA: A263, ALBUM. [Online] Available: uncommonlives.naa.gov.au/dhakiyarr-wirrpanda/enlargements/dr-cecil-cook-and-jw-bleakley-1928.aspx [Accessed 4 March 2013].

2   Personal communication (by email) 2005, 2006.

3   Personal communication (by email) 2006.

4   Herbert spread other rumours about Cook, including that he was a philanderer, an alcoholic and a mismanager of Aboriginal affairs (see Suzanne Saunders 1990). De Groen writes that Herbert constructed a 'romantic smokescreen of legend' (xi) that he built not only around himself but also others. Thanks to Frances de Groen for help in attempting to track down sources for the idea of Cook's albinism.

tural movement different to that planned; not 'breeding out the colour' but 'breeding in the Indigeneity'. But perhaps these visions of Australia's white future were not so radically different.

'Into the white' or 'into the black'

Cecil Cook was a student of medicine at the University of Sydney until 1930 when he graduated with a specialist interest in leprosy, a disease manifesting in the skin as hypopigmented white spots: 'the polite name for leprosy was "the white skin" ' (Achebe 1958, 54). As Chief Medical Officer, Chief Health Officer and Chief Protector of Aboriginals and Quarantine Officer in the Northern Territory (1927–1939), his interests in race and health coalesced, making him a powerful voice on issues of race, health, population and the best ways to control all three simultaneously. Cook arrived in the Northern Territory when it was administered by the Commonwealth Government. This is why the policy of breeding out the colour – where Aboriginal or 'half-caste' women were to be married to 'men substantially of European origin' (Cook 1936, 2) – was so important in establishing that the Commonwealth Government bore responsibility for the policy of biological assimilation. As Tony Austin points out, the Commonwealth Government appeared to have been happy to let Cecil Cook proceed with his plans (1997).

Cook's report, 'Marriage of white men to half caste women' (1936) prefaces many of the commitments made at the 1937 Canberra Conference. Cook saw marriages between 'half-caste' Aboriginal women and white men as being able to arrest the 'deterioration of the white'. Cook believed that, if these white men were 'prepared to marry half-caste females and make decent homes', there could be 'no objection to such a mating' because the result would be 'the white man rearing a white family in good circumstances instead of a half-caste family under degrading circumstances' (Cook 1936, 3). This would, Cook argued, reverse the situation he currently envisaged: that 'in 50 years, or a little later, the white population of the Northern Territory will be absorbed into the black'. Toni Morrison's observation that whiteness is 'formed in fright' (1992, 59) is apt here. The solution was that marriage between white men and half-caste women, 'decent homes' and 'good circumstances' would turn the black 'into the white' (Cook 1936, 3).

Austin describes Cook's policy to encourage 'half-caste' women to marry white men as 'an ultimate eugenicist solution' (Austin 1990, 113). In his promotion of mixed race marriages, Cook had to sell 'colour' to his colleagues, to the press, to the Territory and Commonwealth because (as Austin points out) in many ways Cook (and Neville in Western Australia) were arguing for racial mixing at a time when it was still seen as racial polluting (Austin 1990, 115).

For some, the plans to allow mixed-race marriages confined the labour of uplifting or breeding out the colour to a particular class of white man. A letter to the editor of the Northern Standard from 'Mother All White' reads:

> Just because the settlers out back, railway fettlers, and bushmen, generally have a hard and oft-times lonely life, are they a lower order of beings than the officials of Darwin, that they should be picked upon to do the uplift? (20 June 1933)

'Mother All White' goes on to ask that Cecil Cook encourage his own son to do the 'uplift job'. In another letter, 'Fair Play' encourages Cook to marry a 'half-caste' girl himself (*Northern Standard*, 27 June 1933).

Cook's policy to breed out the colour made him deeply unpopular with whites and Aboriginal people for very different reasons. His control over the lives of Aboriginal people (to marry, to keep their children, to stay with family, to be imprisoned on reserves) was extensive. Hilda Jarman Muir writes of his paternalistic control:

> Dr Cook, the Chief Protector, played the role of father to us. He liked to arrange marriages for girls from the Home, usually to white men. Everyone knew that Dr Cook arranged marriages for white men and they then got good positions working as domestics for public servants. Dr Cook would choose special half caste girls to line up. Like a police line-up, then men looked at them, and then chose the one they liked. Then the half caste girls and the white man would get married with Cook's blessing and the man would get a good job. It wasn't romantic, but it was a good way of getting out of the Compound. Sometimes he even found a nice house for the white men

as an extra pay-off for marrying a half-caste ward from the Home. Really this was a way of breeding out the colour in us. That was the official policy in those days. (2004, 67)

In Cook's Territory, a white Australia/Territory was not realisable in the present. It could only be made, by mixing and breeding within marriage. The white men and the Aboriginal women that Cook and Neville in Western Australia sought to marry were biopolitically imagined as at home in future white skins without Aboriginality: 'granting of full citizenship to a *generation* of persons who may *fairly* claim it' (Cook, 5, emphasis added). They were to be future whites to be made by 'realising an objective' (Cook, 5). Cook argued that the children of 'mixing' possessed many strengths:

> the aboriginal inheritance brings to the hybrid definite qualities of value – intelligence, stamina, resource, high resistance to the influences of tropical environment and the character of pigmentation which even in high dilution will serve to reduce the at present high incidence of Skin Cancer in the blonde European. (Cook 1936, 3)

Cook surmises here that 'Aboriginal inheritance' meant biology only, neatly separated from culture. Skin, stamina and intelligence would make a better type of future white Australian, one who did not look at his or her Aboriginal inheritance as anything other than providing key biological traits for tropical survival. Cook's view of white cultural superiority, while acceding to white biological inferiority, was underwritten by medical expert opinion at the time.

During the 19th and early 20th centuries, governments and medical experts worried that the white race was not going to be able to populate the tropical northern regions of Australia. Susceptibility to the heat and tropical diseases were blamed for the white man's inability to labour as effectively as his coloured counterparts. It was for this reason that 'Kanaka' (Pacific islander) labourers, who were brought in throughout the latter half of the 18th century to work on the sugar plantations of northern Queensland were then later deported en masse by the third Act of the newly federated Commonwealth. Kanakas would compete with and overstrip white workers in the tropics. This made Aboriginal inheritance for white Australians all the more desirable.

Warwick Anderson (2002) points out that while the Act of Federation made Australia white by parliamentary decree, politicians and
leaders worried that the north would always be 'less-than-white', a situation that would have been attractive to Herbert, and a mere issue of
inheritance to Cook. In contrast to Cook's strategic (eugenic) plans
to use colour for white adaptability, many contemporary views were
strictly segregationist. In 1929, Billy Hughes (prime minister of Australia, 1915–1923) wrote in his book *The splendid adventure: a review
of empire relations within and without the Commonwealth of Britiannic
nations* that Australia was a 'white island in a vast coloured ocean'
and needed to 'build dykes through which the merest trickle of the
sea of colour cannot find its way' (quoted in Anderson, 164). In 1911,
Professor Edgeworth David (1858–1934) of the University of Sydney
argued that the white race in the tropics would eventually become black
but that it might take a few thousand years. In the meantime, he con-
cluded, it was necessary to sacrifice 'comfort, health and even life' to
keep Australia as white as possible (quoted in Anderson, 95). For Cook,
these sacrifices could be compensated for by incorporating 'aboriginal
inheritance'. With the inadequacy of white skin came its biopower, for
then it had to be managed, corrected and selected to survive by the incorporation of other skin colours, and here incorporation of others is
simultaneously depicted as elimination and expulsion, a 'breeding out'
that is also a 'breeding in'.

This substantiates Ahmed's point that some forms of expulsion are
based upon 'prior acts of incorporation' (2000, 52). Aboriginal people
who chose to, or who were compelled to, identify as white took on
the inadequacies associated with white skin. Henry Reynolds recalls his
father 'keeping out of the sun so his status as a white man could not be
doubted' (2005, xxi). To be a white man was to be afraid of the dark, as
Toni Morrison suggests (1992). Such fears and doubts would have been
cause for celebration for Xavier Herbert. Or should I say, Herbert might
celebrate such fears and doubts about the specific inadequacies of white
skin, then quickly turn to lament his own all too ordinary whiteness.

'I love them and envy their nationality'

Xavier Herbert was generally supportive of Cook's ideas ('my old friend') but, because of Cook's refusal to employ Herbert as a patrol officer or to work at the Aboriginal reserves, he became Cook's harshest critic ('my old foe'). Herbert wrote to Elkin that Cook was an 'overgrown, clever, bumptious, boy' (Elkin Archives, 23 January 1937) and four months later wrote, 'The man is a monster in his attitude to the unfortunate people he is employed to protect. He not only does not understand them, but detests them. Small wonder they hate or fear him' (Elkin Archives, 21 May 1937). Herbert spread many rumours about Cook, including that he was a philanderer, an alcoholic, a mismanager of Aboriginal affairs (see Saunders 1990 and de Groen 1998) and also, possibly, that he was an albino. Herbert wrote to Elkin, 'I have been trying to plumb the strange fellow's character for years' (6 September 1937). Cook appears far less interested in being plumbed or even returning or engaging Herbert's attentions: 'Mr Herbert's muddled prolixity, in which lies half truths and distortions of the truth are so inextricably mixed as to render categorical denial ineffective' (Cook to Abbott, 24 May 1937, quoted in Saunders 1990, 62).

Herbert's novels *Capricornia* (1938) and *Poor fellow my country* (1975) demonstrate a fascination with skin colour, which in his work also signals a politics of belonging, heritage, as well as an allergic, sunburnt foreignness as well as suntanned at-home-ness. Skin is described throughout his work in a way that highlights, for the contemporary reader, the differences between 1930s Australia and today. Gillian Cowlishaw points out that today there is a notable 'silence around skin colour which, like a trace element, marks the presence of anxious denial' (1999, 12) and Maureen Perkins doubts 'that the colour of skin often goes unnoticed, though it often goes unremarked' (2004, 174).

In Herbert's fictional world of the Northern Territory during the 1930s, there is little reticence when it comes to describing skin colour and how it embodies a person's place within colonial hierarchy which situates a small number of whites, who are themselves 'internally differentiated', at the top (Frankenberg 1997, 4). Aboriginal people's skin is described in *Poor fellow my country* as yellow, black, 'cream caramel' (9), coloured, and as 'perfection' (10). In *Capricornia* it is described as 'honey coloured' (27) and 'the colour of the cigarette stain on his finger' (27). Whiteness is not 'undefined' or invisible (Dyer 1997) but is red, yellow, brown, 'carroty' (*Capricornia*, 3), purple, dusty, ruddy, crimson, like 'pale faced cows' (512). Whiteness is propped up by solar topees 'more a badge of authority than a hat', suits of 'bright white linen everyday' (9), a mincing talk (9), a walking stick, and of course the exclusion of non-whites and the 'low' whites who consort with them. In Herbert's work and in his letters, one can observe a certain skin politics where, as Perkins puts it, 'seeing *all* colour, including white, and challenging colour's power to demarcate boundaries of community goes hand in hand with naming hypocrises of the past' (2004, 175, original emphasis).

Herbert also paid attention to Aboriginal perceptions of whiteness, as did Bill Harney in *Brimming billabongs* (1947) where Marmel, Harney's Aboriginal 'I', recounted the

> strange white man – but he is not white. Your people look what we call them, murundanee, which means 'red', or kumadip, which means 'half cooked'. Their skin is red and peels from their hides in the sun, just as a goanna's does when it is thrown into the fire. (17)

A bit like Harney, Basil Sansom argues that Herbert brings 'Aboriginal constructions to whitefella perceptions … like two filmstrips secretly running in parallel. Herbert then cross-edits' (2006, 94). This cross-editing, this seeing of colour and positioning of skin, underwrites his particular political vision for Australia.

Herbert's nationalism positions Aborigines as being 'essential', according to Mudrooroo (1990, viii). They are essential to Australian-ness and form the basis of the 'perfection' required for a 'new' Australian body politic: a 'light-skinned breed, even tanned Caucasian … Surely a beautiful creature to any eye but the most prejudiced in the matter of race' (Herbert 1990, 9). But what he is also doing, by implication, is tending towards a different conception of skin found in indigenous epistemologies. This is explained by Stephen Kinnane: 'My grandmother was placed by her skin, *Nangarri*, and then taken away to a place where her skin meant nothing more than colour' (2003, 11). For Herbert, skin became more than colour and was imbued with nationalist dreams of belonging. By comparison with the images of 'tanned Caucasian' perfection embodied by Euro-Australians, white bodies, particularly those made red rather than brown, are sources of fear, foreignness and mal-adaptation. In *Capricornia*, Jock Driver, a 'North-country Englishman' (53) was perceived by Nawnim/Norman in terms of his strange body:

> What troubled Nawnim was his [Jock's] colouring. His mouth was as *red* as fresh raw meat, and thick lipped and wide and constantly writhing. Nawnim was used to lean-faced, *brown* faced, thin lipped, small-eyed *white* men. Jock's face was as *red* as a boiled crayfish, even *redder* than it usually was in this climate in which it was as foreign as a gumtree in his native fogs, because it had lately been put under the blood rousing influences of salt-wind and grog. The *redness* of his face set off the *blueness* of his bulging eyes and the *blackness* of his hair and the *whiteness* of his large prominent teeth. His teeth looked like a shark's to Nawnim, his eyes like a crab's. When he approached the bedroom Nawnim turned sick with fright. Jewty must have been given a turn too. She rushed to the bed and snatched up her baby and trod on Nawnim's little hand. Nawnim yelped, heaved away, struck his head on the underneath of the bed, and rolled into view bawling. Diana screamed and clutched at her mother's hair. (55, emphasis added)

If the tanned Caucasian Euro-Australian, 'the light skinned breed', was perfection, then the red, sun-scorched, wind-burnt white skin that belonged to the foreigner, particularly the English, was disturbing, laughable, and ridiculous. Jock's colouring in the above excerpt is primarily red, white and blue, familiar and yet as 'foreign as a gumtree in his native fogs'. Here Herbert achieved in fictional terms what he imagined the Euro-Australian league might achieve politically: to 'sweep the Pommies back into the sea' (Herbert quoted in de Groen 1998, 104).

Those whose whiteness warranted comment and evoked fear included Dr Cobbity in *Poor fellow my country*:

> a biggish man, but with a little round head and very red face that looked like a tomato on a long stalk. So striking were his blue eyes in the red face that when he looked straight across at girls, they cringed visibly. (230)

He had 'intense blue eyes ... [set in his] brick-red face' and a 'glassy stare' (252). The character of Dr Cobbity was based on Cook. Herbert ridiculed Cook as Cobbity in *Poor fellow my country* and Dr Aintee in *Capricornia* (Saunders 1990):

> Dr Aintee held no high opinion of the great black and brindle family he fathered ... he regarded them merely as marsupials being routed by a pack of dingoes ... Most of the dingoes hated him for interfering with their rights as the stronger animals; the marsupials regarded him as a sort of devil devil, and trembled at mention of his name. (1990, 272)

Cecil Cook appears to have been startling, striking and shocking to other whites too. Tom Cole describes him as being excessively white, 'a figure of somewhat striking appearance, standing over six feet in height, and although barely forty, displaying a shock of snow white hair above eyes of an almost startling blueness' (Cole 1992, 101). The attention paid to the whiteness of the other (albino) white body is particularly interesting in that it is made strange and odd within a perceived normal range of whiteness.

Albino

What can we make of all this attention to Cook's whiteness and rumours of extreme white skin? Sara Ahmed points out that skin is not 'simply invested with meaning as a visual signifier of difference (the skin as coloured, the skin as wrinkled and so on)' (2000, 44) but that it functions 'as a border or frame' (45) that separates the self from the Other and is analogous to the ordering of social spaces or 'homelands' (46). Unmarked bodies belong and strange bodies threaten, are expelled and incorporated. In the context of Herbert's novels, the excessively white bodies are strange (compared with the lean and brown whites) and the extremely white body marks the brown and lean white body as closer to home, closer to the ordinary.

In literature, the figure of the albino is sometimes deployed to unsettle racial categories and white privilege. The South African writer Breyten Breytenbach, imprisoned for his anti-apartheid activism, uses the figure of the albino to encapsulate the freakish nature of his political existence. In *The true confessions of an albino terrorist*, Breytenbach is not 'seen' by other Afrikaners who do not feel his difference because his white Afrikaner body is marked as 'same':

> I was the faceless face in the crowd, I was the invisible man. Around me there was the space of death. I was a zombie only, a visitor from another planet – painfully aware of pretending to be regular and accepting as normal the ways of the unruffled bigot. (1984, 94)

Breytenbach utilises the figure of the albino to contextualise his disguise, passing for white in a society where whiteness was ideologically built upon accepting apartheid as norm. Here Breytenbach's depiction of albinism signals a critical distance to those he resembles in corporeal terms, and also his proximity to the black South Africans who are the terrorists according to the terror within Afrikaner nationalism.

Bonnie Tu Smith argues that the figure of the albino functions as a form of racial 'disorientation' and that 'ethnic writers like Wideman seem well aware of the benefits of such inescapable regrouping'. She points out that the albino 'transcends or circumvents the polarities of black and white … it moves us to the fluid of "both/and" ' (1993, 89). With deconstructive potential, the attribution of albinism to Cook draws attention to his problem with whiteness in his role as Protector, turning him into his own ideological ghost. But this also taps into an older tradition of perceiving albinism as a rather sinister manifestation of excessive whiteness, whiteness that is out of place. Melville's discussion of the 'Albino man' in *Moby-Dick* (1851) situates him as 'more strangely hideous than the ugliest abortion' and ends with the question of '[w]hy should this be so?' The quandary of albinism conjures up the quandary of whiteness. In Toni Morrison's reading, this is the value of Melville's text: Melville critiques whiteness in its ideological form as much as its corporeal form. In American literature, Morrison finds that 'Whiteness, alone, is mute, meaningless, unfathomable, pointless, frozen, veiled, curtained, dreaded, senseless, implacable' (1992, 59).

Richard Dyer points out that whites are often represented as the 'living dead' (1997, 211) as profound ambivalence is attached to the absence that is associated with whiteness. Such ambivalence haunts people with albinism. The absence of whiteness (which is also the privilege of invisibility) is cast upon the body of the albino, who is the hypervisible, the extraordinary white-white.

Albinism is intensely racialised, while not being particular to any racial group. In Western countries it is often associated with white people. In the US, NOAH (National Organization for Albinism and Hypopigmentation) states that African-Americans with albinism are sometimes accused of trying to 'pass as white'. Their website (www.albinism.org) points out that Hollywood often depicts people with albinism as villains, for example, the nasty sidekick in *Cold mountain* (2003), the twins in *Matrix reloaded* (2003), and more recently Silas in *The Da Vinci code* (2006). There is also the very white Lucius and Draco Malfoy ('mudblood haters') in the Harry Potter films. Activist Luna Eterna catalogues the negative accounts of people with albinism in literature, film and other popular-culture texts. The Skinema website (set up to show how skin is depicted in Hollywood films) also criticises the stereotyping of albinism in films that situate people with albinism as vampiric, with red eyes,[5] and as associated with death, sadomasochistic cruelty, fascist eugenicism and evil. Utilising the science of melanin theory, African-American writer Frances Welsing situates white people as 'albino mutants' with 'defective skins' (1991, 122) and argues that the source of white suprematism is the inadequacy of white skins to produce colour, which is both desired and loathed.

It seems that people with albinism can be made to be scapegoats for a fear of ideological whiteness or extreme whiteness, about which both Morrison and Richard Dyer write. Dyer points out that extreme whiteness, by which he means 'taut, tight, rigid upright, straight (not curved), on the beat (not syncopated), controlled and controlling' (222) whiteness, lets 'ordinary whiteness' off the hook:

The extreme image of whiteness acts as a distraction. An image of what whites are like is set up, but can also be held at a distance. Extreme whiteness is, precisely, extreme. If in certain periods of derangement – the empire at their height, the Fascist eras – white people have seen themselves in these images, they can take comfort

---

5 See the homepage of the International Albinism Center at the University of Minnesota for discussion of albinism's signs and symptoms (which do not include pink eyes). Available at: www.ophthalmology.umn.edu/patientcare/albinism/.

from the fact that for most of the time they haven't … The combination of extreme whiteness with plain, unwhite whiteness means white
people can both lay claim to the spirit that aspires to the heights of
humanity and yet supposedly speak and act disinterestedly as humanity's most average and unremarkable representatives. (1997, 223)

Cook's alleged albinism collapses the difference between ideological
whiteness and albinism (turning one into the other) and perhaps this
is why I laughed when I first read about it. The other side of the joke is
that it releases 'ordinary' whites from connection to 'abnormal' whites –
scientific racists like Cook (and Neville) whose extreme whiteness contrasts, disconnects and distances my ethics, my time, and my whiteness
from theirs. In drawing attention to the abnormal, we assert our own
presumed normalcy.

Here albinism functions as a highly visible substitute or a scapegoat
for things about whiteness that are unsettling (and therefore might remain unseen, ordinary and invisible). Richard Dyer again: 'the extreme,
very white white image is functional in relation to the ordinary, is even
perhaps a condition of establishing whiteness as ordinary' (1997, 222).
Perhaps this explains the usefulness of albinism to Herbert's ridicule
of Cook. Cook's freakish whiteness made Herbert less so. It made him
more ordinary, closer to the perfect 'tanned Caucasian' Euro-Australian
than Cook would ever be.

Herbert built his own public persona on 'larrikinism, violent con-
troversy and a hyperbolic masculinity' (de Groen 1998, 180). He saw
himself as a neglected champion of Aboriginal people in the north: 'I
have slaved and suffered and impoverished myself for the cause of the
Aborigines' (quoted in de Groen & Hergenhan 2002, 86); as singularly
heroic in his concerns: 'who but myself in all this wide country dares
a curse about the heart burnings of a boong?' (quoted in de Groen &
Hergenhan 2002, 89); and as singled out for contempt by fellow whites:
'I have won nothing but suspicion and contempt from everyone for
my sympathies for the Abos' (Elkin Archives, 22 December 1937). Self-
aggrandising in his devotion to the 'cause', he wrote to Elkin of his
suffering:

I suffer from the plight of these unfortunates all the time, till there
are moments when I feel like spending my last few pounds on rifles

and ammunition and leading a mob of them forth to die nobly taking their revenge on the stony hearted swine that oppress them. (6 September 1937)

In his letters, Herbert typically positions himself as expert diagnostician (like Cook) of the problem, but as not part of the problem itself: he is on the side of organising Aboriginal deaths by political sacrifice (theirs not his). Their suffering becomes his; he is the 'slave' and the impoverished one. As de Groen points out, 'His paternalistic and sometimes racist rhetoric suggests that he was unaware of the contradictions between the roles he was playing as a "blackfella", as the saviour of the Aborigines and as a white bureaucrat' (1998, 104). These positions were not contradictions if we think of Herbert's promotion of a white-Australian nationalism that was founded on Aboriginality (without Aborigines) and on a specific form of 'native' whiteness (without paternalistic Englishness).

His attempts to position himself as expert on Aboriginal affairs (to win him work) is accompanied by a slippage where, instead of representing the Aborigine, he became the Aborigine: 'I have a blackfella's mind'; 'I can see things in a blackfella fashion' (quoted in de Groen 1998, 104). He played up this image as well. Writing to Arthur Dibley, he recalled that he had sent a wire to publisher PR ('Inky') Stephensen 'with a few encouraging words in Abo in it – just to prove that I am the Blackfellow he said I was' (de Groen & Hergenhan 2002, 88). De Groen observes that this 'man of many masks' (1998, xii) strongly identified with 'half-castes' in terms of his own illegitimacy and in his perceptions of Australia as a 'bastard nation, comprising rapacious white colonisers and dispossessed indigenes' (1998, xii). This identification with 'half-castes' like Norman Shillingsworth may well have complicated his championing of Aboriginal rights, given what he wrote to Elkin about 'half-caste' 'hate' for Aborigines:

Halfcastes invariably hate Aborigines, the imagined cause of their debasement. I know of very few halfcastes in this country who can be anything but cruel to a blackfellow … Halfcastes are a deep study in themselves. Except for a few who have been reared in camps, they have nothing in common with the natives. Psychologically they are

just white orphans with a special sort of shame in their race that
drives them mad. (Elkin Archives, 22 December 1937)

If anyone had a 'special sort of shame in their race' then it was Herbert,
who saw himself as a 'white orphan' when it came to his identity as a
white man. An identification with 'half-castes' led Herbert to ponder
his own inferiority as a white man. He wrote to Stephensen, 'I love them
and envy their nationality. Curse the fates that arranged that I should
be born a colonial pommy' (de Groen & Hergenhan 200, 70). He wrote
to Dibley, 'Is he [Dan] not a born bushman? Is he not infinitely superior
to me in his knowledge of moving boulders & shoveling earth and split-
ting logs? I find that my comparative ignorance in these matters irks
me' (de Groen & Hergenhan 2002, 26).

Aboriginal heritage and his whiteness continued to provoke him to
question his belonging: 'Truly, I've come to envy these half castes their
heritage, so much so that, for all my love of the soil & all my pride in
being born of it, I must confess that I'm simply an invader' (de Groen
& Hergenhan 2002, 71). Herbert's conclusion here, that he's 'simply an
invader', confirms Tony Birch's stunning observation that if 'the white
Australian tries to find his Aboriginal face in the mirror, he may come
to see his own face as the face of the oppressor' (2004, 177). In Herbert's case, his failure to find his 'Aboriginal face' also inspired in him an
apparent desire to 'assert ... [him]self in other ways'. Later he wrote to
Arthur Dibley that 'there is no hope of my ever being able to claim the
right to live in this land unless I infuse my very blood into the Aboriginal race' (de Groen & Hergenhan 2002, 71). He wrote to Stephensen
that 'Some day I shall father a Euraustralian so as to truly root myself in
this dear earth and so as to legitimise my bastard white fella genius' (de
Groen & Hergenhan 2002, 71). Rather than looking for his own Aboriginal face in the mirror, he sought legitimation by reflecting back the
gaze of a 'Euraustralian' child. Herbert presented himself as a mirror, a
tool by which to capture, narcissistically, a national gaze.

Had Herbert's desire to father a 'Euraustralian' been known to
Cook, he would have come under some suspicion, as it was Cook's
job to manage white–Aboriginal relationships. Herbert once described
himself as 'the biggest gin-rooter in the Territory' (Richards quoted in
de Groen 1998, 63). If he did have relationships with Aboriginal women, then he would have been one of the white men that Cook sought

to domesticate through marriage (marrying them and their families to the white nation) or warn off. Herbert presented himself as one of the many dingoes that the Protector had to fend off. He 'hated him [Cook] for interfering with their rights as the stronger animals' (1990, 272).

Breeding out/breeding in

While Cook was campaigning to 'breed out the colour', Herbert was dreaming of 'breeding in' the Indigeneity. This conjunction allows us to question what the differences might be between these apparently opposite strategies (particularly when, as Ahmed points out, each expulsion of the Other is simultaneously an incorporation (2000, 52). Both strategies sought to secure a white presence in the Northern Territory; both were based on a sense of the natural (either in science or in law) illegitimacy or precarity of the white presence in the Territory; both sought to use Aboriginality to improve whiteness, to provide it with roots, heritage, stamina of skin and intelligence; both were biopolitically interested in the maintenance of white-Australian life in some triumphant form.

Herbert's 'son of the soil' nationalism was not so far removed from Cook's state-sanctioned future vision of a white nation, since both placed Aboriginal people at the source of white belonging. Cook was paternalistic while Herbert wanted to father 'Euraustralians' – a dialectic that does not unsettle or displace whiteness but articulates it. The two are conjoined by opposition, an opposition that maintains power over what it excludes from the dialectic – Aboriginal voices in the matter. Between the two white men, Cook and Herbert, was a relationship of homosocial intimacy (Sedgwick 1985) rather than a enmity that is often (melo)dramatised: 'I have loved him too much in my time & have only suffered for it' (Herbert quoted in de Groen & Hergenhan 2002, 120).

Herbert's identification with Aboriginal people as their superior interpreter and possessor as well as his imaginative insertions of himself as the figure of the 'half-caste' renders his whiteness both critically self-conscious and blind to its appropriations, as de Groen and Hergenhan point out (2000, xi). Basil Sansom describes Herbert as 'self-consciously expert in the grammar of Aboriginal cultural practice', and describes his work as follows: '[t]his whitefella author takes over (appropriates, steals, purloins, pirates, lifts, liberates or loots) the dynamic that inheres in Aboriginal ridicule stories' and then demonstrates 'a purloining author's consequent discomfort and haunting unease' (2006, 88). The 'haunting unease' that Sansom finds in Herbert's work is detectable in relation to Herbert's desires to 'wreck' Cook: 'I shall wreck Cook ... & all of his cronies' (de Groen & Hergenhan 2002, 130). It was Cook who was Other: he could not survive under the Northern Territory sun and was really white-white, whereas Herbert aspired to be something else.

The red (burnt), white (skin) and blue (eyes) depiction of Cook in Herbert's work (and in what follows it) operates as oblique criticism directed at Cook's controversial policies and severs him from the kinds of whiteness that Herbert perceived to be deserving of a voice in the nation – a kind of whiteness that was informed by Aboriginality, if not appropriative of it. The rumour about Cook being an albino works through the maligned figure of the albino (and his/her status as social outcast) to insist, spectrally, visually, that interest in Aboriginality said more about a threatened and threatening form of whiteness – or, to be more precise, two different threatened and threatening forms of whiteness that were on the surface opposed (one whiter than the other) and yet conjoined by their commitment to make something of Aboriginality in the name of a white Australia.

Herbert's depiction of white skins and bodies can tell us something about the competitive nature of white belonging in Australia, by which I mean not principally the white competition with Aborigines to belong, but more its other manifestation, the white competition with other whites to see who belongs more than the other: who is more at home and who is more foreign in relation to Aboriginality. Such competition to be 'at home' in Australia requires encounters with 'strange bodies' to act in contrast, to be precisely not 'at home or in place' (Ahmed 2000, 46). This competition between whites (to be less Other, less strange, less foreign, less 'the invader', less white) requires a possessive interest in Aboriginality itself, which represents a promise of true belonging that, like a prize, is symbolic and squabbled over.

Such an observation holds true today. Mary Ellen Jordan notes that amongst whites in the north there 'was a covert, relentless competition among Balandas [non-Aboriginal people] where each tried to prove that they were better at talking to Aboriginal people than the others –

more ethical, less racist, less patronising, more egalitarian … I was disgusted with myself for buying into it and made an effort to stop' (2005, 139). Kim Mahood, a white Australian writer, recalls that her skin name

> gives me a link, a way of being here that circumvents my whiteness. It has allowed me to claim a kind of belonging that I have never felt. I have used it to claim a certain credibility among urban friends for my knowledge of Aboriginal society … I have invested myself with its glamour. (2000, 125)

Cook and Herbert's relationship (sometimes friendship, sometimes enmity) was also an example of such tensions. Cook the albino, came to stand for that which is outside of the political community of Herbert's 'son of the soil' future. Cook's allergic, extreme whiteness contrasts with Herbert as father of Euraustralian perfection. In this way, whiteness competes with different accounts of itself for access to a legitimacy conferred by other strangers brought in as familiars. Herbert promoted himself and his access to Aboriginality as a source of difference from men like Cook and ideological forms of whiteness that threatened and excluded him. 'Breeding out the colour' brings into perspective a desire for breeding in the colour, with colour signalling the red, white, blue, cream, caramel and yellow combinations that whiteness could ideologically swallow up and call true belonging.

Colour and Indigeneity

Colour, in Herbert's fiction, slips into meaning Indigeneity. Colour in Cook's work is predominantly used to describe a biological trait of the skin. But it was also much more. If Cook wanted to see it bred out, then it must have been more to him than merely biology; it must have also had a cultural significance too. He also saw it as a desirable trait to breed in to white Australians. And as Patrick Wolfe observes, other coloured groups were not targeted for breeding out or in in such a way (Wolfe 2001, 2).[6] Why only Aboriginal people?

Wolfe argues that the reason why the 'white authorities have generally accepted – even targeted – indigenous people's physical substance (synechdocally represented as blood) for assimilation into their own stock' is that Aboriginal people had/have something that whites want, something that no other racial group has, which is 'rival claims to the land' (2001, 2–3). For Wolfe, incorporation served to reduce this claim to the land. While other 'coloured' groups were excluded from the nation, Aboriginal people were 'shifted from exteriority to one of interiority … since no external homeland could plausibly be assigned to Aborigines' (2001, 12). Aboriginal people could not be deported (like the 'Kanakas') or restricted on entry (like the Chinese, Malay or Japanese, for instance). They could not be Othered in the same way as those with a plausible homeland were. They are at home already. This represents both threat and opportunity for a white settler culture that was and is anxious and adamant about its belonging. As Irene Watson explains:

> In the process of absorption we are to be consumed by the state and its citizens and in their consumption of us, they are to become us. They anticipate coming into their own state of lawfulness through the consuming of our sovereign Aboriginality. In this colonising process of us becoming white and white becoming Indigenous, white settlement deems itself as coming into its own legitimacy, as whites come into the space of our freedom to roam as Aboriginal peoples all over our Aboriginal places and spaces. (Watson 2005, 41)

Watson demonstrates the connections between terra nullius and the incorporation and consumption of Aboriginality through assimilation. This incorporation is predicated on settler anxiety regarding the illegitimacy of possession, characterised within postcolonial theory as a crisis of belonging, a state of 'inbetween-ness' or 'neither/nor', and elaborated on in the early works of Australian postcolonial critics Bill Ashcroft, Helen Tiffin and Gareth Griffiths (1989). Terry Goldie (1989) and Stephen Slemon (1990) point out that the presence of the indigene marks for the settler a desire for a sense of belonging that is associated with indigenous people themselves, both symbolically and in the very certain terms articulated by Aileen Moreton-Robinson.

---

6   The children of relationships between Aboriginal women and men of other races were not targeted for incorporation into the white nation. They were, however, subject to removal policies and intervention designed to curtail the outnumbering of whites (see Regina Ganter 2006).

Moreton-Robinson explains the difference between the postcolonial migrant to Australia and Aboriginal people:

> Our [Indigenous] ontological relationship to land, the ways that country is constitutive of us, and therefore the inalienable nature of our relation to land, marks a radical, indeed incommensurable, difference between us and the non-Indigenous. This ontological relation to land constitutes a subject position that we do not share, and which cannot be shared, with the postcolonial subject whose sense of belonging in this place is tied to migrancy. (2003, 31)

Moreton-Robinson's articulation of Indigenous belonging as unassimilable into the white nation is a powerful statement of difference and resistance in the face of various strategies of violent inclusion that postcolonial Australia has attempted. These strategies of inclusion are designed, according to Goldie's *Fear and temptation: representations of the Indigene*, to 'erase' the 'separation of belonging' (1989, 12) that the settler feels. The ambivalent feelings that Herbert expressed (a desire to belong and a feeling of inadequacy) attests to the reversals, complexities and projections inherent in postcolonialism where settlers situated themselves as 'not at home', as alien, while attempting to make alienation from land and culture a material condition of Aboriginal people; getting 'them' out of the way in order to claim priority and non-alien-ness. These strategies of erasure, in the case of Australian postcoloniality, take different forms, from the myth of terra nullius, to the containment of Aboriginal people on reserves and within identity boundaries determined by 'blood quantum regulations' (the phrase is Wolfe's, evoking Aboriginality measured and bounded in parts and by degrees: 'quartercaste', 'half-caste', 'octoroon' [2006, 388]).

The argument that Aboriginality ceases with fair skin still circulates, without the use of terms like 'half-caste' or 'quartercaste', terms which would be rejected by many as racist in contemporary Australia. However, the 'fair skinned Aboriginal' or phrases such as 'one-sixteenth Aboriginal' are still employed to query and dispute Aboriginality. Such phrases still ascribe to whites the power to erase Aboriginality, excluding the possibility of their being via consuming and incorporating them within whiteness. This belief is no doubt partly a residue of the policy of breeding out the colour that Cook and others promoted. It makes skin

talk in place of Aboriginal life and culture, a slippage that Cook and
Herbert both learnt to exploit for different reasons, but with a similar
faith in white paternity. Both Cook and Herbert situated white paternity as some kind of solution to white precariousness, inferiority of skin,
stamina and secondary belonging built from invasion. The white fathers would and could, in these fantasies, keep their sons, daughters and
wives in line with Australian whiteness. What Herbert imagined, but
Cook could not, is that the opposite could also happen. In proximity
to Aboriginal wives, kin and culture, white men could be transformed
completely, as Bill Harney frequently claimed. The 'combo', as Harney
proclaimed himself, 'bred' neither in nor out of whiteness or Aboriginality (in the terms that Cook or Herbert might dream them). The
combo claimed something in-between; neither slippage nor uplift, the
combo was, for Harney, 'on a level with the half caste woman with
whom he lives' (1943, 188).

The combo

Strange, is it not, how people in trying to forget or bury the past, will make everyone aware of the very thing which they are trying to hide?
Bill Harney (1943, 186)

The future of the native rests on segregation and control.
Patrol Officer WE Harney, Native Affairs Branch, 6 April 1944
(NAA: F1 1944/275)

Bill Harney (1895–1962) described relationships between Aboriginal women and white men as transformative, and that being open about them exposed the 'sham and hypocrisy' of cruel liars and the lie of uplift:

Talk about the uplift of the half-caste! … what matters is not the raising of the half caste to our supposed level, whatever that may be, but the man's getting on a level with the half caste woman with whom he lives, for in that way alone lies a perfect understanding and a finish of sham and hypocrisy. (1943, 188)

In this, Harney introduced a different spatial claim, that of 'getting on a level with' rather than uplifting. For Harney, what was important was being level and grounded, both of which connote equality, truthfulness and intimacy.

In Harney we find the most comprehensive articulation of what it means to be grounded as a bushman: knowing the land, being familiar with Aboriginal epistemologies, loving an Aboriginal woman and children, sharing the campfire, sharing the stories and the lore of the bushman, and guarding their secrets. And from Harney we also get glimpses of how bushmen positioned Aboriginal women as an integral part of their identity as 'men of the bush', as transforming them from *this* ('strait laced scoffers of "Combos" ') to *that*: a combo with 'a new way of life'. Harney said that he had 'seen that thing happen again and again, and the transformation was complete' (1958, 50–51).

Other terms used to describe white men who lived with Aboriginal women included 'degenerates', 'isolates' (Kinnane 2005) and 'black sheep', all of which are terms usually applied from above, from outside. It is significant that there were so many different terms for white men who cohabited with Aboriginal women. Each term was an indication of something beyond normative whiteness, hinting at mixture, combinations, and hidden, secretive lives, but also, particularly in relation to Harney's use of combo, an identity – distinct and self-defining, with a 'way of life' that marked a difference. A combo was, in Harney's work, more of a self-description by a person making strategic choices about his identity, rather than someone whose identity had slipped (as in 'degenerate'), or become obscured in the margins, as in 'black sheep', or 'isolate'.

Bill Harney: bushie and teller of tales

Anyone writing or speaking about Bill Harney would be acutely aware that Harney, if he were here, would be 'itching' to have his say and give the subject, apparently any subject, 'hell' (1943, 56). Barry Hill wrote that Bill Harney was 'simply always speaking' (2002, 281). When he wasn't speaking, Harney was writing. He was one of the most prolific writers of the 20th-century bushmen of the Northern Territory, author of ten books including *Taboo* (1943), *North of 23 degrees* (1946), *Brimming billabongs* (1947), *Life among the Aborigines* (1957), *Content to lie in the sun* (1958), *Tales from the Aborigines* (1960), *Grief, gaiety and the Aborigines* (1961), *To Ayers Rock and beyond* (1963), *Songs of the songmen: Aboriginal myths retold* (with AP Elkin, 1968) and *The shady tree* (with Douglas Lockwood, 1963). His books are largely reminiscences of his time in the Territory. The *Oxford companion to Australian literature* describes him as a 'skillful raconteur, [who] coloured his writing with wealth of bush lore and bush humour' (1994, 344).

Leaving school at the age of 12 in 1907, Harney started out as a drover but worked a variety of jobs, especially during the Depression. He worked as a ringer, beachcomber, salt pan miner, soldier in World War I, boatman, trepang trader, fence maker, road builder, patrol officer for the Native Affairs Branch (1940–1947), the first park ranger at Ayers Rock (as it was then called), and of course as a writer, or rather a teller of tales in written form, but also on the radio, at the campfire and wherever else there was a conversation to be had. Because Harney died before completing it, his last book, *The shady tree*, was finished by Douglas Lockwood who had been a friend of Harney's for 20 years. Death had the final word, but only just. Harney's last words in his notebook read:

> As I sat at my neighbour's table, I felt queer. The next thing I knew, Dr Winn Fowlles was leaning over me and gave me an injection. As in a dream I heard him say, 'He has had a heart attack. He must have rest'. (1990, 241)

He was found dead the next day, New Year's Eve, 1962, aged 68, having almost written up his own death.

Over his 20 years of writing, Harney contributed to a youthful Australian anthropology with early drafts of Aboriginal legends and culture, and also critiques of European culture that many would have found difficult to swallow. The influence of his friend and supporter, AP Elkin (professor of anthropology at the University of Sydney from 1933 to 1956) is obvious in earlier texts like *Taboo*, for which Elkin also wrote the introduction. Elkin's comparatively stiff and formal academic prose explicitly seeks to authorise Harney's text, represented as 'accounts' but structured like short stories. Though Elkin's anthropological credentials might have brought academic validity to Harney's stories, it is likely that the reverse was also true, that Harney taught Elkin more than a thing or two about Aboriginal culture. Morphy writes that 'Most anthropologists, if they are honest, have their Bill Harneys' (1996, 173). By the time Harney had published his first book, he had been living and working in the Northern Territory for over three decades and had amassed considerable knowledge of Aboriginal culture.

Elkin promoted the view that Harney's work described Aboriginal people 'as they were', a phrase that rankles today, and one that seemed out of step with Harney who was less likely to make such grand claims. It would have been difficult for him to write of his friends, his lovers, his wife and his children, as a singular people in Elkin's anthropological sense. Not that he didn't sometimes try. He did so especially when he felt his outsider status keenly, for instance: 'although I was married into *these people* and a part of my family's life, I was just "nothing" to the women who sat and chanted their life giving songs to my ailing wife' (70, emphasis added). Unlike Elkin, Harney had Aboriginal friends to remind him daily, if necessary, of the limitations of his knowledge – friends like Ruby, whom Harney wrote about as teasing him for his supposed expertise: 'I … claimed, as she put it, "to know a little of their customs", – this last part was always said with cynicism' (1961, 116), or Jununju whose 'smile' at his constant questions Harney interpreted as Jununju seeing him as a 'silly whitefellow who think[s] … [he] knows everything and know[s] nothing' (1961, 182). Jununju gave Bill Harney one of his nickmames – Ebumbarboo – meaning 'rock head', which implied that his constant questions revealed his limitations, his 'proper humbug', rather than his all-encompassing knowledge. That Harney included in his writing those moments when he was perceived by his Aboriginal friends as a rock head, ignorant outsider, or even as 'one of the hated conquerors', and by his wife's family as 'nothing', is evidence of a different sort of claim to know based not on abstraction or distance but on intimacy and proximity: he was close enough to know that he didn't know. His intimacy with Aboriginal people legitimised his knowledge in the eyes of Elkin (and others who sought to make use of his knowledge, especially as patrol officer), but it also exposed him to white racial insecurities.

'bushie-cum-combo-cum-beachcomber'

In Darwin in 1923 Harney perceived that to whites he was 'just a bushie-cum-combo-cum-beachcomber, and in a bracket akin to the Aborigines who wandered over the town' (1958, 95). Harney was caricatured by others over the next 20 years, as shown by this entry in society column 'Diana's diary' (a who's who of town gossip) in the *Northern Standard*:

> Two well known beach-combers, Bill Harney and Ossie Jensen, for-sook grilled goanna and dingo steak one day last week. They came to Darwin – with their boots on – and accepted an invitation by Captain Paterson to dine with him on the 'Culcairn' and ate off real plates. Capt Paterson's ears are reported to be still burning, or at least, they were when he left Darwin. ('Diana's diary', *Northern Standard*, 13 May 1949, 10)

When this was written, Harney was on to his fourth book, and that was *Songs of the songmen* with Elkin, which came out in 1949. The books were popularly received and well reviewed, and perhaps the tone of this particular entry above reflected not just Darwin's class-conscious fron-tier society, but also acted as a check on Harney, pulling him back into his place, lest he got all high and mighty with his new-found fame and recognition. His books were perceived to be sympathetic to Aboriginal people, as a review of *North of 23* in 1947 indicated: 'Harney misses no opportunity in his books of plugging the cause of black brother, and in *North of 23* he makes no exception to this rule' ('Book reviews', *Northern Standard*, 14 February 1947, 4). This outspokenness placed him at odds with many white residents in the Northern Territory, par-ticularly those who would measure his racial loyalty in terms of white civility, eating off 'real plates'. Bill Harney had been a critic of this social column in previous years; the following letter to the editor from Har-ney demonstrated his contempt for its class commentary:

> Sir, as a reader of the *Northern Standard* and reading your par. Re. 'criticisms', I offer one with reference to Diana's Diary. This much read and appreciated topical sheet, in my opinion, should be kept free of any cliché, idiom or hackneyed words when dealing with sec-tions of our community. It should be absolutely free of suggestions regarding class, so that all sections of society could read it without feeling it is attacking them. In other words, it should be, as I would like to see it, a newsletter or diary giving out social and topical events of the town and bush. – Yours etc, WE Harney. ('To the editor', *Northern Standard*, 20 June 1947, 6)

Harney was by this stage a keen observer of white racism and its up-lifting class dimension. He was a critic and observer not as one who denounces from outside (that would have been impossible), but one who wrote from a sense of being implicated in presumptions of white cultural superiority, while also subject to censure by other whites, especially after his marriage in 1927 to Linda Beattie, an Aboriginal woman. Harney pointed out that white men who married Aboriginal women at that time 'met the full pressure of the colour conflict' (1961, 46). To some, Harney would always be, in the words of Jessie Litchfield in a letter to Elkin, 'a filthy little combo who goes native because he is a dis-grace to his white skin' (September 1934). For Harney, such views could only be expressed by an 'ignorant bigot' (1958, 50). Contradicting and qualifying this 'sentiment' (as he called it) that saw white men as degen-erate and the Aboriginal women they lived with as degraded, became one of the main driving forces, I believe, in Harney's writing. His mem-oirs were uniquely shaped by a range of responses available to him as white man, bushie and combo who 'met the full pressure of colour con-flict'. This chapter seeks to understand those pressures on a white man like Harney and also his specific responses to them. The pressure he felt was, I believe, implicated in the silence-shaped gaps in his memoirs and his keen ear for public secrecy, a skill honed at the campfire and the oral tradition of the bushman.

Harney: teller of tales

For such a popular Australian author, it seems surprising that Harney's writing has not received much critical or scholarly attention. Jan Wos-itzky's radio documentary 'Bilarni' was aired on Australia Day 2011, reprising Harney's story for settler nationalism, which is still seemingly attached to the white bushman as its surrogate Indigene. Harney's Aus-tralia Day airing echoes how easily he seems to slot into place as, in Manning Clark's words, a 'Dinkum Aussie', 'the very essence of Old Australia' (1983).

The idea of Harney may be popularly embraced, but his writing is less well received. Barry Hill's assessment is indicative. For Hill, Har-ney is 'no great writer and his sentiments were as raw as a socialist realist' (2002, 279). But Hill reserves admiration for Harney's tenacity in writing 'against the grain of dominant views in the Territory' and as producing 'really, a setting down of what could not be written in the official records, a laconic revelation of the hidden life of the Territory' (2002, 280) and for placing 'white secrets in the open as much as the anthropologists were prone to place black secrets' (2002, 281). Tigger Wise describes Harney as the 'uncomplicated Territorian ... short, stocky, paunchy, usually dressed in shorts' (1985, 173). Nicholas Jose describes Harney in highly romantic terms: 'He came to identify with Aboriginal people and it changed him. He spoke with their voice' (2002, 103). These views position Harney as uncomplicated, frank, raw, authentic. In part this view is the result of taking Harney at his word, which is to say that he downplayed the writerliness of his writing.

In fact, Harney attempts to construct his texts as yarns told at the campfire, where his stories appeared raw, real, true, authentic and unambitious. Harney wrote: 'I am only a bushman, who does not claim to be a writer, but only a teller of tales. You must imagine us as around a large fire' (1946, 263). The distinction between the writer who had a claim and the bushman who was only the teller of tales is significant for both how Harney wrote and what he wrote about. Harney's trick was to obscure how this campfire was a cooking of the books while simultaneously making a claim for rawness.

Harney was not 'orientated' as a writer, to use Sara Ahmed's phrase. In *Queer phenomenology*, Ahmed analyses how the orientation of the writer at the writing table itself situates the writer within a 'familiar order', with certain objects and their histories placed tellingly in the background or foreground depending on that orientation. Harney did not write self-consciously of himself at a writing table. There is no mention of him taking up a place in the house he eventually owned, where he might write, be 'writerly'. He was more interested in imagining himself back at the campfire, the bush camp, at places without tables at all and the groundedness that is implied by that absence: 'Sitting here as I write these lines, my mind returns to my mates in the bush' (1972, 122). He did of course 'write' on something, sometimes on his swag in a tent, leaning on his leather bag of notes, or in a chair overlooking the water at his camp at Two Feller Creek, and probably also at a table of some sort, but he didn't discuss writing, rather storytelling. He referred to this often in his books; that is, he was self-conscious of his method in producing rambling yarns that placed him and the reader at the campfire. The full quotation situates us at the campfire, with Aborigines in the background also telling stories within earshot:

> My tale is like a piece of fine silky cotton, which bursting from its pod in a cotton bush, has floated away to be carried by the light breeze over the land, to come to rest at last in some spot to live or die, according to its own quality or on the soil in which it lies. And should you, patient reader, have come thus far with me on these rambles, remember that I am only a bushman, who does not claim to be a writer, but only a teller of tales. You must imagine us as round a large fire. The billy is nearly boiling and the Blackman is chanting away down by the creek. Old Billymuk is down at the camp, telling his people a good story about an incident which happened this day. He tells his story, as I tell mine. (1946, 263)

Like Ahmed's writing table, the campfire orientated the body tellingly, with a 'familiar order' and 'gendered form of occupation' (59). But when I imagine myself as 'the patient reader' in this text, at the campfire with Bill Harney, there are also unfamiliar orders within earshot (and not least my own presence as a white woman in a place where white women were not 'talked about' [1946, 174]). Harney tells us that Old Billymuk 'tells his story, as I tell mine', and this provides literal background to his yarn but also a parallel and different oral tradition that Harney brings in to authenticate his own.

Stephen Kinnane and Glen Stasius (2010) point out that in Aboriginal cultures, the campfire is the traditional site for knowledge transfer and for enacting knowledge in specific places, places which are known as and by storying, and stories whose telling legitimates a connection with place. Blagg notes that campfire storytelling also reflects Aboriginal etiquette and a style of conflict resolution that deflects direct aggression: 'the fire itself absorbs some of the potential conflict, and allows people to avoid direct eye contact' (Blagg 1997, 488, footnote 18). The oral tradition in which Harney 'wrote' was drawn into dialogue with an Aboriginal tradition, even though it located it at a different campfire, doing something similar but not shared.

It is tempting to see Harney's rejection of writerliness in favour of the campfire as a rejection of boss culture, city culture, national culture and its pretensions, and also a reification of the groundedness of his narratives (leading to Hill's sense of the rawness and truth of his writing). It is also possible to read this invitation to the campfire, this incorporation into campfire culture, as an attempt to keep an eye on us, to bring us in in order to protect the bushman's many secrets. As much as the campfire may have been romanticised as a site of sharing knowledge, it was coded with its own orientations, not least being the siting of Aboriginal people in the background within earshot and women, especially white women, preferably neither seen nor heard, especially when the best stories, the ones that couldn't be printed, as Harney repeatedly tells us, were being told. The effect of this was to authorise those stories that he did tell, but also to highlight the fact that we readers were not at those campfires but in the company of a writer who had felt it necessary to censor.

Linda Harney was attentive to the censorious presence of a woman, even if Harney might have sometimes pretended not to be: 'Linda often warned me that if she happened to be in bed and my mates visited our camp, to stress on them that she was fast asleep. By doing that she would be on to the taboo tales from the storytellers' (1961, 30–31). He referred to the bushmen's tales as the 'outlets of a robust life free from inhibitions. They were the bawdy stories that belonged to our early literature which came from the earth-people, and the pity is that so few have been recorded in full detail' (1961, 50).

The Borroloola Library's magic spell

Harney's writing was full of literary references from Jane Austen, Banjo Paterson, Henry Lawson, Rider Haggard, Herodotus, Marx and Freud. Harney had only three years of education in a state school, leaving school at age 12 to go droving. His education came from the campfire, the Aboriginal knowledge told to him by his Aboriginal friends and co-workers, and from his time in the Borroloola jail. Three months in the Borroloola jail in the 1920s (awaiting his appeal on cattle-stealing charges) was described by Harney as 'one of the turning points in my life' (1946, 106). Borroloola in the 1920s was a town with a police station, a jail, a courthouse, a sly-grog shop, some shanties, a handful of white and mixed-race residents in the country of the Yanyuwa, Mara and the Garrwa people, and a library with 3000 leather-bound books up for borrowing by anyone who could read.

The 'Carnegie Library' (as it was known, inaccurately) at Borroloola was started when in 1895 the first policeman, Cornelius Power, decided it would be a good idea to set up a learning and arts institute for the whites in that remote 'wild west' town. The Governor of Victoria, Lord Hopetoun, soon to be the first Governor General of Australia, responded to Power's requests for help and organised a shipment of 1000 leather-bound books delivered by boat to Borroloola in 1901. By the 1920s when Bill Harney was imprisoned there, there were around 3000 books. In that 'little cell' for three months, Harney read and read, only stopping to eat and at night when the light failed. When the light failed he and his cell mates discussed the books they had read that day. If they got too loud the police guard would yell at them. That library 'cast its magic spell' over the bushmen of the Northern Territory (1946, 105). In those books he 'sailed and travelled everywhere' (1946, 106). By the 1950s most had been borrowed for good or lost, the rest eaten by termites,[1] leaving only a page of Thomas a Kempis' *The imitation of Christ* behind. This brings a hint of a smile to the young face of David Attenborough in his 1963 documentary called *The hermits of Borroloola*.

Bill Harney's experiences with these books in the Borroloola jail changed his life, the 'magic spell' that turned him to writing perhaps. But the campfire was also significant too. On one of his first jobs, still a young man, he described campfire culture as strictly enforced:

> At night after supper we would gather round the fire and tell stories or sing songs. Each one had to sing a song or recite a poem; failure to do so would mean instant ducking in the bore drain or water hole. All had their turn, for on those plains washing was at a discount. Lawson, Ogilvie, Paterson would be recited. Strange too, most loved of all was Gordon's 'To my sister'. My favourite song was 'Taps'. I didn't like singing, but I dreaded the cold water, so I sang. (1946, 38)

---

1   For a very interesting discussion on the Borroloola Library, see Ramona Koval speaking with Jan Wositzky, Ted Egan, Nicholas Jose and Peter Forrest, 'The ants that ate Plutarch' on Radio National, 15 June 2002.

Decades later, campfire culture appeared more voluntary, though still competitive, even combative:

> You see we had few books, and in our packs would only carry those full of meat: Shakespeare, Herodotus, Plutarch, Emerson, Marx. Each of us became a disciple of his tome and in the arguments at night would try to slay his opponent with excerpts from his book of knowledge. (1946, 80)

He never said which book of knowledge he embodied, but he mentioned that his 'tattered Shakespeare', his *Othello*, whose 'tender parts' brought tears to his eyes, was his 'wandering friend ... I carried that book for years' (1946, 17).

Yarn spinning, nicknames and protection

Mary Ann Jebb reads one of Harney's predecessors, Ion Idriess, and emphasises how Idriess wrote to disguise and shelter his mates and his informants from any accusation of wrongdoing (2002, 21). Harney also obscured his mates and their wrongdoings in his yarns; indeed it is the very nature of the yarn to obscure and reveal simultaneously. One example of this is in the consistent use of nicknames throughout his books. From one period when he was camped in Katherine with his wife and children we get the following nicknames of fellow doleites and bushies. There was The Student, so called 'because of his retentive memory and vast knowledge' but who was also called Billy Goat to the Aboriginals 'in reference to his past performances with the native girls' (1961, 99). There was Keep It Dark, so called because as a conspiracy theorist his speech was littered with that phrase. There was The Spotted Wonder with his freckly face, One Spud Gus, Big Ned, Bull Tosser, Paddy Lame Leg, and Trotting Cob, who walked at a trot and was mentally unstable (1961, 127). There was The Baron with his posh, affected speech. There was Tarzan, writing a book called 'The ethics of utopian philosophy'. There was Dugong because of his 'fat appearance and his never-ending talk about that sea mammal' (87); The Brain Specialist; Long John the Russian peanut farmer; Crocodile Bill, so called on account of his 'eating ability' (157); and The Roma Terror, 'given his name from the tales he told of his pugilisitic days in that Queensland town' (163). There was Stallion Joe, 'an appellation given not for his sexual tendencies but because he was an Italian' (140) and the Aborigines were not able to pronounce 'Italian'. There was also The Anthropologist, who waxed lyrical about different cultural belief systems. Harney tells us that the nicknames 'are a survival from the natives, who always pick out a suitable name for a newcomer' (1946, 45).

But in a later book he also wrote that 'most of the doleites went under some nickname as a sort of protective instinct' (1961, 84). It's not clear whether or not Harney even knew what their 'real names' were – suffice it to say, having a nickname made it easier to obscure whatever terrors, whatever horrors, they might have witnessed or been part of. Billy Goat/The Student had come to the Territory when, according to him, 'the tucker was just damper and salt meat … our wages – the pick of the "Studs" ', adding, ' "if I done anything wrong to the Blacks in the past I'm sorry" ' (1961, 99). We don't know who this man is, where or what he refers to here, but we read his 'sorry'. The campfire was no place for culpability. This 'sorry' in its anonymity is a little like other apologies written in blue skies and sorry books. Like the 'sorry' uttered at the campfire, tracked by Harney, we are left without details, dates, places. Then again, Harney was probably able to reveal more by not naming. It is a device that Harney uses to put white men on trial, in lieu of that happening in real life.

In *Taboo*, he told the story of a particularly sadistic white man who murdered an Aboriginal man because he wanted his wife. Harney named the white man 'Jim Crow'. He wrote, 'Jim Crow (the name is false)' (1943, 94), and this is the only time that he explicitly tells us he uses a false name. So, the name is true in a different, Harney sense. For Harney, the most sadistically cruel white men were those who in public were segregationist but in private claimed rights over Aboriginal women. I take up Harney's proposition in a following chapter, 'Jim Crow', named after Harney's observation.

In relation to names given to Aboriginal people by whites, Harney was especially critical. He wrote in *Taboo* that 'people who believed firmly in the stupidity of the aborigines [sic] called them names such as this – Daylight, Brumby, Frog, Billy-can and of course, Pumpkin.' He put it down to slavery: the 'pride of possession in man, possibly a survival of the days when people were bought and given a new name by the owner, was perhaps the cause' (1943, 179).

Given the prevalence of nicknames in the Northern Territory, a man who did not have a nickname was 'special'. Like Roger Jose, *just* Roger Jose. And then Bill Harney, mostly known as Bill Harney, or 'Bilarni', an Aboriginal pronunciation of his full name. But then there was also 'Ebumbarboo', a name given to him by Jununju who Harney pestered for explanations of a particular myth. She was annoyed by his questions, his 'proper humbug', so she named him Ebumbarboo, meaning 'rock head'. And then there was another sort of nickname: the sandstone dibbler, *Pseudantechinus bilarni*, a carnivorous antechinus (marsupial) discovered by a team of American and Australian naturalists on expedition to Arnhem Land in 1948, accompanied by Bill Harney. The species name, *Pseudantechinus bilarni*, incorporates the Aboriginal pronunciation of Bill Harney's name. Like other antechinuses, the sandstone dibbler dies at the end of the mating season: they rut themselves into such a hot sleepless frenzy that they overheat and die.

Sexual economies

Harney was understandably sensitive to the ways that his own class of bushmen would be likely blamed for the ills of a systemic 'clash of cultures' (Pitt-Rivers 1927). Writing in the late 1950s, he was aware that the conversations he had with other white men about Aboriginal women would attract scorn today and this explains some of his reticence, self-censorship, and also his occasional attempts to distance himself from its worst aspects. The following paragraph is a good example of Harney's attempts to explain the sexual economy, while also positioning himself alongside an incredulous listener or reader:

> Strangers listening to our conversation might well have believed it was about stock exchange reports. 'Par' was a fixed fee, and the woman's value was based on that market price. Little consideration was given to the wishes of the Aborigines; the right to interfere with their lives was never questioned. To the doleites, the Aborigines' plight was on a level with their own: all were victims of the Depression. In later

years I heard much criticism about the treatment of Aborigines, and
in most cases this was justified, but at the time we were as the slum-
dwellers of the city who have become immune to their environment.
Tales such as how a doleite received a favour from one of the girls,
got her to wash his clothes, cart wood for his campfire, and give him
one of the many pups she had with her, all for sixpence, were not
treated with the scorn they would get today, but were regarded rather
as the feat of legerdemain ... Looking back on those days, I somehow
cannot believe that they ever existed, yet men, women, and children
lived through it all; night life at the Katherine never ceased to pursue
its dismal course. (1961, 140)

The inequalities, the labour of the Aboriginal women, the receipt of fa-
vours all for a sixpence, these things, Harney told us, had been a great
trick back then. But writing this looking back he could barely believe
it. Hilda Jarman Muir's account of her life in *Very big journey* recalled
Harney and his co-worker Horace Foster entrapping Aboriginal women:

I remember luggers with two masts anchored or coming up the river
while I was living at the Malarndarri Camp. Mr Harney and Mr
Foster used them to bring cargo in from Burketown. Bill Harney and
Horace Foster used to invite some of our people on board, including
women. They used to grog on, you know, and then at about lunch-
time the men would end up overboard. Whether they were thrown
or not I don't know, but the white men always kept the women.
(2004, 12)

Harney did not write about these episodes. He expressed great admiration for Aboriginal women, from 'budding belles' (1958, 59) to superior
trackers and drovers, and wives who enabled a 'perfect understanding
and a finish of sham and hypocrisy' (1943, 188). He was also prone to
monumentalise sexuality as an invited conquest, as the following Rider
Haggard-ish image suggests. Arguing that 'Australia owes a deep and
lasting debt' to the Australian Aborigines, Harney suggested that a

suitable plaque to be inscribed to them would be that of a young native woman walking into the setting sun, beckoning, beckoning to a

group of men coming on – settlers, mariners, prospectors, following on into the unknown, lured by the promise of an Eldorado. (1946, 83)

Colonialism is here depicted as an embrace, alluring, something to be beckoned. Such an image is in keeping with Harney's bushman ethic, caught between paying tribute to Aboriginal women as central, crucial to the genesis of the bushman, while also obscuring complicity in colonial power behind an image of a loving embrace.

During the Depression, at the dole camps the stories were 'an outlet for our emotions in that place of despair' (1946, 144). Favourite stories that he did repeat were those that showed white authorities to be hypocritical regarding sexual relations with Aboriginal women:

the one about a bushman who was sworn in as a local constable. He liked the job until he was ordered to go and arrest his bush mate on a charge of cohabiting with a female Aboriginal. As he was living with one himself at the time his mate loudly protested, so he excused himself by proclaiming that he was all right as he was the law. (1961 49)

Then there was the one about an

overgrown tadpole (the bushman's term for a conceited official) who crept one night into the servants' quarter after his Aboriginal girlfriend, and, finding his rival curled up and asleep beside her, he promptly arrested him, charging him with the very act he was about to commit himself. (1961, 49)

These tales were passed on without identifying markers, with no names, and they served to ridicule the authorities (especially when the bushman became an authority) and to declare the public secret of white man's relationships with Aboriginal women. They also indicated tactics by which those in authority (like Bill Harney when he himself was a patrol officer) could openly cover their tracks.

Harney retold other stories with caution and shame, and again they appeared in the form of hazy reminiscences, changing names, locations and giving no dates. He told the story of 'Old Marlboo with station at X creek' who used to 'lock up the girls … Each night they would be counted in by the blind old cook – one, two, three, four, five, six, etc.; click would go the lock and all was well' (1946, 77). This man would lock up 'the girls', Harney explained, because he was what was known as a 'gin shepherd'. The gin shepherd was a white man who sought to fix a claim on Aboriginal women and keep them from other white men. The 'gin burglar' was a white man who sought out one of those women for himself. Harney wrote about this with a mixture of shame, with a sense that those were the times, and sometimes with a sense of humourous disbelief. He observed that such a system of gin shepherds and gin burglars was reflected in government policies of child removal and institutionalisation: 'in the north we find two methods of watching women: the first is to watch the girls, who are kept apart and live in dormitories: the other is to watch the stranger' (1946, 151). This was just as much a description of the Aboriginal Ordinances, designed to watch the stranger, the white man, and also remove, institutionalise and possess Aboriginal women under the rhetoric of 'protection', a word removed but no less related to its bush cousin term, 'gin shepherd'.

Campfire secrets

By the time the reader is interpolated into the campfire as a patient reader (rather than listener), we can be sure that what we are reading has already passed through Harney's myth-making – disremembering, to borrow Stanner's phrase (2009, 189). Bilarni, Ebumbarboo, rock head, the 'famous author and raconteur' was not merely a revelator of Territory secrets. He worked hard to reveal and conceal simultaneously. The campfire was crucial for both revealing and concealing those territory secrets that Hill speaks of, and Harney's art was in knowing a few sides of an argument simultaneously but not letting on:

> Imagine the scene if you can:
> A station homestead, or a native camp, where amidst laughter, swimming, or maybe out hunting with their father or mother, these little half-castes would live among their own people, tended by all the tribe, and particularly by a mother who ever watches over her child and tends to its wants … Then one day that child would be taken away, and great would be the wails which came from the camp.

Blood would flow from the head of the mother, as she gashed it with stick or stone in anguish for her lost child. Yet after a few days all is forgotten, as most people forget. Nevertheless that mother still yearns for her lost one and carries little bits of its clothes around in memory of her child.

Now I saw the mission and all the people who lived there: church, garden, school – a tedious round, ending only when the young folk married and drifted out to work on the stations. With little funds, times were hard for the folk at those places. The food was rice and water, with now and then a little bread and beef. The dresses were of jute and made from flour bags. Barefooted and without hats, those girls worked in rain or sun.

The first time I saw my wife, Linda, she and other girls were hauling on a rope, dragging a jinker that carried a log of cypress timber for the sawmill. As I looked at the tense muscles of those straining forms, heaving and hauling so that timber should be cut to build a church for the glory of God, I became ashamed of all this mad, misplaced energy. Far better a hundred times that these children should be left with their mothers to grow up around the stations. (1946, 154)

Harney published this critique of the policy of child removal back in 1947, as his own seven-year stint working as a patrol officer in the Native Affairs Branch drew to a close. He described seeing his own wife Linda Harney, whom contemporary readers would now recognise as a member of the Stolen Generations, as one of many 'straining forms' depersonalised and dehumanised by hard labour at a mission. Linda Harney was an inmate of the Groote Eylandt mission where she was sent as a child, against the wishes of her mother and her white father, a man who 'to his eternal credit', Harney wrote, 'never denied her' (1961, 15). Harney described Linda's removal as happening when her father was away from camp with a herd of cattle. On his return he was 'told by a wailing Lena that the police trooper from Borroloola had taken the children away from her side and was sending them to a mission station' (15). Harney described Linda as 'one in an institution with other waifs controlled by a religious people who looked upon their charges as the offspring of low mothers and degenerate fathers' (15). Again, this is the sentiment that Harney saw as a principal source of 'colour conflict' in Australia.

Child removal and the 'happy Harney patrol'

Harney's perspective on the policy of child removal was unique and complicated in a way that he never fully explained to his readers. As a patrol officer, employed by the Native Affairs Branch between 1940 and 1948, Harney was empowered to remove 'half-caste' children from stations and send them away to designated 'half-caste institutions', and Harney was named by Lorna Cubillo in the first Stolen Generations court case which began in 1999 (*Cubillo and Gunner v. The Commonwealth [2001]*)[2] as the man who allegedly forcibly removed her from her grandmother. It could not be established during the court case whether or not this was in fact the case.

Patrol officers often left the task of removing the children to local police. Patrol officers did, however, build up the lists of names of those felt to be eligible for removal. In 1947, Harney criticised the policy of child removal from the perspective of one who might have been asked to deploy it, but also from the perspective of someone who had already experienced its cruelties in relation to his personal history: his wife's story, and also because he was himself the father of one Aboriginal daughter removed in 1940 and a son whom he had helped to hide or encouraged to be hidden from authorities. This is on the public record by virtue of Bill Harney's son Bill Yidumduma Harney, Wardaman senior elder, Songman and renowned Aboriginal cosmologist. In his biography, *Born under a paperbark tree* (1996) written with Jan Wositzky, Bill Yidumduma Harney recalls:

old Bill was frightened that the Welfare would take me away, and we were frightened too, because my sister Dulcie was taken away, around 1940, by old Bob Wood, the policeman from Katherine. According to what I was told from my mum, the policeman couldn't take me. 'He's too small' he said, 'we just take his sister'. Old Bill Har-

---

2 *Cubillo and Gunner v. The Commonwealth* (2001) AUIndigLawRpr 36; (2001) 6(3) Australian Indigenous Law Reporter 61.

ney was on a holiday at the time – somewhere, Brisbane, Sydney, I don't know where. There was no aeroplane at that time and they used to ride a boat around, and the boat dragged a bit, and by the time old Bill got back Dulcie was gone. He was upset a bit, and of course he couldn't do anything about it because of the law. He couldn't bring her back, and he reckoned 'Oh well, it doesn't matter, just leave Dulcie over there, and we'll keep Bill under cover' … So my mum was very strict and careful that I didn't get taken away. She used to get this blackcurrant plum from the bush, and it makes your hair go black.

My mum always used to crush the black plum together with a big heap of charcoal and put it all over my skin to make me go black, and when the Welfare would come along I'd be sitting right in the middle of those other blacks, and the Welfare bloke would call out, 'Any yella kids? And half-caste kids around here?'

'No, nothin' 'ere', but I'd be sitting there with them all painted up black … I was the only half caste kid that wasn't taken away from my mother to the islands, and when they were taken away they were put right outta sight for good. (Wositzky & Harney, 1996, 75)

Between approximately 1934 and 1937 (and possibly earlier) Bill Harney was with Bill Yidumduma Harney's mother, Ludi Yibuluyma, and her family, working on a project to upgrade the road. They had two children together, Dulcie and Bill, but Bill Harney was careful not to admit, in front of other whites, that they were his. Ludi Yibuluyma was not named in any of his memoirs, although it is possible that she did appear, with a different name, as one of the many Aboriginal women about whom Harney writes. This part of Bill Harney's story is known today only because Bill Yidumduma Harney wrote about his white father in his biography (Wositzky & Harney 1996), and again, though very briefly, in *Dark sparklers* (Cairns & Harney 2003). Bill Yidumduma Harney is, like his white father, a storyteller: 'it started to build up on my mind to make a book of my own' (1996, vi) because his dad had 'written a few' and 'probably his spirit flew straight across the land and over my mind' (1996, vi). Bill Yidumduma Harney's account of his father forms a relatively small part of his own life story, but what he tells the reader contextualises the significance of the gaps in Harney's memoirs. It certainly puts to rest any notion that Harney was himself 'uncomplicated' or that he casually revealed the Territory's white secrets. His insistence on incorporating the reader into the campfire, his twinning of disclosure with anonymity, indicates his own complicated weave of protection.

Protecting his secrets involved more than Harney alone. In 1990, Ruth Lockwood published a biography of Bill Harney called *A bushman's life*, which was based entirely on things that Harney wrote about himself and therefore maintained the secrecy of Dulcie, Bill Yidumduma Harney and Ludi, their mother. His friend Douglas Lockwood started the biography and when he died his wife, Ruth Lockwood, finished it. Harney and Lockwood had a friendship that spanned more than 20 years. Harney was godfather to Lockwood's daughter Dale.[3] Despite the apparent closeness of their friendship, Lockwood only learned about Dulcie and Bill Yidumduma Harney in 1961, and decided to keep that secret for him. Bill Yidumduma Harney recalls meeting with Doug Lockwood and his father for lunch one day in Darwin. He describes Lockwood as:

> surprised that I was Bill's son, and Bill was very proud of me there talking to him. Anyway, Old Doug Lockwood said, 'By jeez, he does look a bit like you all right. How come you didn't put him in the book?' Old Bill said, 'Was one of those things. I was in the Welfare and didn't want to bring it out because you know the rule they had, because the Welfare was not to be associated with any Aboriginal lady' (Wositzky & Harney 1996, 158).

The Lockwoods kept Harney's secret well after the time that he could have been in legal trouble for cohabiting, associating with or 'being within three chains' of an Aboriginal woman not legally his wife. The secret they kept thus produced an image of Harney as a childless bush-

---

3   He 'completely identified with' the Lockwood's family and was 'welcomed as though a son was coming home' (1990, 38). The 'bond was so strong' that when they went to England for two years, Harney went over to stay with them for five months (38). These are not necessarily Bill's own sentiments. *The shady tree* was a posthumous 'collaboration' with Lockwood, where Lockwood admits in the preface to doubling the length of the manuscript Harney left behind and then having 'discarded his language and substituted my own … rewrote every paragraph, adding where appropriate, his anecdotes from my memory' (Introduction).

man, the end of a line. This is in stark contrast to Bill Yidumduma Harney's account of continuity and pride in the Harney name:

'Look at me', I said, 'I didn't go to school, your grandpa old Bill Harney he had the knowledge of everything and he wrote a book about what he saw, and he didn't go to school'. I said 'He got on well with Aborigine, he left a good reputation, you gotta have a good reputation'. That's what I told the boys … And I said to Billy 'I'm Bill Harney number two, and you are Bill Harney number three. We can't throw that name away. When you grow up and have another, you can call him Bill Harney four. We got to carry that name on'. Now he's got a little baby, and he's Bill Harney number four. (1996, 196)

This pride seems so poignant in contrast to Bill Harney's non-disclosure to his reading public, his reticence with his best friend, even well after the time when he could have been in 'trouble' with the law, or with his Welfare bosses. It is possible that his white bosses and colleagues in the Native Affairs Branch knew anyway. Harney's account of his first day of work as a patrol officer is:

My first job was to acquaint myself with the laws affecting Aborigines and to read the office files. Naturally I looked to see whether I had a file. Yes, assuredly. I was interested to discover that I had been reported for things I had long forgotten, and surprised at the number of people who had grievances to settle. It soon became apparent that the people who were loudest in their condemnation of improvements in native welfare were those who had the most to lose by it … I read in the Aboriginal Ordinance that cohabiting with an Aboriginal woman was an offence punishable by law. I smiled at that attack on established custom, for I really believe that if a Kinsey report were written about the hundreds of men who have lived most of their lives with the natives it would be discovered that they were divided into two groups: those who admit it and those who don't. (1990, 122)

In Harney's view, those who didn't admit to cohabiting with Aboriginal women were likely to also hold the most racist separatist views, their shame twisted into self-loathing and hate. While admitting to cohabiting with Aboriginal women was 'healthy' and 'normal' in Harney's book, admitting to illegitimate children was clearly not something that he was prepared to do. So it would probably be more accurate to say that there were three groups of men: those who admitted it and those who didn't, and those who did or didn't, depending on who was listening. In terms of prosecutions for cohabitation, or the pursuit of maintenance, the same ambivalence would have likely applied.

It seems highly likely that Harney's relationships and his children were already subject to speculation if not actual report. When Patrol Officer Gordon Sweeney, with Cadet Officer Ted Evans in tow, listed Bill Yidumduma Harney as 'Billy Willeroo' in his patrol report dated 1947 with 'alleged father' listed as 'European', did he do so to protect Bill Harney, his fellow patrol officer (Sweeney 1947)? Or did he genuinely not know that Harney was his father? Prior to this, Cadet Patrol Officer Ted Evans had spent five months with Harney on a 'happy Harney patrol' (Evans 1990, 3) in the Gove Peninsula, Arnhem Land, where he was impressed by Harney's 'considerable ... knowledge' and the 'depth of understanding and mutual respect that existed between Bill Harney and the Aboriginal people' (2–3). Harney described Ted Evans, with whom he met up again in 1961, as his 'old mate Ted Evans' and recalled that when he was a patrol officer, 'Ted and I had worked together for several years; we had spent months alone in the bush near Yirrkala, and elsewhere in Arnhem Land' (1972, 43).

Between 1948 and 1955, Ted Evans worked on patrol in the Wave Hill and Victoria River Downs district 'and other areas' including Willeroo Station where Bill Yidumduma Harney grew up. Ted Evans' patrol officer reports from 1950 listed Bill Yidumduma Harney as 'Bill Harney', and expressed concern that those employing him as a stockman and who say that he is treated like a white man show no evidence of doing so. Bill Yidumduma Harney wrote that Ted Evans had been targeting him for removal. Twenty years later in 1971 they met up at the Dolphin Hotel in Darwin and Bill Yidumduma Harney recalled this conversation:

'Hello Ted, how are you going?'
He looked at me, he said, 'By jeez, I've seen you somewhere'.
I said, 'yeah, I'm Bill Harney'.
'Oh you, you mongrel!' he said. 'What are you doing in here? You should be back out in the bush. You're not to be anywhere near

the town. When I wanted you, I couldn't find you, now you're right on top of me, standing up right here. You're too late, everything's gone now, Welfare's all finished'. That's what old Ted said. 'God, you were a very hard man to catch! Every time I come you weren't there, always been hiding. God, you're a very hard man to catch!'

I just laughed at him. I said, 'You know your name is "Wudu wurren wujban"?'

He said, 'What's that?'

' "Wudu wurren wujban" means you was a bugger for kidnapping the kids.'

'Oh jesus, I was really going to put you right away, but I couldn't catch you', he said. 'Oh well, you're right', and that's the last I see of him … Anyway, I think they were still knocking the kids off in 1960, and that why old Bill Harney was frightened to say he was my father, because he was in Welfare, and it was against Welfare rules to be my dad! So in front of others he would say nothing, but he was still my dad, and he used to come around and treat me like he was my dad. (1996, 79–80)

It seems highly likely that Ted Evans knew that Bill Yidumduma Harney was his old mate's son. It's not clear whether or not he knew Bill Harney's views on child removal and that he had supported the hiding away of Yidumduma so that he might grow up with his culture. This is how Bill Yidumduma Harney understands the situation, that Bill Harney wanted his son to grow up with his culture, and that he feared being fined for cohabitation, and for these reasons he did not admit his paternity. Bill Yidumduma Harney recalls:

Alf said, 'That your son there?'

My dad would say, 'No, no, no, not mine'.

But in private he was my dad alright. He knew where I was, and every time he came back to Willeroo district he said 'Hello son', and say to my mum, 'How's that boy? Show him your history and the story, keep the cultural side going' …

Anyway, in front of the white man and with the Welfare blokes my dad didn't want to claim me. He was frightened because in that time Europeans weren't allowed to be associated with Aboriginals. If you were married it was against the law: 'No European was allowed to be associated with an Aboriginal lady.' You could get married if you went into the court and everybody in the government agreed, but for just associating with the Aboriginal lady it was six months jail and £1000 fine. Anyway, the European bloke couldn't go without it because there was no other white women in the country, but if the Aboriginal woman had a kid to the white man, the Welfare used to go to the Aboriginal camp and shoot the dogs off the camp, and if the kid was there they asked the Aboriginal lady, 'Who does that kid belong to?' (1996, 73)

This was the kind of question that Bill Harney, during his stint as a patrol officer (September 1940 to February 1947), would have had to have asked: 'Who does that kid belong to?' Patrol officers were employed by the Native Affairs Branch in Darwin to check on the welfare of Aboriginal people and to try to act as a 'go between' for police, station owners and Aboriginal people. They had been introduced as part of the Native Affairs Branch in the years following the Coniston massacre (1928), where between 30 and 300 Aboriginal people were massacred by a group led by Constable Murray. In 1934, there was also talk (that reached the prime minister's office) of an organised reprisal to 'teach the blacks a lesson' over in Arnhem Land, after the deaths of Japanese trepangers and the white officer sent to investigate. The trial of Dhakkiyari for the murder of the officer (Constable McColl) saw him acquitted. Within a month Dhakkiyari was dead, most probably at the hands of a lynch mob led by bitter police, as Ted Egan (himself once working as a patrol officer) argues (1996). Patrol officers working for the Native Affairs Branch came in at this point because police were seen to be incapable of acting in the interests of Aboriginal people. Olive Pink argued somewhat enigmatically that they were supposed to be 'defenders and protectors of the aborigines, as it was impossible for police to play a dual role'.[4] In other words, the police were criticised for acting only for whites. Bill Yidumduma Harney recalls the accidental death by strychnine of between 40 and 50 'wild' Aborigines. In a chapter called 'A pile of bones', Harney explains that the poison had been meant for dingoes, but the bones laced with the poison had been intercepted by

---

4 'Native Affairs Dept. Inefficient Police', Letters to the editor from Olive Pink, *Northern Standard*, 3 April 1947, 6.

Aboriginal people living nearby. The two men responsible reported it to the police:

> old Jack Mahoney at Daly Waters, and old Jack has a look, and sure enough there was a lot of dead wild Aboriginal people. In those times, if any whites got speared, the copper would be on the ball, but if Aboriginal people got shot or poisoned they just used to let it go. 'That's all right', they used to say, 'just leave it. Dingo can eat him.' (1996, 63)

The police buried the story with the pile of bones.

A patrol officer, who was supposed to have more expertise than police when it came to Aboriginal people and culture, was supposed to work as an advocate for Aboriginal people. The role had been something that Elkin was particularly keen on, and it wasn't until the late 1930s that they were brought in under the Native Affairs Branch. Elkin gave Harney his approval, as did Michael Sawtell, chairman of the committee for Aboriginal Citizenship, who published a critique of Chinnery's welfare policies in the *Northern Standard* on 31 May 1940, and ended his letter by recommending WE Harney be chosen as an 'ideal patrol officer' (Sawtell 1940, 3). Four months later, in September 1940, WE Harney took up a 'temporary position' as a patrol officer, temporary because he lacked higher education qualifications: 'I was simply a worker with a long record of living in the bush amid Aborigines and for that reason apparently I had some value' (1990, 121). He recalls that 'Chinnery and his deputy, Vincent J White, subsequently became two of my best friends' (1990, 121).

In his capacity as NT Director of Native Affairs (1938–1946), Chinnery took over from Chief Protector Cecil Cook, and he made the prosecution of white men consorting with Aboriginal women a specific target of his reforms. In 1941, Chinnery introduced amendments to the Aboriginal Ordinances that saw white men targeted for 'consorting, associating or keeping company with, an Aboriginal woman or half caste other than his wife, between the hours of sunset and sunrise'. Chinnery had tightened the ordinance because the previous law was deemed inadequate. Chinnery explained in the *Northern Standard*, 25 July 25 1941 that 'The police would catch men with native women, all intoxicated, at three o'clock in the morning ... but we could not prove a charge against the men' (1941, 3). With the aid of the new provisions, a man 'discovered with an Aboriginal or half caste woman late at night could be brought before a court and required to prove his bona fides' (1941, 3). He added that those men 'whose reputation was good, and who wanted to take a half caste girl out, say to the pictures, could get a permit from the Director who would entitle them to be out until 11.30 pm' (1941, 3). Chinnery also vastly increased the penalties for those found guilty. Harney would have been expected, as a patrol officer, to have made this ordinance part of his brief. The contradictions, the 'humbug', must surely have made his nerves jangle. He was to enforce an ordinance designed (in part) to monitor a racial line that he himself crossed many times.

'consorting, associating or keeping company with'

Going back to the period when Bill Harney was employed as a patrol officer (September 1940 to February 1948), we get a sense of the patrol and breaching of regulations designed to 'protect' Aboriginal women. In the 1940s Darwin was a segregated town, with Aboriginal people forbidden access to prohibited areas at night. On Tuesday 22 April 1941, the *Northern Standard* reported on the arrest of six Aboriginal people at Hospital Beach at 2.40 am. The charge was being in a prohibited area at night. Harney, whose job it was to assist the court when it came to prosecutions of Aboriginal people, explained that their presence on the beach was a corroboree and that Hospital Beach was a traditional meeting area. The six were convicted of the charge, without penalty, and told that 'they must not corroboree in the town'.[5] Directly underneath this report is an advertisement for an event held at the Botanical Garden five days later, featuring the regimental band of the Darwin infantry battalion alongside an 'Aboriginal Corroboree, spear throwing and musical turns'. Corroborees were acceptable in the town, but only as white managed events in the context of other cultural performances. The *Northern Standard* reported regular arrests and enforcement of segregation of white men and Aboriginal women. A white man

---

5   'Arrests at Beach Corroboree', *Northern Standard*, 22 April 1941, 12.

in November 1940 was fined five pounds with costs 'in default three weeks' imprisonment' when he was found 'within three chains of an aboriginal encampment without lawful excuse'. The white man defended himself by saying that his car had stalled, and that he had tried to 'hunt her away, but she would not go'.[6]

By far the most common concerns reported at this time involved the mistreatment of Aboriginal women and the consumption of alcohol – and the illicit trade in both women and alcohol between Aborigines and whites. One court case that got a lengthy write-up in the *Northern Standard* concerned the prosecution of a white man for committing 'grievous bodily harm' to an Aboriginal man. It was reported that the white man had approached and 'asked him for a lubra [an Aboriginal woman] but he said he was a single man and could not get one'. The white man alleged that the dispute was over the Aboriginal man asking him for drink, and that 'he had no conversation with any of the blacks about a lubra'. The white man alleged that the Aboriginal man was angry at being refused a drink, resulting first in swearing off ('he had twice called [the Aboriginal man] a black B— before [the Aboriginal man] called him a white B—') and then a savage attack that saw the Aboriginal man in hospital with lacerations and abrasions on his face and forehead. The court sentenced the white man to six months of hard labour.

Bill Harney frequently appeared on behalf of Aboriginal people on trial in Darwin: the *Northern Standard* reports that 'WE Harney, of the Native Affairs branch' was heard by the judge 'on the effect of tribal lore in mitigation of the sentence'.[7] In *Taboo*, he argued for 'tribal offences' to be kept out of the courts: 'offences other than tribal [should] be tried by the white man's court' (1943, 206). Harney's work in explaining customary law to the court, or acting as surrogate witness for the defence, put him in an unenviable position, one which often brought him and the Branch into question. In March 1941, the *Northern Standard*[8] reported criticism of the way that the Native Affairs Branch conducted its defence: ' "There seems to be far too much casualness in the Native Af-

---

6 'Found near black', *Northern Standard*, 19 November 1940, 4.
7 'Mercy Shown to Native Murderer', *Northern Standard*, 28 March 1941, 3
8 ' "Native Affairs Branch casual" says bench', *Northern Standard*, 25 March 1941, 4.

fairs Branch" Mr Leydin remarked after hearing the evidence.' Leydin argued that 'because the native is frank, he admits the charge' whereas 'in similar circumstances a white man might not have been convicted'. The court relied too much on Harney who 'examining the native, got him to admit the charge', which Leydin suggested was inadequate: 'If you merely ask the boy to admit the offence, it is not equivalent to a plea of guilty or not guilty'. Leydin was quoted as saying, 'I suggest to Mr Harney that he discuss this with the Native Affairs Branch, and sees that accused black boys are given assistance in their defence' (4). Harney was not directly quoted in the article, but it gave the impression that he and the Native Affairs Branch were criticised for presuming to know, through talking with defendants, the guilt or innocence of the accused, thereby acting as prosecution and defence simultaneously. In 1947 Olive Pink asked 'is there a "war on" between the Police Department and Native Affairs? If so, it is the aborigines who suffer for it.'[9]

It would have been in Harney's interests not to have been caught up in any such war. None of his books cover the time that he spent working for Native Affairs, though he writes in *North of 23*: 'What a story there is to tell of that time!' (1946, 262). As a patrol officer, he was a member of a group that the bushies traditionally despised, the 'khaki gentry' and, in contrast to the many years Harney, Linda Harney, and their children Bill and Beattie, had spent on the road as doleites during the Depression, he was in a position to eat at the tables of the cattle bosses over whom he had significant bureaucratic power. He could revoke their licences to employ Aboriginal people, and he could inquire into their sexual habits, as Patrol Officer Strehlow sometimes did. But Harney never did eat at the tables of the cattle bosses while a patrol officer. He explained that 'I somehow felt in my heart it would be an insult to my loved ones who have now passed on' (1961, 67). Harney never forgot that he and his wife Linda Harney had, the decade before, been denied hospitality by such cattle bosses on the basis that they were a mixed-race couple.

---

9 'Native Affairs Dept. inefficient police', Letters to the Editor from Olive Pink, *Northern Standard*, 3 April 1947, 6.

The combo

Linda Harney

Bill Harney married Linda in 1927 after a courtship that took two years. He had made the decision to get married and he and his friend Horace Foster went to the Groote Eylandt mission to effectively choose a wife. To do so, they exchanged sulus for trousers, shaved and cut their hair with a knife and spent nights on the mission, escorted at all times by the missionaries. It is not clear how Linda and he got together: 'I never spoke to my wife, who was a quartercaste, till the day after we were married. She would listen to what I had to say and then either nod her head or send me a letter in reply' (1946, 152–53). In order to marry Linda in 1927, Harney had to seek permission from the Chief Protector of Aborigines in the Northern Territory. This was not only because Linda was an inmate of the Groote Eylandt mission, but also because, as an Aborigine, she came under the *Aboriginal Ordinance Act 1918* (NT) which regulated all aspects of her life to a degree that would not have been tolerated for whites. If she had lived in Darwin she would have needed permission to work, permission to be in certain areas after dark (for instance, to go to the cinema), and of course permission to marry. The missionaries married them and, when Bill and Linda Harney returned once for a visit, they discovered that the mission had deliberated on whether nor not they would be welcomed back. Bill Harney wrote that the missionaries

> compromised by letting us sleep on the verandah, and naturally, this showed the other mission waifs that the social prestige of the mission people had not been lowered. When we heard of the proceedings of the mission later, Linda was bitter, and I never went near the place again. (1961, 159)

Harney wrote in allegorical terms about his marriage in his first book *Taboo*, in a short story called 'The complex', named after the inferiority complex that the mission generated in its wards, and the protection complex that sought to justify their own interference. In the story 'Rosie', the mission girl was afraid to speak to whites because of her shame over her 'pidgin English', which was itself attached to the shame of Aboriginality that the missions had 'slowly matured' (1943, 188). Harney wrote:

73

throughout her life she had been told that her mother was an aboriginal, and, from the way they said it, a person very low on the social scale. Her father too, must have been a low type to have brought her into the world; so springing naturally as she did from such a union she must be a low type herself. (1943, 185)

In this story, it was not until Rosie was married and reunited with her Aboriginal family that she threw off the inferiority complex. To Rosie, her marriage 'was no love affair, but just a safe harbour to shelter her from the cry of "Abo!, Abo!, Abo" ' (186). He represented Rosie as 'happy in her new life, with her two children, a boy and girl' (188). But still Rosie and Bill, like Linda and Bill in real life, ran up against the 'colour conflict'. Rosie eventually died of tuberculosis and her last words 'coming clearly as in a low whisper' to Bill were: 'Whatever you do, Bill, never, never send these children to a mission' (190).

Linda and Bill's four years of marriage was marred by tragedy and constant movement. While pregnant with their second child (their children were Beattie, born in 1928, and Billy, born in 1932), Linda was diagnosed with tuberculosis and advised to go down south, away from Darwin to avoid its damp and humid air. The doctor also implied that Linda, as a 'coloured' person, was more vulnerable to such an illness. The second reason that they were on the move for most of their married life was due to the Depression that set many thousands on the road looking for work. The structure of the dole at that time forced men to shift from town to town to pick up dole cheques, the idea being that men on the move could not form large organisations or flirt with communism:

Everywhere we travelled were wandering travellers carrying swags. By lagoons and shady trees those unemployed camped, living on the few shillings a week which was handed out to them by a government that insisted they keep moving for the next hand-out … the bosses laughed in their faces when they asked for toil as though they were wanderers in hell looking for blocks of ice. (1961, 33)

Harney described the 'melancholy decay' of those times, camping with fellow doleites in and around Katherine and then further south-west, where money had dried up: 'how terrible men can become as bosses over their fellow men in poverty' (1961, 62). He saw 'Cattle too old for droving into the markets ... [being] put – as I once saw – into a dry paddock and left to perish as a cheaper method of slaughter than using bullets which cost money' (1961, 64). He described the isolation and fear of that time:

> we 'out of works' were an untouchable caste. The ones in work became furtive in our presence, their conversation died down at our approach, and they would move into their huts as though we would taint them with the curse of the road. (1961, 35)

Chasing news of further work, Harney, Linda and the kids packed up the Chevrolet one-tonne truck and headed off to a station near Barrow Creek. When they approached the manager whose name was also Bill, Harney could see that 'he was embarrassed and that we were not wanted around'. Harney, who had waxed lyrical about the generosity of his mates across the land, was shattered: 'it was as though the world of mateship had gone up with a bang' (1961, 45). Linda, in tears, had reminded Harney that these 'great mates' he had spoken of were not so great after all. Harney described this episode as 'a stab in Linda's heart, aimed by whites who were then keeping black concubines' (1961, 45). Harney came back to this issue of white hypocrisy often as his way of trying to understand the colour conflict and the contempt to which he, Linda and their children were exposed. His account of this event shows how prescribed white male mateship was, and how it could rely on participating in the lie of racial segregation:

> Bill's [the manager's] attitude, that of the cattle-drover-station owner, reflected the attitude of most people to the half caste Aboriginal people. They were treated at that time as were the Aboriginal people, they lived in native camps and were rarely paid wages. Their lighter skins made them in greater demand as concubines, and the white man who married one, as I did, met the full pressure of the colour conflict. Should I be invited into a cattle station homestead for a feed or drink of tea, I would pass some hint that my wife was coloured and she must be invited too. Should I notice a slight hesitation, I must ask to be excused. In one instance I omitted to inform the host of her situation and this was regarded as an insult. Yet I found that most of

the people who frowned on my wife were the ones who had many half-caste children throughout the land (1961, 46).

This lack of civility shown by the cattle bosses determined Harney's relationship with them in the following decades: 'I never ate at the tables of the cattle bosses when I was a patrol officer in the Native Affairs Branch afterwards' (1961, 67).

In September 1932, Linda died in a segregated hospital ward in Katherine. Harney took up what he called his 'maternal duties' in the care of their two children, Beattie, who was aged four at the time of Linda's death, and Billy, who was two years old. He described taking on the 'chores which belonged to the mother of a family. The children themselves somehow realized my predicament and pulled their weight, and I was ever amazed how well Linda had house, or should I say, bush-trained the kids' (1961, 91). He wrote,

> as the male mother of the family, I soon became aware that any move of the children might mean something, and it would have me alert in a drowsy sort of way; as in a dream I would attend to their wants, then return to sleep again and forget all about the incident. (1961, 91)

He slept with the children curled up around him: 'I wished to be near them should anything happen in that era where drunken white men and black men were always getting bushed and stumbling into other people's shacks' (1961, 91).

The death of Linda brought many offers of help from residents of The Ghundi, an area of Katherine where doleites and mixed-race families were mostly camped. Ruby, Harney's close family friend, and Ruby's family ended up looking after the children if Harney had some work, and eventually their households become intertwined by the constant movement of children between them. He called the 'Ruby method' one of his main guiding principles on how to 'rear the children' (1961, 92). When he got home after his work fence-making or road-building, either for the dole or for 'real money', Harney 'always cooked a hot meal with dessert' (1961, 89) and often these meals included Ruby and her family too. Harney wrote that 'Modern mothers would no doubt shudder at the method I used, which was but a carry over from pioneering days and the Aboriginal way of life' (1961, 112). He was proud that Beattie and Billy were learning about the bush from their Aboriginal friends in the camp, and commented that Beattie had learnt to tell stories in the 'Aboriginal way', and that Billy had learnt 'finger talking'. He wrote: 'I had lost Linda, but I had my two children to remind me of her' (1961, 154). On Christmas Day, three months after Linda's death, they visited her grave on the banks of the Katherine River. He wrote that Beattie was 'full of questions' and so he told his children the story of how he and their mother met and married at the mission, and how the missionaries had deliberated on whether or not they would be welcomed back on a return visit. Harney told his children that 'those who looked down on people because of colour could not complain if they, too, were despised by others. Perhaps I was a fool to tell them such a thing, but that was how I felt at the time' (1961, 159).

Some time later, Harney saw that 'something was wrong with Beattie. She was not so bright as before, and her little back was slightly arched, as though it were having to bend beneath some heavy load' (1961, 168). He took her to the doctor 'repeatedly' (1961, 168) who told Harney it was asthma. Harney took her to another doctor 'passing through, but he brushed us aside' as another doctor's patient. Eventually a white woman who had trained as a nurse diagnosed Beattie with tuberculosis spine and berated Harney for not seeking treatment earlier. Beattie and Harney made the trip to Darwin and she was examined at the hospital clinic by Cecil Cook, who confirmed the diagnosis and admitted Beattie to the hospital. Harney stayed three days in Darwin, after which he had to return to Katherine to work, and to Billy. Leaving his daughter who 'looked very cute against the white sheets', he rose on hearing the hospital bell signalling the end of visiting times 'still holding my little girl's hand. Afraid to kiss her for fear that I would be overcome with emotion, I just waved her goodbye' (170).

During that stay, Harney was approached by a Roman Catholic priest who offered to look out for Beattie, and who also suggested that Billy could be taken in at the nearby convent. He discussed this idea with Ruby back at The Ghundi. Her response was: 'Why the hell did yer never get hooked up again, so that someone could look at the kids'. Harney's reply turned Ruby's demand on its head; he replied that he was 'not looking after himself, but rather the children' (1961, 185). Ruby's argument seemed not to be that he, Harney, needed looking after, but rather that having a wife, particularly an Aboriginal wife, would have allowed the kids to stay with him and stay connected to Aboriginal culture. Either Harney missed this point or chose to ignore what Ruby was suggesting were his responsibilities. Harney agreed to leave Billy with the people at the convent 'until a suitable boarding school was found for him in the South' (1961, 185).

On the trip to Darwin, Harney reported mixed feelings of joy and sorrow because 'I was going to see Beattie [she was still in hospital], but I was also sad for I realized that when I left my children this time, it would be a long time before I could see them again' (1961, 186). He left Billy at the convent: 'he cried a lot as I left him, and my heart was heavy within me as I walked away' (1961, 186). The next few months Harney was out doing road work which, he said, 'took my mind away from the children' and the losses he had experienced over the last four years. Soon after, Harney received a telegram telling him that Beattie had died while being operated upon. He 'cried bitterly into the ashes of my campfire' while his 'native friends', the Waddaman who worked with him on the road, 'resumed the light tapping of their boomerangs and an old man began to chant a ritual song of his people. It was a sad song' (1961, 187).

It is possible that the Waddaman friends he wrote of here are Bill Yidumduma's family, his mother Ludi Yibuluyma and her father Pluto and mother Minnie. Between 1933 and 1937, Harney was in Willeroo country to lay down a road (the Victoria Highway), with Pluto, Ludi and Minnie. Bill Yidumduma Harney recalls that

Old Bill Harney treated them all right; employing them, but with no wages. There was never any money. Old Bill used to clothe them and feed them, and old Pluto was happy to get his shirt and trouser and a bit of feed. (1996, 15)

With the money that Harney saved from the road job, he was able to send Billy to a boarding school in Brisbane in 1934 and then Adelaide: 'I visited him now and then, and together we made plans for the future' (1961, 188). Tragically, Billy drowned aged 15 in the Todd River, on a visit with his father. Bill was sent his son's things from the school in Adelaide and took some of them to a 'deserving church home for children'. The lady receiving them consoled him but then added these shocking words:

> 'perhaps it was best he went now. This is a hard world and, as you know, he was coloured'. The superior white, I thought – not principle but colour … I did go away wondering why such genuine sympathy could at the same time be so cruel. Then I remembered that at Linda's first illness also, the doctor had informed me that her colour could deter her from getting well. Now, at the end of the road, the same argument was being used in sympathy to show that my son was better off dead than alive. (1961, 190)

'their fathers were a race of hardy pioneers'

The characterisation of coloured folk as better off dead, and their parents as degenerates and degraded is something that Harney criticised frequently in his 20 years of writing, with varying degrees of anger and resentment: 'A lot has been written about the "low heel" white man mixing with the native women. Such sentiment is only for the ignorant bigot' (1958, 50). In place of this sentiment, Harney saw an alternative. In *North of 23* he imagined a 'new future' for 'half-castes', where they would 'build up a national sentiment, learning that their fathers were a race of hardy pioneers, and their mothers women of a race whose traditions stretch back into the dreamtime' (1946, 154–55). Ten years later he made a similar argument: 'Each country is full of these men who laughed at society yet became the ancestors of people who are proud that their stem goes back to the original tribes' (1957, 164). If there was an overall theme in Harney's tales, it was to imagine pride in place of shame, and to engender a future Australia where his children would not be considered 'better off dead' (1961) because they were 'coloured'. Harney romanced the bushman as worthy of holding up one half of a better national future, and his writing was testament to his desire to beget that future for his children even while, or perhaps even because, he did not publicly acknowledge (some of) them. If he spent time polishing the pedigree of the bushman, it was perhaps because there was some kind of hope there that the image of the good bushman might 'uplift' him and the children he left behind, in the background.

Harney never really trusted his white audience, though he cared very deeply about trying to educate them to appreciate Aboriginal culture and legends. Ultimately it seems that he did not have much faith in white people's capacity to see beyond racial classifications and superficial notions of civilisation and progress. In his last book, finished off by Douglas Lockwood, the narrator (who we can't quite say is Harney) wrote: 'a man tires of talking, of being always classified as an earbasher' ([1963] 1972, 70). This tiredness was inspired by another white audience made up of 'people who didn't care, who really didn't want to know' and who couldn't or wouldn't appreciate 'aboriginal people whose intelligence surpassed their own – and then some!' (1972, 69). The narrator also knew that a white audience that could not appreciate the richness of Aboriginal culture would also judge him to be a combo in the derisive sense of 'degenerate', and not in the sense of 'transformation' that Harney celebrated. Championing a view of the combo as an anti-racist, Harney sought to outmanoeuvre those who would characterise all interracial relationships as degenerate. In doing so, he was also caught up in mythologising and its twin term of disremembering, closeting stories and narratives – including his own – that he could not entrust to his readers, or even to his best friends, for many years.

As a patrol officer who helped hide his son from Welfare (or wanted his son hidden from Welfare), Harney protected himself, his Aboriginal partner and his son. It seems that it was while he was working as a patrol officer that he was most often able to stop by and visit. Such visits might have confirmed for Harney the rightness of his decision not to 'own' his son. 'Owning' him would have meant removing him from his mother's people and culture. Not 'owning' him in public, and suggesting that he be hidden, meant keeping his son with his Aboriginal mother and father. Kept hidden and able to remain with his Aboriginal family, Bill Yidumduma Harney recalls that he grew up knowing both laws, European and Waddaman, through his mother, her husband Joe Jomornji,[10] and his grandfather. Evading removal, being taught stock work by other white men who supported him when his own white father did not, Bill Yidumduma Harney's early life was precarious, under constant surveillance by Welfare. Even when he was a

---

10   A western understanding would refer to Joe Jomornji as Bill Yidumduma's stepfather.

grown man, Welfare questioned his traditional marriage to Ida, his first wife, on the basis that she was 'full blooded', and when she died, they threatened to remove his sons. Bill Yidumduma Harney refused to let them be taken away, and decided to be 'mother and father by myself'. Later, he married again, saying that he 'needed a mother to look after those two boys' (1996, 178). In the early 1980s 'Bill Harney Dreaming' became the basis of his land claim in the Upper Daly near Scott Creek Station. The land claim came through in 1981; Ludi died before seeing it settled.

The important thing to note is that Bill Yidumduma Harney credits his Aboriginal father Joe Jomornji, not Bill Harney, for much of his successes, his knowledge, his law. Harney might have had limited knowledge about some of those things, but it would never have been his to pass on. What Harney did attempt to pass on was the legend of the bushman which was put to use, in his writings, to counteract the dominant view of white men and Aboriginal women as the degenerate in pursuit of the degraded. Such a view, Harney believed, did nothing but produce inferiority complexes and white protection complexes and sham, hypocrisy and humbug, something of which he himself was not entirely innocent. Harney's silence about his Aboriginal children is directly related to his constant speech and prolific writing. That he could not tell his personal story in his words, in his campfire books, reflects also on his audience and its orientations, on what it could hear. And reading through all his work, I get the sense that the audience he courted was never really quite what he wanted. The bushman legend, it seems, was the best the storyteller and the readers could come up with between them, a 'dinkum Aussie' myth poised to disremember as it orientates a white bushie and his readers at the campfire, perhaps staring into a fire, avoiding eye contact, with Aboriginal stories in the background. The next chapter examines the bushman legend more closely and, in particular, examines the effects of re-situating the white bushman in dialogue with his Aboriginal partners, sons and daughters.

Black sheep

Every privileged class tries at first to whitewash its black sheep.
Richard Adlington (1932, 76)

They must also cease to believe their own myths.
Stanner (2009 [1938], 130)

In this chapter I look at the narratives of white bushmen besides Bill Harney, including Matt Savage, Daryl Tonkin and Roger Jose. These men married or were in de facto relationships with Aboriginal women and were and are (in contemporary readings) positioned as 'black sheep'. There is Nicholas Jose's *Black sheep: journey to Borroloola* (2002), an account of his 'mystery relative' Roger Jose, who lived 'beyond the pale' with his Aboriginal wives in Borroloola, Northern Territory (itself the black sheep of Australia according to Ernestine Hill [1970, 2]). There is also Daryl Tonkin, 'father of nine active, articulate Aboriginal children who were proud of representing their people in this country' (Landon 1999, xv), who recalls that his sister regarded him as the 'black sheep of the family who deserved nothing' (Landon 1999, 236).

In biographies and autobiographies written decades after the times they describe (set in the 1920s–1940s but written between 1971 and 2001), these black sheep are reclaimed, with the men themselves now positioned as 'heroes' (Landon 1999, xiv) and 'neglected visionaries' (Jose 2002, 38) of the 'Australian legend'. As Adlington suggests above, the black sheep was liable to be 'whitewashed' by generations who understandably sought comfort in imagining 'good ancestors' who bestowed, passed on and provided positive stories by which to navigate the present. Here I discuss how the life stories of Daryl Tonkin, Matt Savage and Roger Jose are presented by *white* writers as providing exemplary origins for an anti-racist white belonging. I emphasise here how these bushman narratives/legends are far from settled. The white men had moved in and out of white *and* Aboriginal kinship networks, making the idea of 'whitewashing' them, as exemplary forebears for any postcolonial nation, highly fraught. What I want to highlight in this chapter is some of the differences represented by these white men, built on by their white interlocutors, and then, in the best example I have come across, complicated yet again by their Aboriginal daughters. It is vital to highlight these competing claims on the black sheep/white fathers because, especially when it comes to the legend of the bushman, he so often slips onto the national stage as embodying something quintessentially (white) Australian. This 'dinkumness' is something, I venture, that might have made many a black sheep laugh.

The white men whose stories I examine here identified as bushmen and were critical of the expectations of middle-class, norm-aspiring whiteness, a form of aspirational whiteness that distinguished itself partly by a rejection of whites who consorted with Aboriginal people (particularly those they were related to). Suzanne Parry notes that white men who fathered Aboriginal children in the early 20th century were scorned, 'but the greatest derision was reserved for those who attempted to incorporate an Aboriginal woman into a nuclear family' (1995, 144). White men who moved into Aboriginal kinship networks were perhaps even more of a threat; they did not uplift or move Aboriginal people 'towards the white rather than the black' (Neville 1947, 68). Such a directive was undermined by men like Tonkin, Liddle and Savage who, instead of moving their Aboriginal families into whiteness, were themselves 'transformed' (Harney 1958, 51), to adapt Bill Harney's term. While they were 'transformed', so too was (and still is) the cultural vehicle that carried them, or should I say 'elevated' them, to centre stage over and over again: the bushman legend.

The bushman legend

Graeme Turner observes that 'one would be hard pressed to name contemporary versions of "the Australian" that have the cultural currency of the bush legend' (1986, 107). The legend of the 'Australian bush-man' is kept alive today by politicians (Keating 1994; Howard 1996), film-makers, popular culture celebrities (like the late Steve Irwin and Malcolm Douglas), and characters like Crocodile Dundee, and the drover in Baz Luhrmann's *Australia* (2009). Turner's observation of its cultural currency also attests to the multiple readings this legend can withstand: it is subject to constant critique, qualification and renewal, as if there is a kind of obligation to keep returning to the legend of the bushman, to keep opening it up to further scrutiny, in spite of the fact that it was of course never 'closed' in the first place. For example, Ward claims that it is usually associated with the 1890s (Ward 1958). John Docker suggests that the legend privileges 1950s nationalist nostalgia (Docker 1991). Marilyn Lake discusses the bushman as the 'Lone Hand', rejecting the 'idealisation of the Domestic Man which was integral to the cult of domesticity, imported to Australia in the cultural baggage of English immigrants' (Lake 1993, 2). Others argue that it reveals predominantly European influences (Astbury 1985), or manifests envy for indigeneity (McLean 1998), grounding a backlash against reconciliation (Curthoys 1999) and providing justification for selectively 'reconciled' settler belonging as I suggest here.

Ann Curthoys' reading of the Australian legend highlights the political imbalances of the bush legend. She argues that the bushman/battler resurfaces in the late 1990s as an obstacle to white Australian recognition of 'indigenous perspectives, of the trauma of invasion, institutionalisation, and dispersal' (Curthoys 1999, 18). Curthoys writes that the bushman legend celebrates 'hardships endured by white people, especially British and Irish white people' (7–8) and that these hardships, often celebrated as failures, meant that white Australians were and are unable to see themselves as responsible for the injuries and victimisation of others. In other words, sympathy for the black sheep redirects or blocks sympathy for Indigenous dispossession. The black sheep becomes white Australia's fetish Indigene, already incorporated (as once shamed, then proud rebel) into the white nation. While I agree with Curthoy's reading, I also want to emphasise how some black sheep complicate reinscriptions, and how they are already reinscribed within Aboriginal life histories. What the legend of the bushman obscures is how the bushman is himself positioned by Aboriginal onlookers (in these cases family) around him; that is, how they live inter-subjective lives, as Moreton-Robinson's work emphasises. Moreton-Robinson's work highlights how different, indeed incommensurable, Aboriginal and white perspectives can be from each other and that it is this very difference that constitutes the intersubjectivity between black and white subject positions (2003).

Bob Randall's account of his white father Bill Liddle in his autobiography *Songman* (2003) is a case in point. *Songman* describes Randall's white father's relationships with the local Indigenous people on Angas Downs Station, a sheep, then cattle, station in Central Australia. He is careful to distinguish his father from other white men who abused Aboriginal women:

> My people formed a close relationship with Bill Liddle because he was good to them, but many white people were very prejudiced against white men such as my father who formed close associations with Aboriginal people. I think it is important to distinguish between those white men who just used and abused Aboriginal women, and retained their racist attitude to Aboriginal people and others who, like Bill Liddle, sought to relate to Aboriginal people in a way which integrated Aboriginal and European ways. (Randall 2003, 123)

Such a view contrasts with another reading of Angas Downs Station written by white anthropologist Frederick Rose, who visited the station in 1962. *The winds of change in Central Australia* is Rose's anthropological study of the Indigenous community living on Angas Downs. Rose wanted to study Aboriginal practices of polygyny and gerontocracy, and Bill Harney suggested Angas Downs Station as an appropriate base. But what Rose found there was a community that was no longer 'authentic' in their 'original socio-economic condition' and so he decided to study 'the factors making for their disappearance' (Rose 1965, 6). His conclusion was that it was the white man and his white-flour economy that led to the disappearance of polygyny and gerontocracy. However, according to Bob Randall, who was born on Angas Downs and removed from it 21 years prior to Rose's study, what was significant about Angas Downs was the way that his white father, Bill Liddle, was incorporated into an Aboriginal polygynous kinship network. Bob Randall was probably a child of Bill Liddle, the white man owner of the station, with one wife married 'whitefella way' and four other wives married Yankunytjatjara way. While Rose positioned the white man and his economy as causing the loss of polygynous and gerontocratic social relations amongst the 'authentic' Aborigines, Bob Randall saw the situation differently, as the incorporation of the white man into Yankunytjatjara society:

> During the early years of dispossession, when the establishment of cattle stations was disrupting our traditional way of life and access to food sources, men would offer their wives to the white men within this system of reciprocal hospitality ... We just incorporated these new white people, with their superior wealth and weapons, into our system of kanyini. It is true that many white men did not understand this, and so did not fulfil their reciprocal obligations, causing such events as that which led to the Coniston massacre. However, Bill Liddle did, and that is why we respected him and why today the many children who are descended from him from a number of different women, all recognise each other as brothers and sisters. We do not distinguish between the children of his Arrente wife, whom he married whitefella way, from the children of his Yankunytjatjara 'wives'. (Randall 2003, 113)

Both Randall and Rose's readings illustrate the different politicisations of Aboriginal and white interactions, and the broader epistemological and cultural issue of the 'limits to knowing an "Other" be they black or white' (Moreton-Robinson 2003, 185). Frederick Rose's study is indicative of an anthropological approach that situates 'authenticity' in bloodlines as central to cultural continuity; the implications of which are that Bob Randall (a 'half-caste', in the language of the day) is then situated on the side of 'decline' and 'disappearance' of Aboriginal culture, while his father, Bill Liddle, is the archetypal 'demolisher of tribes' whose whiteness is made to matter too much. That Aboriginal culture could withstand, incorporate, continue and even expand via the white man, regardless of his whiteness, was not imaginable. That white men would also want to have connections with their Aboriginal kin on their terms was also rarely countenanced. Eugenicist views of a 'dying race' that position only 'full blooded' Aboriginal as 'authentically Aboriginal' would necessarily see Bob Randall and his other 'half-caste' brothers and sisters as emblematic of a cultural contamination that made anthropological objects decidedly slippery, hybrid and lacking in authenticity. This discourse of Aboriginal authenticity, which Povinelli astutely describes as constructing Aboriginal people as 'failures of indigenousness as such' (2002b, 23) also situates white men like Bill Liddle as the cause of such failure.

In a country where white men were once positioned by white authorities as 'breeding out the colour', such a view is not surprising. What gets left out of this very instrumental view of what constitutes culture (as 'colour') is the very unpredictability and specificity of culture: 'the cultures that we create do not mirror those represented by anthropologists' (Moreton-Robinson 2003, 89). White men who might have been seen to have caused decline were also capable of moving into Aboriginal kinship networks, making whiteness neither so predictably administrable nor equivalent to genocide. Kim Scott's novel *Benang* (1999) illustrates such a tension. The narrator Harley describes himself as the 'first white man born' and worries that 'I myself represented the final killing off' (1999, 446). His abusive grandfather, who subscribes to the genetic mathematician's view that denies Aboriginality past the 'octoroon', fails to 'breed out the colour' because colour is not (only) where Aboriginality resides. Moreover, the grandfather's sociopathic project provides the (albeit fascistic) archives for the reclaiming of Indigenous culture – archives that, as Stephen Kinnane notes, represent colonial control, but can be utilised, against the grain, to track a suppressed history:

> They did not think we would one day be leafing through the personal files they created about our grandmother, watching back, as her life was tracked and controlled across those pages for almost half a century. Cuts leave scars. Scars leave tracks. Tracks can be followed. (2003, 12)

Kinnane's metaphor of the shadowline is also a methodology. It highlights the existence of parallel lines of thought that are 'difficult to reconcile', unassimilable into each other. One challenge (of many) for the white critic is thus to imagine how legends obscure, downplay and overshadow the fact that the black sheep discussed here were always already visible and under scrutiny by their Aboriginal families, friends and critics.

Going native, natives going

The literature on how the bushman as a legend appropriates and mimics Aboriginality is substantial. Emphasising the appropriation and mimicry inherent in the bushman legend is Ian McLean's reading (of Russel Ward's celebration of 'indigenous influence' on the Australian legend) as a 'type of Aboriginalism which, in the manner of the day, displaces Aboriginality within a white indigeneity' (McLean 1998, 88). The 'radical nativism' that McLean identifies (1998, 87) in Australian art (like that of Margaret Preston) is also seen in the literary work of Charles Barrett, Katherine Susannah Prichard, Ernestine Hill, and Xavier Herbert, and indeed these artists and writers were working in the same period as the bushmen I examine here. That movement coincides with the biopolitics of 'breeding out the colour', to produce white 'stock' wherein 'a combination of novel environmental influences and absorption of other stocks would eventually produce a unique white Australian type, a new amalgam of blood and soil' (Anderson 2002, 256).

That novel 'type' found expression in the legend of the Australian bushman, the white man who was often characterised in terms of 'going native', a phrase that alludes to a 'dominant feature' of settler colonisation which, according to Patrick Wolfe, is 'not exploitation but replacement' (Wolfe 1999, 163). The settler seeks to replace the Aboriginal. Ernestine Hill comes close to indigenising bushmen when she describes them as 'something new in the rank and file of mankind, civilised man with no need of civilisation. He could live like the blacks in a black man's country, and build a white man's empire' (1970, 422). The bushmen were always there before anyone else:

> There ain't no such thing as the first white man missus, they was everywhere ... There ain't no creek or gully or hill or pocket of country in the island where a bushman hasn't been before you. (1970, 428)

It is not difficult to find accounts of a white settler belief that the white bushman had 'gone native'. But it is impossible to find evidence for an Aboriginal belief that the white man had 'gone native'. Tonkin's Aboriginal family, for instance, are described (by Tonkin) as being well aware of Tonkin's whiteness, and he is told by his father-in-law that he 'was considered a white blackfella by most of them' (1999, 86), signalling his difference as much as his similarity. Even Bill Harney, who wrote a book 'as' the Aboriginal man Marmel, and who told Aboriginal legends and stories in a way that today appears appropriative, did not do so because he had 'gone native' (even if he might flirt with this idea for the benefit of his southern white allies, like Elkin). Harney's writings reveal that his proximity to Aboriginal people, family and friends is such that he knows enough to know his outsider status. Bob Randall is also adamant that Bill Liddle 'sought to relate to Aboriginal people in a way which integrated Aboriginal and European ways' (123), but not that he became Indigenous or went 'over to the other side completely', to quote Nicholas Jose on his putative kin, Roger Jose. Nicholas Jose's reading of his putative black-sheep kin seems to collapse the differences between the bushman and the Indigene.

Black sheep: journey to Borroloola follows Nicholas Jose on a journey to find out if he is related to Roger Jose, 'a labourer who lived "blackfella", in the policeman's disapproving words' and who by the 1950s had become something of a minor celebrity in folk stories and travel writings of the period. Roger Jose lived in the infamous town of Borroloola, in the Gulf of Carpentaria, described by Bill Harney as 'combo heaven' and by Matt Savage as 'a kind of heaven' with 'plenty of queeais', a term he uses to refer to Aboriginal women (Savage quoted in Willey 1971, 75). But Nicholas Jose (some 40 years later) describes it as populated by old white hermits infused with the values of 1960s culture: 'existentialists, hippies, anti-racists and anti-consumerists before their time' (2002, 147). In Roger Jose, Nicholas Jose sought a direct link to someone who 'might turn out to be the most exemplary of forebears, a neglected visionary' (38). In the most explicit statement of personal longing ('I wanted ... I wanted') for 'connection', Jose wrote: 'I wanted the connection because I wanted to join myself to someone who had earned his belonging in this country' (38). What had 'earned' him this belonging? Principally, Roger's life as a combo. The memoir re-reads the term 'combo' and makes it central to an economy of contemporary reconciliation:

> The stigma of the combo was not merely that he [Roger Jose] consorted with an Aboriginal woman, but that he found degrees of mutuality and equality between black and white. The combo showed

that the two communities could sometimes mix contentedly. He challenged the myth of white supremacy and Aboriginal inferiority that social Darwinism had bequeathed, exposing the falsehood of the idea that the two ways of life were incompatible. Combos were despised because they undermined the orthodoxy of values the new society was determined to impose. I'd heard 'combo' used as a way of dismissing Roger Jose. Living 'blackfella' was even worse, since it amounted to going over to the other side completely. (88)

Jose's desire to connect to Roger Jose reminds me of Marcia Langton's suspicion towards white readers of Sally Morgan's *My place* (1988). That hugely popular book, Langton suggests, raises the possibility that

> the reader might also find, with a little sleuthing in the family tree, an Aboriginal ancestor … he or she would thus acquire the genealogical, even biological ticket ('my great-great grandmother was Aboriginal') to enter the world of 'primitivism'. (Langton 1993, 29–30)

Nicholas Jose's sleuthing after his 'mystery relative', great-uncle Roger Jose, promises Jose a connection to legitimate belonging, a white man 'gone native', 'living blackfella'. But looking a bit more closely, it seems that it is not Roger Jose himself that bestows the possibility of belonging on his ancestor Nicholas Jose. It is Roger Jose and his Aboriginal wives Maggie and Biddy that do this. Nicholas Jose implies that Roger Jose had 'earned his belonging in this country' by living with an Aboriginal woman in a relationship of 'mutuality and equality'. In fact, Nicholas Jose knows little about the relationship that Roger Jose had with his Aboriginal wives. What he knows about Roger and his wives is gleaned from researching the town of Borroloola and writers like Harney and the biography of Savage, men who 'laughed at society', but not necessary *with* us, as Jose's celebratory prose implies, but *at* us, I would suggest.

Harney's jocular sentimentality for Borroloola as a 'combo heaven' was not consistent with his other observations, particularly later when he returned as a patrol officer in the 1940s. There he described the town not in terms of its freedom for white men but in terms of its feudalism, its child stealing, and the forced movement of Aboriginal workers in and out of the area. In other words, he described Borroloola in terms that do not necessarily support an image of 'mutuality or equality'. Harney wrote: 'The residents of this place are unique, each living on his own hill as it were with his own group of natives' (Harney, Patrol Officer Report, 6 November 1944). He went on to say that he was amazed at the requests of natives to have their children returned from places where 'policeman been send him [sic]'. He noted that drovers and the local mailman routinely took Aboriginal men out of town, what he called 'blackbirding', as a deliberate means of securing Aboriginal men's labour and separating them from their wives. He described Aboriginal women working at the local hotel as in 'need of protection' and was critical of white men for not taking steps to protect their own 'half-caste' children. He described a 'systematic clearing' of the Yanulao, Kurawa and Mara people out of Borroloola, and indicated that a 'war' was underway:

> If ever a tribe of people felt the full weight of this war then that one is the Yanula tribe who, not five years ago, lived together, and who are scattered over four hundred miles of plains country, far from their tribal lands, and their old folks, living beside the McArthur stream, loyal natives if ever there were natives that could be called so. Today they ask the Native Affairs official, 'Where are our children? Where are our daughters who have married into different tribes?' I ask that this movement be stopped. (Harney, Patrol Officer Report, 6 November 1944)

Harney described a town in which Aboriginal women had to make strategic decisions to align themselves with white men 'living on his own hill' with their 'own group of natives'. Despite not knowing much about Roger Jose's relationships with his wives, Nicholas Jose's reading posits an equivalence between a long-term relationship with an Aboriginal woman, imagined in terms of 'mutuality and equality', and 'living blackfella' itself. Nicholas Jose does not claim Maggie or Biddy as his 'mystery relatives' (aunts), but only claims Roger. He doesn't need to; Roger fulfils the role of being that genealogical link to indigeneity that Langton suggests white Australians crave.

In Jose's memoir, Biddy and Maggie's stories are unknown but they retain a powerful symbolic status, ostensibly having the capacity to confer 'belonging' on Roger Jose, which he then passes on to Nicholas Jose 50 years later. Maggie's role is thus puzzlingly sublimated, but actually central. This symbolic role for Aboriginal women is a consistent feature of settler literatures, as Terry Goldie points out. Aboriginal women possessing 'the power to confer indigenisation' on white men emerges as a consistent theme in Australian literature, and in New Zealand and Canadian settler literature (1989). This is clear in Katharine Susannah Prichard's *Coonardoo*, where sex with Coonardoo makes Hugh appear his 'old self' and 'attached to the earth' (1990 [1929], 71; see also Elder 2001, 138). Their symbolic status is here consistent with Partha Chatterjee's point that although nationalism is a 'discourse about women; women do not speak' (1993, 7). They do of course speak, did always speak, but in Jose's text (like Herbert's and to an extent also Harney's), the women are allotted largely symbolic power to reproduce the nation (Anthias & Yuval-Davis 1989) and provide redemptive genealogies for an anti-racist white belonging. His black sheep is a 'genealogical, even biological ticket' (Langton 1993) to enter a postcolonial dream of 'mutuality and equality' between whites and Aboriginal people, counterposed by a colonial nightmare of violence, denial and segregation.

Kim Scott articulates the same desire for good ancestors, a desire kept in check by his Auntie Kayang Hazel and co-author of *Kayang and me* (2005) in the following exchange between Scott and Kayang Hazel:

> I [Scott] prefer to see John Mason as a commendable man, even if the birth and wedding certificates only ever refer to his female companion as 'Fanny – an aboriginal' ... I wanted to find something like love, something like equity in their relationship, even if Mason, like Dunn and Moir and many others, was initially just another white man who grabbed women and took them away, 'Always did that, if they could', said Kayang Hazel. So maybe J Mason was a good man, lusting and loving; maybe he was a villain. And Bobby Roberts? I'd prefer all my ancestors to be heroes, but Kayang Hazel seems less sentimental than me in that way. (2005, 81)

Biographers are themselves implicated as witnesses to stories that in their retelling take stock of brutality, and the ordinariness of that brutality. Much of Harney's campfire yarns were, for instance, testimony to what Gillian Cowlishaw has described as 'extreme and vicious cruelty

… without remedy' (1999, 149) regarding the treatment of Aboriginal women by white men: Aboriginal women chained up at night, locked into rooms, kept on verandahs strung up with tin cans by 'gin shepherds', husbands poisoned, tricked, removed; all events recounted with a mixture of disbelief and something like humour at having got away with it. It is the 'getting away with it' that is of particular interest here, because many of those stories that Harney related included names that were changed, locations obscured, motivations trivialised or explained away as part of the 'system'. Such stories, like legends, were also smokescreens that can be fanned into textual life by biographers who appear, at times, to struggle with how to account for and do justice to, some men's stories.

'an ordinary sort of bloke'

Keith Willey's biography of Matt Savage was one such example, where there was also a cross purpose at work between the biographer and his subject. One sought to redeem while the other presented himself as irredeemable: 'They say the road to hell is paved with good intentions. Well at least I could plead not guilty to that one' (Savage quoted in Willey 1971, 8). Savage was inclined to view himself as a conquerer at a time when the Kimberleys were lawless. He depicted the Kimberleys of the 1910s as a place where Aboriginal women were not only 'half the stockmen' but were also part of their wages:

> I had been told that the queeais, native girls, up that way were mighty willing, and I wanted to test this for myself. At that time half the stock riders in the Kimberleys were women recruited – or simply snaffled – from the local tribes. They seemed to have more brains than the men and were more reliable in the mustering camp. As the saying went, they would 'work all day with the cattle, then work all night in the swag'. (Willey 1971, 12)

Savage contextualised this by arguing that

> The system was there when I arrived and I was all in favour of it. Later it became unfashionable: I think the government stepped in

and made a law that Aboriginal women could only work around the homestead ... it didn't really make much difference. There had been at least one station owner who had kept a harem and boasted that he 'bred his own stockmen' (Willey 1971, 12).

Savage described the attitudes of white men and white women towards Aboriginal people as 'rather like that of a medieval baron towards his slave and serfs'. (Willey 1971, 19)

He recounted one example after another of sexual violence and murder:

Another old-timer – and I have only heard this on hearsay – was said to have had a lubra, a native woman, chained up with some other prisoners. He took her off and slept with her that night, and in the morning he shot her dead. I met him years later and he seemed an ordinary sort of bloke, and a really good stockman. I suppose he did do it. (Willey 1971, 15)

As a counterpoint to the recollections of extreme violence by 'ordinary' white men, Savage was presented in this biography by Keith Willey as a family man: 'At a time when so many men were ashamed of the native women they slept with, and disowned their children, Matt loved a Mudburra girl, married her, and educated his three pretty daughters as well as he was able' (Willey 1971, iii). This image of the 'family man' works to strategically complicate the representation of violence around Savage presenting him as exceptional in relation to this ordinary violence. Willey emphasised his marriage to Ivy: '[h]e has kept his family together; his Aboriginal wife Ivy and their tribe of children and grandchildren' (Willey 1971, i). Like Harney, Savage associated bad white men with those who pretended not to associate with Aboriginal women, or accorded no value to them and their relationships. Savage would have had to participate in the lie as well. In her biography of Olive Pink, Julie Marcus described a chance meeting between Pink and Savage:

Matt Savage had a fearsome reputation as a brutal station manager, though this was probably not known to Olive Pink at the time. She asked about the young girl travelling with the two men and was told that he was a boy. (2001, 139)

Drover's boys (as the Aboriginal women who rode with the men were called) were often 'snaffled' from the local tribes, as Matt Savage himself explained in relation to 'the system'.

Willey hoped his biography of Savage would 'help a new generation to understand their forebears without judging them: balancing the bloodshed and injustice against the courage, endurance and stoical humour which contributed so much to the Australian legend' (Willey, iii). This was of course a judgment in itself – that in this history of the Australian legend there is some kind of balance. The 'good father and husband' image that Willey constructed around Savage helped to position him as legitimate source of the nation's legends, something which, I venture, might actually have made Savage laugh: Savage offers the reader a far more complex picture of himself. Willey and Savage collaborated on this book, though perhaps with different moral purposes; it was not Savage who mentioned the nation or its legends, he was more circumscribed by his allegiance, primarily to the 'bushies', the men of the outback who were identified by their ambivalence towards the 'nation'. It is in the retelling of these stories that they became genealogically linked to the 'nation': the white nation, that is. How would his legend be written from the position of the drover's boy, for instance? Moreover, which legends become 'Australian'? And given the propensity for national sentiment to favour upstanding pride, what would be left out of such an elevation?

Narrative interventions: Jackson's Track

Daryl Tonkin's biography is a case in point, using the bushman as suitable vehicle for the 'Australian legend' and then also, crucially, undoing that fantasy as a result of the intervention of his Aboriginal daughters. The Tonkin biographies (the first written by Carolyn Landon with Tonkin, the second by Landon alone), complicate the approaches in texts discussed up to this point, none of which really consider the role of Aboriginal women beyond her being 'recruited' and incorporated into white belonging. *Jackson's Track* (1999) and *Jacksons Track revisited* (2006) do something far more interesting. Taken together they elucidate Stanner's prescription for white Australia: 'They must cease to believe their own myths' (Stanner 2009, 130), and also illustrate Moreton-

Robinson's call for whites (feminists specifically) to render whiteness visible and in intersubjective dialogue with Aboriginal people (2003).

The first biography, *Jackson's Track* (1999), situates Tonkin as part of the bushman legend, while the second, *Jackson's Track revisited* (2006), undoes much of this mythology in favour of alternative stories brought to the fore by Tonkin's Aboriginal daughters and sister-in-law. In doing so, attention also shifts from the bushman to the story of the Aboriginal people who lived at the track. This shift has a number of ramifications, which are noted by Carolyn Landon in her self-reflexive mode of address in the follow-up text (*Jackson's Track revisited*). These texts, taken together, highlight the cross-purposes at work in telling the story of bushmen, and highlight the importance of the 'response-ability' of Aboriginal relatives in these (his) stories, and also the importance of white interrogations of dominant cultural myths through dialogue with Aboriginal witnesses.

The original text, *Jackson's Track* (1999), is more traditional in structure (and framing) than the follow-up (*Jackson's Track revisited*). *Jackson's Track* is narrated in the first person, and there Tonkin recalls his life in a series of vignettes about living at the track as a bushman, as father and husband, son and brother and, in his own words, as a 'villain in the eyes of most' because he chose to live with his Aboriginal wife, their children and extended family. In the introduction to *Jackson's Track*, white woman Carolyn Landon recounts meeting Tonkin's Aboriginal daughter, Pauline Mullett, at the local school (where they both worked), and agreeing to her suggestion that Landon help her father write a book about his life (xiii). Landon describes her surprise when she found out that Tonkin, Pauline's father, was white: 'A white man among Aborigines. A million questions leapt into my brain' (xiii). On meeting Tonkin, she thinks of him as a 'hero' (xiv) and as 'understanding way before his time' (xiv–xv), and wants to know 'how Tonkin had come to throw his lot in with the Aborigines' (xiv). Landon describes the process of writing: Tonkin would talk, prompted by questions, sometimes reassured by his daughter Pauline that now, these days, it was alright to talk about his life with Euphemia (Tonkin's wife), and Landon would 'go home to … write up his story each week' (xiv). I'll now turn to aspects of Tonkin's life story, and then return to the question of framing further on.

Just before the Depression, Daryl Tonkin and his brother Harry took over a large parcel of land (Jackson's Track) in Gippsland, Victoria, and invited the families of their Aboriginal workers to live on the land with them. His (de facto) wife, Euphemia, was the daughter of one his workers, and her parents lived close by, also on Jackson's Track. Euphemia died before Tonkin's biography was written, so what the reader knows of Euphemia comes to us from Tonkin and through Carolyn Landon's writing. Tonkin says of his life with Euphemia:

> It was good to be with a natural person. That was the beauty of her. No matter how rough it was, she loved it. Being in the bush was what I liked and she was a marvellous person in the bush. She was an ideal companion. A jewel. (1999, 111)
>
> I knew she was honest, kind and generous; I knew she was a good mother; I knew I liked her and that I wanted her to share my camp with me. That was good enough for me. It didn't occur to me to use the word love then, but I know now that I loved her. (1999, 86).

Their nine children (two of whom, Pauline and Linda Mullett, play a vital role in expanding the narratives that Landon and Tonkin produce) did not share their father's last name. They took the last name of Euphemia's first husband. This was because, Tonkin tells us, Welfare was more likely to intervene and possibly remove the children if he was known to be their father. In this case, the lack of (white, public) acknowledgment was geared towards keeping the family together, rather than denying it, or perhaps using denial strategically to avoid scrutiny.

Obscuring their family connections to outsiders was also made possible by the fact that Jackson's Track was isolated from the main town centres and even from main roads, such that the Aborigines Protection Board and missionaries would have had to go looking for them. Tonkin aroused suspicion: 'They [Welfare] were especially suspicious of me because I was a whitefella in amongst the blacks' (1999, 216). Although Jackson's Track was private property, Tonkin was conscious of the threat that the Aboriginal Protection Board posed because it could determine where Aboriginal people could and could not live. When Tonkin and Euphemia went to town for provisions, they would walk at a distance from each other, to avoid public scrutiny. He also recalls the 'ill-treatment and disrespect from local clients who ... were not happy to have to deal with the fellow who had Aboriginal children' (2006, 05.17).

'No brother of mine'

Jackson's Track operated as a large tree-milling property, managed by both Daryl Tonkin and his brother Harry, and then also by his sister Mavis. When Tonkin got together with Euphemia, his white family expressed different opinions. While his own father did not mind that he had chosen to live with Euphemia, saying to Tonkin, 'in my opinion, colour has nothing to do with it' (1999, 102), his brother Harry disapproved and indeed tried to remove Euphemia, as I will discuss later, while his sister Mavis told him 'You'll be an outcast with your people, with your family, with all white people!' (1999, 96). Tonkin's father had to suppress laughter at the reaction of his daughter. Mavis is depicted in the biography as the one who was most interested in maintaining a respectable whiteness that did not include Aboriginal nieces, nephews and sisters-in-law: ' "What if there are children?" said Mavis with a look of horror on her drained, by now almost blue, face' (1999, 97). Mavis went on to say, 'No brother of mine is going to live with a black woman' (1999, 95). Tonkin explained Mavis' attitude by saying: 'she is not a bush person, she doesn't understand what is right and natural' (1999, 106). His brother Harry, who was a 'bush person' like Tonkin and also shared Mavis' views about Tonkin and Euphemia, avoided becoming a target of Tonkin's criticisms. Mavis' gender set her apart.

Tonkin was adamant that Jackson's Track is 'no place for a woman' (1999, 48) by which he meant a white woman, his Aboriginal wife fitting in perfectly well. There was no sisterhood between Mavis and Euphemia. Although we don't get to hear what Euphemia might have thought of Mavis, what is depicted in Tonkin's account is very little interaction between the 'sisters out-law'. When Mavis comes to live at Jackson's Track she moves into the main house, which only Tonkin seems to have visited. Mavis is represented as a monitor of the racial line and mistress of the main house, consistent with Rowley's observations on the private/public gendered spheres of bush mythology (1989; see also Lake 1986).

When his sister Mavis arrived, Tonkin felt that she was the only one that didn't fit in: 'We all got on, gave each other room, accepted each other. Except Mavis' (1999, 70). Her misfitting introduces the chapter about Mavis called 'People talk', which opens with a photograph of a smiling Mavis, in a fur coat, hat with lace, shiny dark gloves, a lip-sticked smile and a strong resemblance to Tonkin. Mavis brought with her the outside world and the gossip of neighbours, a hypocritical white world closing in on the freedoms that he had up until then enjoyed. When Tonkin and Euphemia moved in together, it was Mavis who was most upset and worried about the colour line and the implications for the white family. She never recognised her Aboriginal nieces and neph-ews (in the period of time that she is discussed in the narrative), and never visited Tonkin and Euphemia's camp. Tonkin's heroism in his personal fight against racism is established in contrast with Mavis' vil-lainy: 'Mavis let the blacks know she didn't approve of them, by being bossy with them, ordering them around and not being friendly' (1999, 72).

Mavis had a financial interest in the timber mill that the brothers had established. She moved onto the land with them to 'look after them', but she also looked after the books, feminine 'nurturance' com-bined with a 'very good head for business' (1999, 49). When Tonkin's father died, it was Mavis who took over the family wealth and effect-ively severed Tonkin from it, his perceived misdemeanours allowing her the greater concentration of wealth: 'I thought she was probably right about me not deserving anything. That thought always stopped me in my tracks' (1999, 207). Tonkin's sense of shame came to structure his relationship to the family business, which Tonkin perceived was shifting more and more in favour of Mavis' plans: 'she would manage to get the lion's share' (1999, 206). Mavis' rejection of Tonkin's family enabled this distribution of wealth. Illegitimacy thus functioned in a traditional way here, to concentrate wealth, though this time in the white woman's favour. This racial dispute, conducted within the family, serves to demonstrate the complex interactions of gender, race, class and the roles played by an aspirational white woman in gaining control over land, finance and lifestyle. Tonkin consistently represents Mavis as a monitor of race and class lines, as she sought to benefit from both: 'She was aware of who owned things and who didn't, who worked hard and who didn't, who was white and who wasn't' (1999, 70).

Harry Tonkin's lack of acknowledgment of Daryl Tonkin, Euphemia and their children was also a significant source of pain for Tonkin:

> I was sure that one day he [Harry] would get sick of living away from the bush and return to the main house, that he would eventually get to know his nephews and nieces and feel relaxed and comfortable in my house with my family ... But it wasn't to be. (1999, 228)

Harry intervened radically in his brother's life by removing Euphemia from their house and taking her many miles away, motivated by his sense that she and Tonkin needed to be separated. Tonkin travelled to find Euphemia and bring her back. Harry died some time later, prematurely, and never recognised his brother's family. It is difficult to imagine sharing the same property with your brother's nine children and wife but not acknowledging them, something which seems particularly cruel given that Harry is described elsewhere as respecting 'blackfellas as equals' (1999, 106). According to Harry, 'equality' must not have meant necessarily accepting an Aboriginal person as an intimate family member. Tonkin was amazed that Euphemia was able to forgive his brother, indicating that he 'had a lot to learn from her' (1999, 110).

Harry's refusal to acknowledge his nieces and nephews did not attract the same level of contempt as Tonkin reserved for Mavis. It is clear that Harry and Tonkin were still able to work together as bushmen despite their disagreements, and Harry's attempts to remove Euphemia from the property. What Harry and Tonkin had in common was the life of the bushman, which Tonkin romanticises:

> we never thought about whether we were black or whether we were white. We were workers, we were bushmen. We all lived together on the same bit of land and we all got on, gave each other room, accepted one another. (1999, 70)

Except Mavis, of course. She is presented as one of those white women matrons and monitors of the racial line (Jolly 1993; Sharpe 1993). Unlike Harry, who was also clearly a racial monitor in his own way, Mavis did not have access to the redeeming ideology or identity of the bushman. Harry and Tonkin had that, at least, in common. Of his and his brother's decision not to enlist in World War II, Tonkin says, 'I'd say we were true blue Aussies, but we were bushmen, and bush people and governments don't mix so well' (1999, 53). Tonkin expresses his antipathy for particular forms of whiteness that are associated with the bosses, the Church, developers and governments, and of course, Mavis.

Whites as a group (but referred to as 'white men') are criticised by Tonkin for their insensitivities:

> In my experience, wherever white men go, they damage things. Look at nature. Blackfellas are satisfied with nature and do nothing to damage it whereas the whites pollute all the streams, making them unfit to drink from ... They look after their own, keeping thieves and murderers in luxury yet not allowing the blackfellas to live together in peace wherever they want in the land they were born in. (1999, 249)

He describes feeling 'chafed and hemmed in by the white man's civilised ways' (1999, 42), similar to Harney's self-description as a 'a nomad who went into the bush after the First World War and stayed there for more than forty years because I wanted to escape from what others called "civilisation", and all it represented' (1972, 151–52). Like Harney, Tonkin learnt a great deal from his Aboriginal friends and relatives, and, for Tonkin, it is Euphemia's father Stewart who is most admired and to whom Tonkin expresses a profound gratitude: 'Here was a bloke living on our property who was brought up to natural living and I had a lot to learn from him ... he had natural skills that were razor sharp, skills I wanted to learn' (1999, 42). Speculating on prior occupants, Tonkin wonders 'about their way of life and wished I knew what they knew' (1999, 11). Stories that he heard 'makes the whitefellas' understanding of things seem small' (1999, 62), and he later couches his respect for Indigenous epistemologies in terms of his relation to his outsider status as a 'whitefella': 'I respect their knowledge and take their stories seriously although I'm only a whitefella' (1999, 226).

The postscript to *Jackson's Track* is co-written by Tonkin and his daughter Linda, and it takes a different turn from the rest of the book. It deflects attention away from Tonkin and onto the story of Aboriginal people in Victoria as a whole (and across two centuries) and to their treatment by white authorities (1999, 293–96): 'we believe that life at Jackson's Track was a very important part of this history' (1999, 293). The difference in the way that the story is framed (between author and subject, who is also a co-author) is important because it links with the sequel, *Jackson's Track revisited* (2006), and Pauline Mullett's role redirecting the story. As it stands, Landon's introduction presents Tonkin as an exceptional bushman, a heroic anti-racist whose life story 'embodied the whole of the Australian experience' (1999, xv). This particular casting of Tonkin as an embodiment of something whole strongly influences the way that the story of the track is initially presented. Landon's enthusiasm for his side of the story is evident in the introduction where she writes that 'I *knew* the central story of Jackson's Track was this white man's story' (1999, xv, emphasis added). Later Landon comes to see this as not something that she knew but something that she had written, foreshortening Tonkin's own intersubjectivity to *his story* only and thereby narrowing the very thing that made him interesting in the first place. In revisiting the story of the track, Landon is drawn to conclude that in many ways the original version of events privileged the singular perspective of one 'witness', as Tonkin calls himself. This was the case even when doubts about the accuracy of his narrative were arising in the process of writing his story: 'Over the eighteen months that Tonkin and I worked together, Pauline and I had become increasingly aware that his memoir was only one version of events' (2006, 01.8). But it was not only that there were different versions of *events*. The differences between Landon's introduction and the postscript written by Tonkin and Linda Mullett point at broader divergences over what constitutes the focus of the story; for the former, it is the white man, while for the latter, it is the broader story of Aboriginal people of the track, of Victoria and over two centuries.

In *Jackson's Track*, Landon accounts for Tonkin's 'guilt and grief over the inevitable tragedy that befell the blackfellas of Jackson's Track' and attributes his reticence to acknowledge, express and discuss feelings to the typology of the bushman: 'Memory, of course, is about feelings, and a bushman is not used to talking about feelings' (1999, xv). In *Jackson's Track revisited*, such reticence is neither a measure of the truth nor a symptom of bush life. Nor is the bushman's story presented as embodying something of the 'Australian experience', whatever that might be, but as a starting point for other stories to emerge. *Jackson's*

Track 'ends' the story with tragedy, but Landon concludes in the sequel that 'It was he who felt the tragedy, not the blackfellas' (2006, 07.11). Prompted very much by the vigilance shown by Pauline Mullett and Aunty Gina, Landon concludes that Tonkin's witness account does in fact underplay the agency of the Aboriginal people in relation to their treatment by white authorities that Tonkin clearly despised and blamed (his hostility was towards white Others). Tonkin blamed white authorities (Welfare and missionaries) for removing the Aboriginal families from Jackson's Track. But his account underplayed the agency of the Aboriginal people around him and the failure of Tonkin's business to provide enough work to justify staying on at the track. In coming to terms with these sides of the story, Landon writes: 'I believe we would now be able to give the Aboriginal people in his story more credit for determining their own lives' (08.4). Moreover, *Jackson's Track revisited* qualifies Tonkin's acceptance by the blackfellas: 'During her interview, Aunty Gina, after giving a quick conspiratorial glance at Pauline, said quietly, "Dora didn't like Euphemia taking up with Tonkin" ' (Landon 2006, 08.3). So it was not only whites who took issue with Tonkin and Euphemia's relationship: Euphemia's mother did too. Tonkin does not mention this in his memoir; white racism is, in the context of his and Landon's hostility towards racist whites an easier, more recognisable (as in familiar) obstacle.

Rejection by his white brother and sister, with the possibility that he might also have been a white black sheep to his Aboriginal family, might have been too much for Tonkin to contemplate. It complicates the view of Tonkin's 'heroic' narrative, introducing a powerful shadowline. Landon notes how difficult it was for her to alter her own view of Tonkin's story and listen to Pauline Mullett and Aunty Gina's accounts, accounts that attest to continuity (rather than tragedy and discontinuity) of Aboriginal occupation and culture. Landon suggests that her own 'righteous outrage' also contributed to underplaying Aboriginal agency: the story of Jackson's Track was not, *is not*, the full story of the Kurnai people who lived there and still occupy the land. There is 'no last word' (2006, 01.12), as Landon concludes. What changes is the privilege accorded Tonkin's story amongst the others':

If Daryl and I were to tell his story afresh, now that time has passed and other stories have been told, would it be very different from *Jack-*

son's Track? We would be better placed to discover the chronology of events, since the archive has been scoured, but I don't know if the facts and events he relates would change much. What might be different is the emphasis he gives them. And this would have as much to do with my ability to hear the meaning in his words as it would with any restructuring of his narrative. (2006, 08.1)

Consequently, the legend of the bushman in *Jackson's Track revisited* is localised and demythologised by virtue of his relationship with his Aboriginal daughters, and Landon's self-reflexive reframing of her own 'righteous outrage', the kind of outrage that can overshadow the problem of speaking on behalf of Aboriginal people unfairly treated by whites. Rethinking the figure of the bushman as a man in dialogue with his Aboriginal daughters opens up further possibilities for this particular figure. It was Pauline who 'got her dad to write' his first pages of the memoir early on (1999, xiii). Landon suggests that 'Just as Pauline had hoped, her father's story seemed to create the space for more stories to follow' (2006, 01.8). Carolyn Landon describes herself as Pauline Mullett's 'tool. She was hoping that more stories, the hidden stories of her people – stories from her mother and aunty in particular – would follow her father's memoir as part of this process' (2006, 01.6). But perhaps it was less a matter of hope and the merely fortuitous than of strategic dialogue and vigilance on the part of Pauline Mullett, who, in the context of Landon's research, is described as actively guiding the research, 'looking over my shoulder' (2006, 06.2). It is also Pauline who guides much of Landon's rethinking in relation to how the story of the Kurnai is one of continuity rather than having a tragic end.

The differences between the two texts (one that celebrates and centralises the bushman and the other that contextualises his views as intersubjectively given) demonstrates how the typology of the bushman operates. In one, there is a tendency to idealise the bushie as mediator, or as having unique access to truths about Indigenous people. This is a position that Tonkin himself occasionally seems to take up and it is also a position that Carolyn Landon's vision of him helps to romanticise. It is a way of reading that prevents other stories from being heard. Pauline Mullett's account demonstrates vigilance in relation to her father's narrative, cross checking his interpretation of events in a way that emphasises the bushman's ongoing dialogue.

Tonkin's self-description as a 'witness' (1999, 281) is useful as a way of understanding his subject position and subjectivity, caught in a network of complicit 'belonging' rather than a choice between pride and shame, hero or villain. 'Witness' is a particularly interesting word to use in the context of his story, especially in light of Kelly Oliver's deployment of the term in *Witnessing: beyond recognition* (2002). Oliver's project to formulate witnessing as 'beyond recognition' situates recognition as assimilative, working to reproduce the Other as the Self's opposite or lack. Oliver argues that contemporary theorists influenced by post-Hegelian accounts of recognition actually repeat (rather than open up) the ways that subjectivity is formed in traumatic antagonism between Self and Other and by doing so their readings 'undermine the deep sense of response-ability implied in claiming that subjectivity is dialogic' (2002, 5). Oliver's project is to outline how this 'deep sense of response-ability' might open up ethical forms of subjectivity not based on normalising hostility between Self/Other. She does this by thinking about subjectivities as formed through witnessing rather than through recognition, where witnessing does not presume that the Other be excluded as threatening or incorporated as same.

In Oliver's terms, if the bushman is a witness, rather than a model or a typology, then he is not closed to the ethical potential embedded in dialogic intersubjectivity. This term helps to redefine the bushman not as maverick isolate or native informant who can speak on behalf of the Aboriginal community, but as someone whose words flow in a network of response-ability. Or, as Deborah Bird Rose puts it, 'witnessing promotes remembrance and works against death and against the comfort of monologue' (Rose 2004, 30). A position of response-ability also highlights the ways that 'bushman', as a self-description, might also have operated as a protective device (as in Harney's 'us bushies'); a means by which Tonkin could himself survive the conflicts in his family and his shaming by whites (and the disapproval of his mother-out-law). It also draws attention to the intersubjective view of the white father held by Linda and Pauline Mullett; that his story would allow more stories to be told, and to highlight the continuity and difference of the Kurnai. The postscript to *Jackson's Track* written by Linda Mullett and Tonkin emphasises from the outset on Tonkin's intersubjectivity, his witness account, his relationship to his Aboriginal family and the Kurnai. The first biography's 'legend of the bushman' emphasises Tonkin's dialogic relationship with white culture as one of its continuously produced hero/villains. The second biography revisits and keeps open the act of witnessing, those who witnessed *back*, and witnessed different things.

Relating witnessing to testimony, Oliver argues that the process of witnessing 'works to ameliorate the trauma particular to othered subjectivity' (2002, 7). Tonkin is, according to his own testimony, an 'othered subjectivity'. After all, he calls himself a 'villain in the eyes of most'. Tonkin, and his Aboriginal family, are rejected by his brother and sister on racial grounds, as well as shunned by whites in the community. He is also shamed by his complicity with whiteness, evidenced by his difference from the blackfellas with whom he identifies but whose tragic fate he laments. One can imagine that Euphemia would have been witness to the ways that Tonkin suffered rejection at the hands of his brother and sister, and in listening to him she would have been able to restore his address-ability and his response-ability. Likewise, Pauline Mullett's encouragement and Carolyn Landon's listening and recording of his narrative may well have contributed to the restoration of his othered subjectivity. In the introduction to *Jackson's Track*, Landon attempts to replace his personal shame with national pride, making him stand in for the 'Australian experience', a sovereignty of self far from the margins: his subjectivity is restored by being universalised and repositioned as a kind of general truth. But, as *Jackson's Track revisited* finds, such restoration risks reducing the agency of those he speaks about.

From *Jackson's Track* to *Jackson's Track revisited*, the so-called 'legend of the [white] bushman' is transformed primarily by the vigilance (address-ability and response-ability) of his Aboriginal daughters, and also by Carolyn Landon and the complex cultural politics of bearing witness to that which cannot be recognised (i.e. assimilated or erased). Landon's critique of her investment in hearing particular elements in her construction of the story is also crucial. The ethical obligation towards the Other's response-ability is maintained, according to Oliver, by 'vigilance'. Vigilance 'in elaborating and interpreting the process of witnessing' (18) opens up the possibility of maintaining an ethical gap between Self and Other that is potentially a non-hostile space where difference is articulated in the form of response-ability and address-ability. Such an approach privileges (rather than exceptionalises) the unreliability of testimony from a singular witness: *the story that I tell of you is not the story that you would tell.* In this sense, the two books,

Jackson's Track and *Jackson's Track revisited*, sit together as a form of postcolonial diplomacy which fails to produce the last word and as such keeps alive the suggestion of words to come. Bushmen like Harney, Tonkin and Savage were not simply observers of what went on and faithful recorders of the frontier, they were also seen by others who told a different story, interrupting in another way the (secondary) polishing or whitewashing of their stories into appropriate/d legends.

Jim Crows

Some of the white men in country towns who would specially discriminate against Aborigines by day, under the cover of darkness
would slip out to the Aboriginal Reserve or fringe camp looking for
sex with Aboriginal women ... This ambivalence, the jangling coexistence within the same individuals of aversion and attraction, desire
and repulsion, itself constitutes one of the raw nerves of race relations.

Denis Byrne (2003, 185)

One cannot make full human sense of the development of European
life in Australia without reference to the structure of racial relations
and the persistent indifference to the fate of Aborigines.

WEH Stanner ([1963], 2009118)

Bill Harney could tell whether or not he and Linda would be welcome
at the table of white station bosses: 'I would pass some hint that my
wife was coloured and she must be invited too. Should I notice a slight
hesitation, I must ask to be excused' (1961, 46). What would it have
meant for the cattle boss to have a coloured woman and her white
husband to tea? Or to put it a different way, in what context might a
coloured woman have been welcome into the homestead *without* any
hesitation? Aboriginal women at the homestead were usually servants,
not wives. As a servant, an Aboriginal woman would have been, as
Moreton-Robinson writes, 'allowed to be in contact with material items'
like tea cups, plates and dinner tables but not allowed 'use of the same
material items' because such 'recognition would have disrupted the on-

tological basis for hierarchy and discrimination' (2003, 28). Hence the 'slight hesitation' that Harney looked for in the expression of the station bosses implies a mutual awareness, albeit unacknowledged, of the precariousness of racial segregation built into the rituals and material culture of 'domestic colonialism' (see McClintock 1995). Refused hospitality on the basis of a mixed-race marriage, both Linda and Harney felt the hypocrisy keenly, suspecting that those who refused were themselves 'keeping black concubines' (1961, 46). Harney's marriage to Linda cemented his critical standpoint, making him keen to 'out' the white men of the north for their 'sham and hypocrisy'. These were the men whom Harney believed to be more invested in the 'race trap' and the 'colour conflict' (to use Harney's terms) because they used segregation as a screen; they were the Jim Crows, capable of extreme cruelty, confident (however nervously) that their own transgressions would be covered over by their public performance of segregation.

While the previous chapter examined narratives of white bushmen who were open (but still guarded like Tonkin, or secluded like Jose) about their relationships with Aboriginal women, this chapter focuses on white men who were not open about their relationships, who hid and denied them, and kept their tables and tea rooms for whites only. These were the men whose 'raw nerves' might have jangled, as they lived with the 'coexistence of aversion and attraction, desire and repulsion' as Denis Byrne indicates in the epigraph above. How did the white men who enforced segregation by day and pursued Aboriginal women by night manage these jangling nerves? How did segregation and sexual intimacy correlate? One thing is clear and that is the sheer effort that went into maintaining control over the public secret that Harney and others wished to out. In his desire to expose the Jim Crows, Harney found himself up against cultivated paternal indifference, brought to the fore, indeed already outed, by the policy of 'breeding out the colour'; a policy on paternity that instrumentalised white sperm (emphasising biological paternity) while making social fathers largely incidental. The role of indifference, and in particular the *cultivation* of paternal indifference, is thus central to the story of Harney's Jim Crows.

Two years after Harney had written of his frustration with the Jim Crows, WEH Stanner argued that 'persistent indifference' towards Aboriginal people was a major feature, if not the definition, of European life in Australia. Stanner wrote: 'one cannot make full human sense of the development of *European life* in Australia without reference to the structure of racial relations and the persistent indifference to the *fate of Aborigines*' (1990 [1963], 118, emphasis added). Rather than talking about Europeans in terms of national character, he wrote of life, as if life itself has come to be defined as European. He also referred repeatedly to Aboriginal fate, stressing the structural relationship between European life and Aboriginal fate, or 'ruin', as in 'there was more than an accidental correspondence between the ruin of Aboriginal, and the making of European, life in Australia. There was, in fact, a functional concomitance'. This was Stanner's biopolitical reading (before Foucault) of power exercised in and by the cultivation of life itself, and the cultivation of Aboriginal fate, to 'un-be' (2009, 21), to let die.[1] Life itself was made in the service of Europeanness, defined into being alongside war ('silent wars' as Pascoe writes, 2007), violence, biological absorption and the unparalleled social engineering represented by what we now know as the Stolen Generations.

The sheer scale of the 'reproductive intervention' (Anderson 2002, 228) that the Stolen Generations represent attests to a profoundly active interest in procuring life for Europeanness, as the Canberra Conference announced: 'all efforts be directed to that end', that is, 'their ultimate absorption' (1937). This was not a 'comfortable and relaxed' attitude (see Bird Rose's discussion of John Howard 2004) towards an historical inevitability or evolution, but rather a social intervention on a grand scale to lay claim to life in the form of a 'biologically homogenous national body and mentality' (Anderson 2002, 256). And at the same time as this reproductive intervention to cultivate whiteness, there was the cultivation of indifference.

Indifference did not simply appear by itself. Like whiteness, or the concept of destiny as deployed by the chief protectors in 1937, indifference had to be cultivated. In terms of the white fathers who denied their kin, it was not simply a matter of indifference alone, or a matter of not caring. Rather, I have come to the conclusion that the policy of biological assimilation, itself modelled more broadly on the appropriation of life for white Australia as Stanner shows, was itself implicated

---

1   All this in the decade before Foucault writes that biopower is 'situated and exercised at the level of life, the species, the race, and the large-scale phenomena of the population' (1990–92, vol. 1).

in the cultivation of paternal indifference, a state of unknowing, disre-membering or denial that made it possible for white fathers to act 'as if they saw the children of their unions with Aboriginal women as not being connected to themselves' (Kinnane 2003, 31). Kinnane's stunning description of white fathers as puzzlingly disconnected from their children encapsulates that state of indifference and also leads me to wonder how it was cultivated. It seems not to have been motivated by feelings like hatred, or even just fear or guilt alone, but also a state of numbed indifference. It seems to me that the policy of biological assimilation exposed, reflected and also cultivated that state of indifference because it positioned white men as, on the one hand, spermatic conduits for future whiteness and, on the other hand, as the white nation's black sheep, degenerate sons who threatened the very legitimacy of white colonial authority.

It is clear that Cecil Cook, for instance, worked towards securing marriages between Aboriginal women and white men, while his Western Australian counterpart, AO Neville, appeared nonplussed about the conditions under which 'white' Aboriginal people were to be born. When Neville told Canberra Conference members that it 'didn't matter if she has a dozen children' because they would be taken away and raised in white homes and institutions, he was also implying that it would not matter to the white fathers either. Indifferent paternal figures were thus paradoxically useful to the program of biological assimil-ation, even while it lamented their paternal shortcomings. Although bemoaned by state paternalists as failing in their duties towards their own offspring, the indifferent white father was also assumed to be un-likely to intervene to prevent the removal of his children from their mother, nor likely to expose the unfair treatment of Aboriginal wo-men and girls by whites, nor was he assumed to be likely to complain of government interference, white 'civilisation' and its pretensions. The indifferent paternal figure was, in other words, a good client of a state that had its own ideas about a future formed by state-sponsored repro-ductive intervention.

But the indifferent paternal figure could also bear traces of those jangling nerves that Byrne describes. Should his indifference wear thin, should he start to show signs of having an interest, there were other mechanisms for denial that were ready at hand. It is the various cultural mechanisms for cultivating paternal indifference that I am interested in exploring here, in sometimes fleeting examples where otherwise silent white men are seen and recorded and described in Aboriginal life histories. Indifference was not something that was a masculine prerogative. White women as well as men were implicated in the cultivation of indifference and denial, as the examples from this chapter demonstrate. It is especially interesting to consider how indifference was cultivated in the home. What fed and sustained indifference was not the melodramatic but the everyday, the mundane habits of cultural life that cultivated normative expectations, such as the seemingly unspectacular question of who was and who was not welcome at the homestead for tea. As Harney indicates and as Moreton-Robinson's reading of the servant's relationship to the white home's material items shows, it was in a segregated domestic sphere that the everydayness of indifference was cultivated, sustained, fed, and served up.

In a number of Aboriginal life histories, the attitudes of whites towards Aboriginal people is symbolised by their exclusion from the dinner table, which is always much more than sharing a meal, as Gladys relates in *My place*:

> I suddenly realised that there hadn't been one Christmas dinner when Mum had eaten her meal with us. She'd had hers alone in the kitchen all those years. I never wanted to be in the dining room again after that, I wanted to be in the kitchen with my mother. (1988, 338)

This kind of exclusion was aimed at distinguishing family from servant, as Glenyse Ward discoverd when working for Mrs Bigelow who specified that she was not allowed into the dining room 'while any member of the family was there' unless the bell summoned her inside to serve (1988, 19). In *My place*, Arthur Corunna recalls that his white father Howden Drake-Brockman

> used to dance on his own in the dining room. He'd be doin' this fox-trot, kicking his leg around with no partner. I used to watch. There was a big dining room then, and a great, huge fan that we had to pull to cool people off who were eating there. They gave us a handful of raisins for doing that. (1988, 226)

Arthur was Howden Drake-Brockman's son but is here positioned as a servant given raisins to pull a fan for those eating in the dining room. Arthur's absence from that dining table, while cooling those sitting at it, is significant. It is part of the puzzle about white fathers that Kinnane raises (2003, 31). Family servants – servants who were family but *not* family – could very well represent the ambivalence of this connection, that 'slight hesitation', those jangling nerves, detected in white men who simultaneously *did* and *did not* want their Aboriginal partners and their children around. The children and partners were necessary labourers after all, and crucial to the success of pastoral stations which were in white hands but on Aboriginal land; fraught and nervous sites of co-existence.

Sara Ahmed's work on the phenomenology of the table (dining table, writing table) is very useful here. Following Janet Carsten's *After kinship*, Ahmed builds on the proposition that the table is a 'kinship object' that expresses commonality and sociality between people (Arendt 1958 in Ahmed 2006, 80). Gatherings at the table are 'not neutral but directive', and being 'at the table' we 'may be required to follow specific lines' (2006, 81). Ahmed examines how the table reproduces certain encounters and desires by 'orientating' the body and its desires towards certain legitimate (straight) objects and away from others that are deemed to be illegitimate. She shows that heterosexual objects (marriage photos, the arrangement of chairs, places at the table, wedding gifts) that surround the family table construct a heterosexual 'line' which the child is expected to emulate. That these objects are often in the background is part of the reason that they seem to disappear into social norms, becoming invisible like whiteness. Ahmed's work helps to bring the spotlight back to the 'homeliness' of colonialism, highlighting what Anne McClintock describes as the 'far reaching clout' of 'domestic colonialism' (1995, 36) (the 'home' writ large). In this 'domestic colonialism', the colonies were not only extensions of the imperial 'family of man' but did their very best to bring Aboriginal people within the white home – but not necessarily *to the table*. Again, what is highlighted is the very 'everydayness' of political, racial and sexual orientations, organised into the very habits and furnishings of domestic life. Bringing Ahmed's work into the conversation with the arrangements at the homestead that Harney and Linda encountered, it is clear that for Harney, sharing a feed at the homestead with the white bosses was literally a matter of sustaining life (and mateship) through food and recognition. Being denied that share also fed and sustained the indifference with which the white bosses treated their own servants, lovers and children. At the homestead the dinner table sustained life and cultivated indifference simultaneously. The question of who sat at the table and who served at it was thus not just symptom but an act of colonial control.

Ronald Hyam's study of sexuality in the British Empire shows that unequal race relations became more entrenched in the 19th century and that this was not (only) because of the scandals of interracial sex, but because such relationships failed to give ground to new political fraternities. He puts it this way: 'it was not what happened in the bedroom that matters, but what did not take place in the dining-room' (1990, 214). Kirk-Greene notes that 'a major hiatus in the colonial race relations situation was the deficiency of the social oil of shared meals or refreshment' (Kirk-Greene 1986, 283). Hyam agrees with Kirk-Greene that it was *this* rejection and not sexual intimacy itself that produced interracial conflict. There is no reason why 'sex in an imperial context' should 'be seen automatically as an act of imperial domination', Hyam reiterates. But *not* coming to dinner should, Hyam implies, be seen as close to an 'act of imperial domination' (1990, 212). Matt Savage recounts this conversation in *Boss drover*:

'Why can't Fred eat in the dining room with the rest of you?'

'Oh', the manager said, 'but he's a half-caste'.

'What does that matter?' Sid Bradley said. 'Out in the stock camp you not only eat with him, but often he's cooking for you. I can't see the difference. Why won't you have him in here?'

'No', the manager said. 'Why, next thing you'd want the lubras in the dining room eating with us. You wouldn't care for that, would you?'

'I wouldn't mind', Sid Bradley said, 'provided they were clean and their table manners were in order. Anyhow you sleep with them don't you?'

'Of course' the manager said, 'But I don't get intimate with them.'

Sid threw his hands in the air. 'How could a man be more intimate with his own wife than that?' he said. 'It's the most intimate act between male and female. What's wrong with you? (Willey 1971, 20)

This exchange reveals very different approaches to what constitutes intimacy and how intimacy can be constituted as a condition for political fraternity. Sid Bradley indicates that if the manager is sexually intimate with Aboriginal women, then there is no reason not to eat with them in the dining room; sex here situated as equivalent to the social contract of marriage: 'How could a man be more intimate with his own wife than that?' For Savage (who would never have had a dining room), men like the manager who saw no connection between sex and intimacy are hypocrites and liars. Harney would have agreed, and added that these men were the real source of colour conflict in Australia; they would not get 'on the same level' as the women in their lives (as Harney deemed necessary) and so guarded their dinner tables, their white domains, closely.

Harney, Sid Bradley and Savage were keen to point out what they saw as a profound contradiction in the life of the managers (the bosses). Sid Bradley even suggested that there was something 'wrong' with the manager. The manager's response, related by Savage, provides a glimpse into a different sort of logic that the manager held, regarding sex and a politics of recognition. His response was more useful than the 'slight hesitation' that Harney detected in confrontation with his cattle boss. The manager's response indicated that, for him, sex was not a matter of intimacy, was not akin to marriage, did not necessitate anything to be shared, and therefore did not provide the basis or the impetus for any realignment of social power. Sex did not *contradict* the racial hierarchy; it did not produce the conditions for recognition, for greater hospitality. Extrapolating further, he might have seen sex as merely part of his pastoral right to women's bodies, akin to his right to their unpaid labour on the station. Sex appears to have been immaterial, a private transaction of bodily fluids, akin to other bodily motions that one does not share in polite conversation or in the dining room. If the manager was to eat with Fred (the 'half caste' stockman) in the dining room, then that *would* endanger his sense of propriety. If Fred was in the dining room, then everyone would have 'known' that he had sex with Aboriginal women and, possibly, that he even cared about them. He would have been serving himself up for dinner.

What this fleeting glimpse into a Jim Crow's logic indicates is that if sex was to be made *immaterial* (of no broad social consequence), then dinner tables could have gained disproportionate material significance, including the capacity to materialise intimacy itself. It is also important to note that the manager was able to decide what was public and what was private and how private affairs could and could not gain public recognition. White bosses were able to control access to forms of recognition (political, social and kin) by monitoring and enforcing a segregated dinner table. Moreover, it appears that the enforcement of a publicly segregated table, while breaching segregation in private, was not a contradiction of the hierarchy, but an expression of it. The manager's logic may well have been wrong according to Sid Bradley (and indeed Harney and Savage), but that logic was nevertheless internally consistent with his position within a culture of slavery and segregation. He was in a position to determine the constitution of the public/private spheres of the cattle station, so he was not breaching that binary, but maintaining it. As Carole Pateman observes in relation to the false binary of private and public spheres, as a station boss Bradley was able to 'properly inhabit and rule within, both spheres' (1988, 120).

Another example can be found in the depiction of station life in Sally Morgan's *My place* (1988) and in the response to Morgan from Judith Drake-Brockman. In *Wongi wongi: to speak* (2001), Judith Drake-Brockman argues that her white father, Howden Drake-Brockman, was unlikely to be the father of both Arthur and Daisy Corunna (as Morgan suggests) because according to Judith Drake-Brockman, her father had made 'a very strict ruling against fraternising at Corunna Downs' (2001, 9). But as we see in Matt Savage's account above, white station owners like Howden Drake-Brockman might have conducted their liaisons not as guilty exceptions within a 'strict ruling about fraternisation' (9). Instead, they might have conducted their liaisons as part of a station complex that gave them the power to make those rules in the first place, to be responsible for those rules, to have those rules attached to their public face, and for those rules to be passed on as family lore, becoming more and more insistent (dependent on ghosts, as we will see) as inconsistencies appear. Howden Drake-Brockman's capacity to make those strict rules on Corunna Downs demonstrates that he was well placed to be able to breach them or maintain them, with impunity.

Judith Drake-Brockman, as a white woman, demonstrates a commensurate sense of privilege in her attempts to demarcate the private life of her white father and mother. As well as Howden's 'strict ruling about fraternisation' on Corunna Downs, her other argument for the impossibility of Howden's wayward paternity relies on her parents' sleeping arrangements: 'happily, happily in the same bed, double-bed always' (2001, 4). Drake-Brockman's rejection of Morgan's account includes an intimate reading of her parent's relationship, a curious transgression of another sort, seeking good conscience through peeping at the parent's bedroom, their sex life, their double bed, the place for 'legitimate' sexuality. The idea of 'the incest, the daughter' so horrifies her that, 'I just want to throw up about that' (Dalley et al. 2004). Understandably, Drake-Brockman wishes to expel it from the body of her family history; her own body and her family's history fused in rejection, private and public spheres articulated together. For women, whose access to public life is limited by their identification with the private sphere, the separation of these spheres is part of their subordination (Pateman 1988).

But as a white woman in a settler colonial context, Judith Drake-Brockman asserts herself in both the public and private domains: her very public defense of her father is based on peeping into the private life of her white father and mother and finding nothing. To her, Howden has no closet, as it were, no part of his life that was unknown to her. Arthur Corunna describes the same man, his white father, as having 'shared my Aboriginal father's two wives, Annie and Ginnie' (Morgan 1988, 223). Arthur describes Howden as caught between recognising his kids and seeking white legitimacy as the white husband and son of his religious parents. Howden was a man who 'owned us, we went by his name, but later, after he married his first wife, Nell, he changed our names' (1988, 200). But this did not disrupt the arrangements with Arthur's Aboriginal parents: 'after marrying his first wife, he was still sleeping with Annie' (1988, 202). Arthur describes a

> lonely man. I know one night at Ivanhoe, we both got drunk together and he told me all his troubles. He used to go down to Daisy's room at night and talk to her. I can't say no more. You'll have to ask her. (201)

Isabel Flick tells the story of her aunt, who at the age of 13 was told by the boss to go to the stockmen's quarters one night. Again, this story highlights the control that the white bosses were able to exert over both the public and private spheres of their station. Flick recalls that her aunt:

> didn't say nothing, because she was a bit frightened. But when she gets down there the stockman was eyeing her off, see. And he's saying: 'They said you was 18'. 'I'm only 13', she said. And he said 'Well, they told me you was 18'. See they must've made arrangements for her to sleep with him.

After being 'terrified all night' the stockman decides 'Well, you'll just have to sleep there. We'll tell them a story in the morning' (Flick & Goodall 2004, 53). What kind of a story was the stockman going to tell? Why didn't he just let her go given that, according to Flick's reading, he 'cared enough not to touch her'? In the morning he tells Flick's aunt, 'Just don't say nothing when you go back up there. You just don't say nothing'. It's not entirely clear if the secret the stockman wants kept is his own, or the boss'. Flick reveals an attitude towards Aboriginal women and girls that saw them as sexual currency between boss and stockman, an attitude that is referred to somewhat approvingly by Matt Savage in *Boss drover*, and with restrained horror by Harney. Flick's emphasis on the story that the stockman wishes to tell ('We'll tell them a story in the morning' [Flick & Goodall 2004, 53]) is also vitally important, I believe, because it highlights the fact that such stories would have been in circulation alongside the sexual trafficking organised between boss and stockman. Such events were spoken about, not hidden. But they may well have been spoken about in different ways, coded depending on who was doing the talking, and with a view to talking it into silence, turning it into a public secret, something that was to be revealed in order that it might be concealed (Taussig 1999, 51).

The cultivation of these kinds of silences would also take considerable effort. Ella Simon describes her white uncle, who never acknowledged her, in a way that recalls the public secret, as well as his own particular, very active expression of indifference towards her. She writes:

> I'd nearly always run into this little old fellow buying a paper. He'd always be looking me up and down out of the corner of his eye. I used to wish I could read his thoughts. I mean, was there ever just a

little doubt in his mind about the family dismissing me out of hand? Did he ever wonder what I was really like? Did he ever think that my father might not have done something so dreadfully bad in conceiving me as they had made out he had? If he did, he never said a word. I didn't speak to him either. I never gave him a chance. (1978, 25)

Ella Simon poses vital questions here. What *was* going through her uncle's head as he watched his niece so closely and so regularly 'out of the corner of his eye'? If he wanted to ignore her, then why watch her so closely? Did he keep an eye on her in order to maintain the silence? His silence seemed purposeful and active, 'as pointed and performative as speech' (Sedgwick 1990, 4). Was he fascinated by her 'secretly familiar' (Taussig 1999, 51) face? Did he perhaps wish to make contact with her but also feared the same disowning that had happened to Ella Simon's white father?

White men like Ella Simon's uncle are of particular interest because their active silence places what Stanner calls white Australia's 'indifference' in the context of *cultivation* rather than simply being inattention or deliberate ignorance. That Ella's uncle watched her so regularly indicates a motivated interest in her. And his watching continually exposes him as well. But they did not speak. What prevented this speech is indicative of what goes into the 'great Australian silence', a 'curious silence' which can be appropriated as a closet, that 'curious space that is both internal and marginal to the culture: centrally representative of its motivating passions and contradictions, even while marginalized by its orthodoxies' (Sedgwick 1990, 4). It resonates with Stanner's 'great Australian silence' in more ways than one.

Stanner's 'great Australian silence' refers to the way that Aboriginal life, culture and kinship is continually overlooked in the writing of history, in government policy, in our national monuments and pioneer myths. He argues that this is much more than 'absentmindedness'; rather, it forms part of our 'cults of disremembering'. He calls it a 'structural matter' like a 'view from a window which has been carefully placed to exclude a whole quadrant of the landscape' (189). Stanner's choice of the image of a window is significant given that it positions the viewer inside looking out, thus the background, the part that white Australia rarely examines though inhabiting daily, is largely unseen. This domestic space of hiding, which Stanner calls a window, resembles a closet. The closet has long been associated with public secrecy (see also Fiona Nicoll's discussion of 'coming out' as white [2002] and Nolan 2004) and sexuality (Sedgwick 1990) and has recently been taken up in Clarence E Walker's discussion of the 'heterosexual closet' in his analysis of US Founding Father (and third President) Thomas Jefferson's relationship with slave Sally Hemings. A familiar tale of subordinated family lines, Jefferson probably fathered all six of Hemings' children (Walker 2010). Walker describes the heterosexual closet as 'more than a place of hiding; it refers to a vantage point from which one looks out, watching as well as watched' (Walker 2010, 109). Much like Ella Simon's uncle: watching as well as being watched and fearful (perhaps) of being exposed as the uncle of an Aboriginal niece, brother to a white man who had crossed the line and recognised and loved his Aboriginal daughter.

It is tempting to read the tension between those who were 'out' and those who were 'in' the white closet along the lines of Sedgwick's *Epistemology of the closet* (1990), and I have found many resonances between her reading of the closet and the closeted relations of white–Aboriginal relationships. Harney's pride in 'comboism' as a transformative identity, a new way of life, parallels a coming out, a reclaiming and renaming of supposed 'degeneracy' for progressive anti-racism. On the other side, the Jim Crows are the outwardly 'straight white' men who would 'specially discriminate' (Byrne 2003) by day while crossing the line at night: 'the man who most electrifies those barriers is the one whose own current is at most intermittently direct' (Sedgwick 1990, 84). But Sedgwick warned that the closet and 'coming out' are 'now verging on all-purpose phrases for the potent crossing and recrossing of almost any politically charged lines of representation' (71), but that while it might be 'vibrantly resonant … for many modern oppressions, it is indicative for homophobia in a way that it cannot be for other oppressions' (75). The reasons that she gives for the specificity of the closet for homophobia is that other oppressions based on race, gender, age, size and physical handicap are 'based on a stigma that is visible in all but exceptional cases' (75). Still, closets and 'coming out' proliferate, and such proliferation complicates (by over-extending) and also confirms (by harking back to) the foundational, original and long-standing relationship between homophobia and the closet (69).

Thinking of how the closet is both useful and not useful to describe the life of the Jim Crows in relation to Harney's combos is productive in a couple of ways. First of all, it reminds us, crucially, that it would be a mistake to assume that all hidden relationships are pathological, or, rather, just because relationships are hidden does not mean that they therefore have something awful to hide; it may be love that perilously crosses boundaries. Daryl Tonkin and Euphemia Mullett's relationship is one example. Hiding their relationship (from Welfare especially) was part of a strategy to keep their family together, not deny it. Bill Yidumduma Harney indicates that his father Bill Harney wanted to keep his son and daughter hidden to prevent their removal from their mother's culture. Bill Yidumduma Harney suggests his father was not open about his own relationship because he feared being fined for co-habitation. While hiding might mean shame, shame is not necessarily the result of individual culpability, but can also be, in cases like Tonkin and Harney's for instance, a result of perceiving oneself to be profoundly out of step with dominant community attitudes. The closet as refuge is relevant here.

But the main problem with the closet as an epistemological device is that it has, as Melissa Hardie describes, a 'deadening logic' (2010) stemming from the 'in or out' binary that energises it. Sedgwick, Butler and Hardie critique the closet as a device for liberation because no neat lines can be drawn between those in and out of the closet, as Harney's own particular story shows, with its not-so-great Australian silences. Harney had an ongoing relationship with the closet at the same time that he celebrated and endorsed comboism as a solution to racial conflict, and as a way of outing the Jim Crows. As a place of hiding, the closet is not a space of consistency; we will not find a consistent meaning for those in the closet. Sometimes it is a place where problematic whites are put by others, and sometimes it is a place of retreat, a sanctuary. The point is not to diagnose those in the closet with any one particular meaning, but to think more strategically about what effects the closet has in different contexts.

The most obvious effect of the closet, the white closet, is that it makes possible a figure of whiteness that is not closeted, that is out rather than in, as Harney implies, that is 'without sham and hypocrisy', that is on a level, rather than banging on about the uplift. All these spatial metaphors ground Harney's claims to sincerity and his distance from sham and other false behaviours particular to the closet. Up/down, new/old, inside/out. These binaries hark back to the problem of the closet, that one is either in or out but, when out, as Judith Butler observes, are we really in some 'new unbounded spatiality?' Butler argues that it is the 'figure of the closet that produces this expectation, and which guarantees its dissatisfaction ... being "out" must produce the closet again and again in order to maintain itself as "out" ' (1991, 16). When used to articulate a 'liberation' from racist belief and practice, one side effect on the insistence on 'outing' is to disavow the contested space (indeed the very ground) in which grounding, or 'getting on a level' with, takes place. Harney was prone to overplay the distinctions between himself and the shamming hypocrites by exaggerating his outrage against the abusers. The previous chapter on Harney's campfire, presumed to be 'on the level', while full of its own codes, secrets and silences, illustrates the false promise of its 'new unbounded spatiality' (Butler 1991, 16). Harney's campfire is loaded, like the dinner table, like the closet, like other social spaces.

Swimming pools, cinemas, streets

Moving on from the 'vibrantly resonant' (Sedgwick 1990, 75) closet, there are other items of the domestic scene of colonialism that can also help to highlight the imbalances, the secretive everydayness of lines of order, orientation, desire and denial. It seems that it might be a case not so much that closets as such proliferate, but that public secrets and hierarchy are capable of attaching themselves to many different kinds of objects: closets, tables, swimming pools, cinemas. Aileen Moreton-Robinson's reading of Aborginal women's autobiographies highlight the material items of the household as markers of social hierarchy (2003). Sara Ahmed's work highlights the work that the table does in orienting desire (2006). Denis Byrne's work on NSW rural towns also highlights the ways that segregation can be built into the very landscape, as well as into buildings, roadscapes, and ways of moving in and around town centres and margins (2003).

At a time when the federal government was pursuing a policy of integration or assimilation from around the late 1930s onwards, many rural towns had policies of racial segregation. This paralleled Jim Crow laws across the southern states of America and apartheid laws of South Africa after 1948. Byrne's work suggests that segregated sites did the work of making sure that sexual intimacy did not translate to a shared public sphere. If consensual sexual relationships threatened the racial hierarchy, then it could be publicly reasserted in the segregated street, the cinema, the swimming pool, the café, the hospital, public spaces where Aboriginal people could be excluded, marginalised, threatened, or cordoned off. Not surprisingly, such nervous landscapes as the ones that Byrne describes, produced the 'Jim Crows' that Harney complained of at the outback stations. For Harney, it was the white men who viciously enforced racial segregation by day while pursuing Aboriginal women by night who deserved the name 'Jim Crow'. These segregated landscapes helped cultivate the paternal indifference at the heart of the policy of biological assimilation; manifesting physically the psychic disconnection that Stephen Kinnane brings into stark relief in *Shadow lines*.

Byrne explains that racial segregation operates as a cadastral grid imposed on landscapes and streetscapes, and that segregation worked to enforce a line between theirs/ours, private/public, modern/premodern. Aboriginal people found ways to subvert 'that system of spatial control, transgressing its numerous finely drawn boundaries, poaching on its preserves, tweaking the nerves of a spatial system which was inherently tense with racial foreboding, paranoia, longing and deprivation' (170). These are much like the 'shadow lines' that Kinnane indicates are present whenever racial lines and demarcations are apparent. Byrne points out that the nervous sites produced emotional and affective reactions that reflect the failure of the 'settler fantasy' of containment (188). He lists the swimming pool as one of those places (along with the space of the town common, the river bank and the picture theatre) for such nervousness where 'racial anxiety arguably becomes most intense and acute when the separating space reduces to zero – when black and white bodies actually touch' (170). These 'nervous sites' are akin to Ann Laura Stoler's 'stress points', not 'metonyms for empire writ large' (2002, 208) but indications of its opening fractures, its shadow lines.

The public secret of segregation

In Australia, racial segregation and its nervous sites constitute another public secret. Denis Byrne points out that often segregation in Australian towns was *not* the subject of explicit council by-laws and that practice of racial segregation was 'something white communities were both hyper-conscious of, but also self-censoring in regard to' (2004, 188). Sometimes segregation operated by tacit convention, as Isabel Flick describes in relation to Crows Corner in Johnson Corner in Walgett, where the Aboriginal community in the 1950s could feel comfortable: 'everywhere we went we had a special place where everybody had to meet ... People didn't feel so welcome in the rest of the town' (2004, 55–56). Tacit conventions could be bricked into public spaces themselves, such as Flick's local cinema, where Aboriginal people were supposed to sit in a roped-off section down the front. When Isabel Flick confronts the manager, he suggests that he was merely doing what was always done in the cinema, as if segregation was bricked into things themselves; things made ahistorical and devoid of responsibility. *It's always been that way*: the 'it' means the cinema, rather than the cultural conventions operating in it.

In relation to the public secret, these stress points or nervous sites principally constituted a form of regulation, revealing and concealing simultaneously. One example of this is the Moree Swimming Pool and what is revealed by the explicit attempts by the council to enforce racial segregation of its use. Bob Brown, who was a member of the local council in Moree, tried to find out just why the councillors sought to ban Aboriginal people from the pool. He was given two reasons. One was a fear of sexually transmitted diseases spread via the waters between Aboriginal and white patrons. The other reason given was that: 'You know how Aboriginal men would love to impregnate white women, well they could ejaculate into the pool and this semen swimming around would make the women pregnant' (Curthoys 2002a, 124). Such a comment is almost laughable for its ambivalent projection. Pat Healy, one member of the group, noted that it was a real challenge for her to

> stand in front of a group of people who can seriously tell you that black kids should not be allowed to go into a swimming pool because if they ejaculate they might impregnate white girls. How did you an-

swer something like that? It's so mind-bogglingly ignorant and so mind-bogglingly racist. (Curthoys 2002a, 124)

But there is a perverse logic that public secrecy brings to this folk story. Like a kind of transitional object (Winnicott 2009), the swimming pool worked to reveal and conceal simultaneously what the white community did not, by and large, acknowledge. The segregated swimming pool was the 'legitimate' public face of the town's illegitimate and largely denied, gene pool. What was being practised privately (mixing of the gene pool) was being manifestly banned in another (the swimming pool). So the role of the local swimming pool was to act as a nervous site or stress point for the public secret of 'wayward' (Weinbaum 2004) white paternity. While Ann Curthoys was concerned that the swimming pool represented a 'trivial thing' (Curthoys 2002b, 10) compared to discrimination in the health and educational systems, the swimming pool was an important site that, once identified, came to articulate fractures between the public and private dichotomy that secured and destabilised (again 'revealing and concealing') the public secret of white–Aboriginal relations.

The racial categorisation of identities at this time also served to further divide social spaces: half bloods, mixed bloods, upper-class and lower-class blacks, and so on, terms reflected in popular and anthropological understandings of identity at the time. Maree Reay and Grace Sitlington's work in Moree (published in 1948) describes a town where 'upper class mixed bloods' discriminated against 'lower class mixed bloods' by reference to dirt and disease, and where the former blamed 'mixed bloods' from out of town for causing the 'townspeople to implement a policy of segregation in education and entertainment which did not previously operate' (1948, 187, 183). Reay and Sitlington's attention is on the 'mixed blood' community, which, at the time, would have been considered radical (most anthropologists then were more interested in what was called 'full bloods'). There is little attention paid to the town's white community, apart from the following statement: 'Sexual promiscuity is practically absent in the upper class of mixed-bloods, because they have developed a fairly rigid moral code patterned on that of the white community' (1948, 196). It's not clear what the source is for this depiction of the white community's 'fairly rigid moral code' regarding sexual promiscuity. Whatever the case, the rigidity of the moral code they identify as belonging to 'whites' flew in the face of what surfaced at the Moree pool.

Seventeen years after Reay and Sitlington wrote that the white community of Moree had a 'fairly rigid moral code' that made 'sexual promiscuity … practically absent', Bob Brown described the Moree pool Freedom Ride protest as unacknowledged relatives pitted against one another: 'a huge number of people in Moree are related, they may not be registered down at the registry office … it was cousins and uncles pitted against their nephews' (Perkins 1993). Nor did the 'fairly rigid moral code' describe the situation at the time down the road in Walgett, when Pat Walford admonished the angry white crowd with:

> What did you say your last name was? … That's mine too … you wanna go and ask your father where 'e used to spend his Friday nights, out there at the mission with *my* mother, that's where 'e was. (Perkins 1993)

Reay and Sitlington's 'fairly rigid moral code' (reminiscent of Howden Drake-Brockman's 'strict ruling about fraternization') is not supported by Isabel Flick's account of growing up around Collarenebri, or Ella Simon in Taree, or Myles Lalor's Uralla (250 km away from Moree) (Beckett & Lalor 2000). I wonder if Reay and Sitlington, two white female anthropologists, knew things to be otherwise but did not say, kept secrets and remained silent about the community that they were part of (as whites), and not expected to interrogate. Might they not have intuited or guessed that the white community was not all it said it was, or appeared to be? Would such transgressions confirm or fly in the face of those racial categories they employed so freely?

Jangling nerves

If sexual intimacy risked de-segregation (as relationships formed in love might), then this de-segregation would be reversed by divided social spaces and divided blood lines and identities. Jangling is a word that Denis Byrne uses to describe the raw and contradictory feelings of fear and desire. I imagine that if public secrecy had a sound, it would be a jangling sound; a jaw clenching, eye pinching kind of sound, manifest on the face as it withdraws towards the neck. Public secrecy, like denial, jangles and makes itself heard as something inarticulate, not exactly silent, but not exactly eloquent either. Public secrecy is similar to denial which Stanley Cohen describes as 'always partial; [although] some information is always registered. This paradox or doubleness – knowing and not-knowing – is the heart of the concept' (2010, 22). Ross Gibson describes something similar in *Seven versions of an Australian badland* where he writes, 'sensing but trying not to see, by fearing and knowing but trying not to acknowledge' (Gibson 2002, 111). This 'sensing' but 'trying not to' produces that jangling effect. It is something that is felt, and also something that is reproduced in literary texts, in words, in phrases that somehow 'jar' or 'jangle' with a poorly executed attempt to cultivate indifference, or to cover up, or both.

Australia has been seen as a country of silences and secrets for so long that in fact it seems more accurate to say that it is more a case of public secrecy, which Taussig defined as 'that which is generally known, but cannot be spoken' (Taussig 1999, 50). It resonates with Stanner's memorable phrase coined in 1968: the 'great Australian silence'. Stanner argued that this characteristic silence represents more than sheer 'absentmindedness': it is more of a 'cult of disremembering' (189) and it began, he suggests, from the very early days of the colony in 1788 when relations between whites and Aborigines broke down in the presence of a 'new element'. That 'new element' consisted of sexual violence: 'several instances were noted of open fear amongst the women, and of their menfolk refusing to let them go near the colonists' (103). And yet, Stanner added, the 'documents were curiously silent about the sexual traffic between Europeans and the "sooty sirens", as one appreciative officer called them' (109). This curious silence over sexual traffic was, Stanner implied, a foundational event in the cultivation of the 'great Australian silence'. Stanner rarely mentioned sexual violence again, though it seemed to him to be central to the ways that Aboriginal and white relations soured in the beginning.

Bruce Pascoe takes up Stanner's silence, and a broad culture of silence surrounding Aboriginal–white relations, in a chapter of *Convincing ground* called 'The great Australian face', where he writes:

Their [white Europeans'] native born Australian sons and daughters soon outstripped the height of their parents and grandparents. The features of their faces were changing too. If you look at pictures of the first squatters and then turn to photos of generations ten, twenty and even 150 years later you see a remarkable transformation. The faces are wider and stronger, the lips and noses fuller and we know from our ancestors that the character became more reticent, stoic and laconic. Sociologists have speculated on the influence of diet and the loneliness and hardships of the bush to explain both appearance and behaviour but the Indigenous influence is always ignored. (2007, 116)

Aboriginal and non-Indigenous scholars including Suzanne Parry, Patrick Wolfe, Larissa Behrendt, Anna Haebich, Vicki Grieves, Hannah Robert, Warwick Anderson, Peggy Brock, Russell McGregor, Marilyn Lake, Anne Brewster, Mary Ann Jebb, Alison Holland, Jennifer Sabbioni, Francesca Bartlett, Ann McGrath, Aileen Moreton-Robinson, Victoria Haskins, Ros Kidd, Deborah Bird Rose, Jackie Huggins and many others, have observed that illicit relationships (both non-coercive and coercive) between white men and Aboriginal women were ambivalently endorsed as part of the policy of biological and cultural assimilation. Generations of Aboriginal and white writers, past and present, have established this.

So, the sexual traffic that Stanner observes to be hidden at the birth of the colony became bureaucratised trafficking by the 20th century, not hidden but harnassed, not secret at all, especially for Aboriginal people, but secreted away in the name of forgetting Aboriginal people and sovereignty. The policy of ultimate absorption was designed, as AO Neville suggested in 1937, to allow white Australia to 'eventually forget there ever were any aborigines in Australia'. Chief Protector Neville's own words highlight the deadly irony of his job title. Critical of what he saw as the protection complex in whites, Bill Harney wrote that 'the so-called protectors increase in direct ratio to the decrease of the natives, so that, when all the natives die out, "killed by kindness", these departments will probably be transferred to protect something else' (1943, 205).

Cadastral words

In 1937, Patrol Officer Strehlow was called on to investigate the claims of the Campbells against their neighbour William 'Nugget' Morton, a man known to Harney, and from 1928 known to anyone aware of the Coniston massacre. Barry Hill, referring to Strehlow's diary of 1937, writes:

> 'Nugget' Morton was keeping a Western Australian lubra there for his stockwork: she had tried to run away – as well as some of the girl victims mentioned below – but Morton had got her back (and the other two) each time and inflicted a severe hiding as a deterrent against further attempts to run away. 'Nugget' was since employing as 'stockmen' (he has no male abos. working for him) one or two other little native girls, 9 or 10 years of age, whom he had raped. Another little girl he had given to his nephew 'Shrimp', who was about 17 years of age. Ben Nicker, who was working for 'Nugget' was similarly using a little girl, and both Ben and the girl were suffering from gonorrhoea. (Strehlow quoted in Barry Hill 2002, 288–89)

Barry Hill records that 'for these offences with Aboriginal girls Morton was never brought to account by Strehlow: the evidence was evidently too difficult to gather' (290). The awkward repetition 'the evidence was evidently' is jarring, deliberately so. 'Evidently' in this context highlights the effort that Strehlow was not willing to make known publicly what he knew about Morton. It highlights the cadastral grids imposed on public knowledge, particularly knowledge collected with the interests of whites in mind.

Cadastral justice

Nine years prior to Strehlow's meeting with William 'Nuggett' Morton, Morton had been involved in the Coniston massacre that took place between August and October 1928 in the Central Mount Stuart region. It began when 'Nuggett' Morton was himself attacked by a party of 15 Warlpiri men, or so he alleged. Frederick Brooks was killed and in both cases it was Morton's and Brooks' mistreatment of Aboriginal women that was cited to be, or rather, understood but not acknowledged to be, the cause. Nuggett Morton's character as revealed in the Strehlow excerpt above would certainly support such an understanding. The words 'evidently too difficult to gather' also highlight the role of public secrecy, where knowledge is both present and absent simultaneously. In response to the murder of Brooks, a reprisal party was organised, led by Constable Murray who had recently returned from Gallipoli. Ernestine Hill described Murray as 'a fine character, quiet, methodical, six feet two in height, and of powerful physique'. Her medal-polishing prose situates him as 'leader of the last of the great punitive raids that alone have made for the safety of the white man in a black man's country' (Ernestine Hill quoted in O'Brien 2002, 36).

The Coniston massacre led by Murray was responsible for the deaths of between 70 and 300 Aboriginal men, women and children, while the official figure put it much lower, at 31. Murray admitted to shooting 17 Aboriginal people, with a shoot to kill policy. The board of inquiry set up by the Commonwealth Government (under Stanley Bruce) in 1929 found no evidence that the settlers had done anything to provoke the attack, and also, in contradiction of this, that the party had acted in self-defence. However, for his indiscretion in talking to Hill about 'police matters' without the permission of his superiors, Murray was threatened with being marked down as breaching the public service code. He was let off. He was then charged with assaulting Willaberta Jack (who had killed Harry Henty), but got off. Later, in 1937 he was reported for making profit from rations intended for Aboriginal people. Strehlow assisted in the investigation. Murray got off. But then he was suspended from duties for six weeks when he was found guilty of stealing a table from the Commonwealth Government. He had converted the table into a linen cupboard. I'd prefer to call it a closet. He died aged 91 in 1975, in Adelaide (O'Brien 2002). The 2003 ceremony to commemorate the massacres – to 'remember all the people that had been shot by the ones with rifles'[2] as Theresa Napurrurla Ross explains – included some of Murray's descendants who offered their profound apologies. In this case, the official lines that covered up and gave unof-

---

2   Available online at: www.nma.gov.au/exhibitions/now_showing/
first_australians/resistance/coniston_massacre/yurrkuru_kurlu_video_transcript/
[Accessed on 11 March 2013].

ficial licence to Murray's actions come into direct conflict with family lines decades later, in the form of their inheritance of 'perpetrator history'.

Knowing and unknowing

The inheritance of shameful white family histories, involving perpetrators of frontier violence is explored in Alex Miller's *Journey to the stone country* (2002), where a white woman confronts her own family's denial and the accompanying cultivation of indifference. *Journey to the stone country* illustrates the complicated entanglement of knowing and unknowing, and the lack of inquiry, passed down within white families from one generation to the next. White woman Annabelle's reaction to hearing Panya's story of the massacre of her Aboriginal family by members of Annabelle's family is significant for its portrait of complicity, and for showing that Annabelle may well have known of this massacre, in some way, without acknowledging the full horror of it, for her whole life: 'Annabelle knew that the truth of Panya's indictment lay behind the decades of her own family's silence' (347). The novel portrays Annabelle's 'knowing' in a way that highlights the difference between knowledge and acknowledgment, the difference being, as Stanley Cohen outlines, central to the concept of denial as 'always partial' (2010, 22). Hearing Panya's story, Annabelle is physically doubled over with her 'head in her hands' and 'sick in her stomach'. She is also psychologically doubled up, 'afraid and ashamed and angry all at once' (Miller 2002, 347). Miller depicts Annabelle's 'double wall of denial' (Bar-On quoted in Cohen 2010, 125), or the 'mutual interest of parent and child in denying or avoiding knowledge of what the perpetrators did' (125) in the following:

> Her grandfather: pastoralist, pioneer, cattleman, Louis Nicholas Beck, eldest son of Nicholas Louis and Marthe Annabelle Beck, form Haddon Hill in the green Vale of Taunton. Had her father known the truth? That gentle, loving man? Had her father secretly known himself to be the son of a murderer and his beloved land the plunder of that crime? She had never thought of herself as the granddaughter of a murderer. The Becks, like all the others, had trusted to their silence

about such things in the belief that their crime would eventually be forgotten. (347)

Annabelle herself never asks until the moment when she is forced to consider how it was that her family came to own the vast tract of land where she is from:

> She thought of all the country town museums she had visited, where there was never any mention of the Murris. And whenever she asked the attendant why this was so he would tell her with a fatuous sincerity. Why, Miss, didn't you know? There were no Murris in this part of the country. For it was either tell her that or tell her that her celebrated pioneering forebears of the district had been murderers and thieves. And that is what they must have been. For in truth there were no other means than murder by which they might have acquired their land. The truth was simple enough, but nearly impossible to deal with. (Miller 2002, 348–49)

These national commemorations of white settlement pride are props for Stanner's 'cult of disremembering'; willful ignorance of the fact that, in Stanner's words, 'every fence in Australia encloses land that was once the sole or the shared possession of a particular group of Aborigines. There are virtually no exceptions to that statement' (Stanner 2009, 220). Cohen describes this kind of 'simple' truth hidden as a collective lie 'neither personal nor the result of official instruction' but as related to 'micro-cultures' where 'a group censors itself, learns to keep silent about matters whose open discussion would threaten its self-image' (2010, 11). Annabelle's participation in her family's secret, the town's public secret and the nation's, is not a simple matter of her lying to herself. It is related to her learning not to ask, not to inquire further, and not being in dialogue with Aboriginal women like Panya up until that point – that learning not to ask is part of that cultivation of indifference, from family dinner tables to national public monuments.

Without public acknowledgment (which is where private knowledge enters into public discourse [Cohen 2010, 13]), the knowledge of atrocity and brutality can reappear as a sublime haunting, shadowing, ghosts, the stuff of nightmares. Annabelle's fears shift, ominously, from the story ('She felt she must surely be haunted for the rest of her days by Panya's story' [Miller 2002, 347]) to Panya herself ('Old Panya persist[ed] like a nightmare' [348]). This also signals a deflection of attention from the horrors of the story to the storyteller herself, or from a potential dialogue to a monologue[3] where 'the articulation of injury comes to be represented … as itself an act of aggression: as if Aboriginal people sought explicitly to destroy White Australians' comfortable attitude towards history' (Bird Rose 2004, 23). Annabelle wishes, above all, to reconnect with her Aboriginal lover, Bo Rennie, and 'reclaim their innocence with each other' (Miller 2002, 347). This is made possible not by anything that Annabelle says or does (in fact, she remains silent and passive, burdened by her perception of the weight of this history and Old Panya), but by what Bo Rennie says. He tells Arner and Annabelle:

> Old Panya's just filled with hatred. She can't help herself. You don't want to blame her too much. She never had what Grandma had … The old people did their fair share of killings too. Them days is over. If we don't live together now we gonna do it all again in years to come. The way my Grandma seen it, brothers and sisters don't kill each other. And that's the way she lived. (360)

By moving into a white family that claimed the land, Grandma Rennie pursued a strategy of survival, of entering 'European life'. Grandma Rennie did not pass on that story of the massacre to Bo; her strategy therefore included 'not telling', keeping those family secrets. Grandma Rennie's silence and secrecy was not a matter of indifference, but a requirement to live through (but not necessarily as a part of) 'European life'. Different sorts of secrets are kept for different sorts of reasons, and this limitation on what we can know about secrets is a further paradox of public secrecy.

---

3   Deborah Bird Rose argues that monologue is one of two (the other being time) 'powerful forms of closure' that are 'embedded in mainstream contemporary practice surrounding the relationships between past and present'. Both can be seen to 'deflect responsibility for others' (2004, 14).

How many publics in the public secret?

This clarification is supported by Stanley Cohen's breakdown of denial into specific forms. There is 'literal denial' by which he means a genuine not-knowing, then there is 'interpretive denial' which he writes 'ranges from the genuine inability to grasp what the facts mean to others, to deeply cynical renamings to avoid moral censure or responsibility' (9). Examples of such renamings abound, starting with 'terra nullius' and all the different terms invented to disguise, camouflage and underplay colonial violence. Gordon Reid notes that an organised police party that shot to kill Aborigines in the Roper River region in 1875 was directed to 'have a Picnic with the natives' by Inspector Paul Foelsche, then head of the Territory Police (Reid 1990). Mrs Aeneas Gunn's 1908 memoir *We of the never never*, a bestseller at the time, originally included the chapter called 'Nigger hunt', which concerned a reprisal party organised to prevent further spearing of cattle. The chapter was renamed 'A surprise party' in later editions (see Katherine Ellinghaus 1997 for discussion of this). 'Half-caste' children were renamed when they were taken away (Bob Randall discusses this in his biography), while many were named after the properties on which they were born (and removed from) in a way that obscured white paternity: Arthur and Daisy 'Corunna', Jess 'Argyle', Billy 'Willeroo'. Dulcie Harney, removed as a young girl, was able to find her way back to her brother Bill because she was able to remember her last name. Arthur Corunna describes Howden Drake-Brockman as a man who 'owned us, we went by his name, but later, after he married his first wife, Nell, he changed our names' (Morgan 1988, 200). For Arthur Corunna, changing the names was an attempt to deny paternity.

After the publication of Sally Morgan's *My place*, there was talk of legal action from the Drake-Brockmans, who were accustomed to having their place recognised: Judith Drake-Brockman asked for and received an audience with the premier of the state when she was upset by the publication of *My place*. Write 'your own', the premier advised. In that memoir, *Wongi wongi: to speak*, Judith Drake-Brockman writes that Morgan 'discredits my family and casts serious aspersions on my father' (138). Drake-Brockman's memoir tells us, in the last section, that those aspersions 'are easily ignored' (138). All it takes is a ghost at the bed:

One September night in 1988, 5 years after Daisy's death, I heard her crying. I looked up to see her standing by my bed. Between her tears she kept repeating that she didn't say all those things about Mum and all those other things in Sally's book. Her face wasn't moving but I could hear and understand every word she was saying. 'I know you didn't,' I tried to reassure her. 'It's alright, I know'. (139)

Drake-Brockman conjures a ghost by her bed, more than once, to reassure her that she need not be unsettled by *My place*. By the time Howden Drake-Brockman had sent his 'Corunna' children away with the name of the family property (but not as 'proper' family), opportunities had been lost. Daisy's account of Gladys' paternity is a reinstatement of public secrecy: 'Everyone knew who the father was, but they all pretended they didn't know. Aah, they knew, they knew' (Morgan 1988, 419). Judith Drake-Brockman recalls that she dreaded telling her mother about *My place*, but was assured when her mother's response was 'simple'; it is 'Dais knows' (2001, 136). Neither Daisy nor Mrs Drake-Brockman confirms nor denies, but each asserts that the other *knows* and that knowing is the benchmark of truth itself. What is revealed here is the concealment of truth via an acknowledgment that it is already out there, that someone else already knows (but pretends not to), because in the past they also knew (and pretended not to). It harks back to 'the social function of secrecy' which is 'not to conceal knowledge, so much as to conceal the knowledge of the knowledge' (Miller 1988, 206). Such logic requires that we see the same ghosts; both gesture towards a 'sublime' knowing that transcends, has no need for, indeed avers, dialogue or public acknowledgment. If everyone knows but nobody says, then how do we know that they're not saying the same absent thing? In other words, who makes up the 'public' in the 'public secret'?

Miller's reading of the 'open secret' (1988) reminds us that just because something is 'open' does not mean that its meanings are understood universally. He writes:

Secrecy would thus be the subjective practice in which the oppositions of private/public, inside/outside, subject/object are established, and the sanctity of their first term are kept inviolate. And the phenomenon of the 'open secret' does not, as one might think, bring about the collapse of these binarisms and their ideological effects, but rather attests to their fantasmatic recovery. (Miller, 207)

What this indicates is that although a secret may be open, that does not mean that it gives up the oppositions that produce the secret in the first place. When a secret becomes a public secret, it still does the job of organising knowledge into those oppositions of private/public, inside/outside that the practice of keeping secrets entails. For this reason, although the term 'public secret' connotes a homogenous public that knows the *same* secret, I want to focus here on the ways public secrets can still be culturally specific; that is, silences do not revolve necessarily around the same subject/object, and when spoken about or 'outed', they are not necessarily outing the same thing. Thus my reading of the public secret here is qualified and limited by my focus on how they circulate in white responses to Aboriginal life histories, and also how Aboriginal writers perceive the keeping of white secrets by whites themselves. Twelve years after the publication of *My place*, Morgan revealed

> When I wrote *My place*, we thought Nan had only one child. We've since found out that she had at least six children, and they were all taken away. We're still tracking some of that stuff. So I think for people like my grandmother, there's nothing that could compensate for that scale of loss. (Laurie 1999)

Judith Drake-Brockman describes Daisy as someone she knew for 63 years, and as having 'wonderful, deep and easy friendship' (135). The incommensurabilities are stark. The scale of denial, of secrecy, trauma and incomprehension are weighty. And in this, Howden Drake-Brockman remains without textual flesh of his own, without direct speech. His silence is passed on/over, not without considerable effort of many (Judith Drake-Brockman, Sally Morgan, and Arthur Corunna in particular) to put his silence into speech.

In the context of stolen children, stolen wages and racial segregation, the exclusion of Aboriginal people from the political table appears as a natural extension of their exclusion from intimate familial lines. But in the context of 'domestication', of bringing them into white homes for 'training' into whiteness, this was an exclusion built upon initial incorporation, a claim on 'half-castes' that they belonged to white bosses and, biopolitically, to future whiteness. While articulated within the realm of the family and its servants, such an exclusion based 'on a prior incorporation' (Ahmed 2000, 52) appears natural. Of course it was not natural at all, but practised and enforced through conventions and props such as ringing bells for service, employing sons to fan hot dining rooms, of not using the nice cups, designations of house natives above camp natives and so on. All of this would have helped to create the illusion that the family line was secured in those being served by those brought up to serve. In an interview on Channel 9's *Sunday* program (2004), a member of the Drake-Brockman family, Ashley Dawson-Damer, recalled that on reading Sally Morgan's book, she

> felt the family had been betrayed because we had loved them and we had looked after them, and they were our family. And I don't say blood family, because we knew we weren't, but we loved them. (Dalley et al. 2004)

Here Dawson-Damer articulates the slippage between the paternalism of Aboriginal–white relations white relations – 'we had loved them and we had looked after them' (*like* children) – and the non-figurative paternity that paternalism conjures up: 'I don't say blood family' (*not like* children).

This one word, 'family', like the dinner table itself, troubles those who wield it to articulate love and care but not the *real, blood family* kind of love that signals the presence of those jangling nerves. That troublesome word 'family' also tends to get swept up – uplifted – by national dreams. It seems to me that from what we know (and don't know) about the Jim Crows, the black sheep, the combos, and the bushies, it is important to avoid rushing to reconcile these incommensurabilities within national fantasies.

Conclusion: embracive reconciliation

> Embracive: Given to or fond of embracing; embracing demonstratively.
>
> *Oxford English Dictionary*

> Genealogy can be harnessed to support racialized and racist versions of nationhood and ethnicities but it can also serve as a way of reimagining the fixity of belonging, culture and inheritance in postcolonial contexts.
>
> *Nash (2003, 188)*

> Racial discourse, for example, accrues its force not because it is a scientifically validated discourse but just its opposite. It is saturated with sentimentalisms that increase its appeal.
>
> *Stoler (2002, 159)*

The last two decades in Australia have produced many examples of a culture of denial being met by calls to embrace Aboriginal people, usually in the name of reconciliation and sometimes twinned with republicanism. Reconciliation is regularly invoked as a familial, fraternal embrace between settlers and Aboriginal people, in contrast to republicanism's 'manly' rejection of the mother country's embrace. The same old gender/race tropes trot out. But as an opposite of, or remedy for, denial, embracement is also problematic. Aboriginal people have not only been denied through lack of embrace, they have been denied by being embraced, through various strategies of assimilation, and again within a certain sentimental form of reconciliation that can reveal the persistence of an entrepreneurial settler belonging. I discuss these aspects not in order to denounce reconciliation as an entire political movement (indeed, I am broadly sympathetic to much of what the reconciliation movement seeks to achieve), but to offer, as Wendy Brown puts it, a 'disturbance of settled convictions' (2005, x).

First some examples of what I mean by reconciliation's tendency to position embrace as an opposite to denial of Aboriginal people. There is *This country*, where Mark McKenna calls on Australians to 'embrace the Aboriginal people and cultures that we have for so long tried to deny' (2004, 21). Germaine Greer, in *Whitefella jump up* (2004), builds her thesis for change on the embrace of long-term histories of Aboriginal and non-Aboriginal intimacy. Also notable is Chief Justice Jim Spigelman (a freedom rider with Charles Perkins) announcing in his 2005 Charles Perkins Memorial Oration that:

> To the extent that I am correct, and that millions of Australians have Aboriginal ancestors, the Reconciliation process will be substantially advanced if persons of whom that is true take steps to identify those origins and take pride in finding them.

This is a form of kin-fused reconciliation where family connections are envisaged as an answer to racial discrimination. While the family can be an answer in some contexts, it is also – and I think this is what gets overlooked – part of the problem, especially where Aboriginal people have been 'targeted … for assimilation' (Wolfe 2001, 2) though a process of bringing them into white families and (other) institutions. Being related might today be seen as a 'beautiful thing that can unite people' (as Rintoul 2003 describes the Dodson and Fegan family connection), but, in the history of 'breeding out the colour', it was also envisaged as a thing that can unite people in forgetting.

The major problem with reconciliation's embracive sentimentality is how easily family connections slip into assumptions about difference (as something to be overcome) and about sharing (of land, histories and identity) and this is where it can get a bit tricky. Newspaper headlines regularly bring up unacknowledged bloodlines along the lines of sharing: 'Shared histories surface at last' announces the *Sydney Morning Herald* (January 2010), detailing a story of an Aboriginal side of the family 'lost' by the white side and recovered decades later. Stories that promote a shared history align with national myths, like that of the 'legend of the bushman', where stories are brought together by obscuring as much as revealing. So many of these 'lost' histories, denied pasts and reclaimed connections rely on rethinking the 'white father' as enabling fraternal embraces. They skip (and sometimes deny) the details (and the difference) in order to embrace the sentiment of sharing. Take, for example, the discourse surrounding Sally Morgan's *My place* (1988), a book which drew attention to the denial of Aboriginal and white relations and the legacy of assimilation. Morgan's work was critiqued for potentially pandering to white belonging (Langton 1993, 29–30), and of race opportunism: 'Instant coffee doesn't mix easily with pure spring water' (Huggins 2003, 62). Critics complained that her work overlooked her white relatives in favour of an essentialised Aboriginal identity (Michaels 1994; Attwood 1992) while in *Wongi wongi: to speak* (2001), Judith Drake-Brockman accused Morgan of generating 'serious aspersions' about her white father. It seems that taking pride in their connections might be an unliveable task for both Morgan and Drake-Brockman. Neither seem to be able to ascribe a positive value to the relationship that brings the families together. Their identities, deeply held family beliefs and loyalties, lie not with both communities/families, but with the one (my place) with which they identify.

The capacity for the Morgan/Drake-Brockman story to do the work of reconciliation lies only in its retelling in second-order myth – where the violence, the shame and disgust are allegorised away, leaving a narrative of redemptive reconciliation, where white and Aboriginal shame is reclaimed as a source for the nation's renewed pride. The institutionalisation of fraternal pride as the nation's possession underscores reconciliation's embracive sentimentality; clinging on and searching for things to share, to embrace, to take pride in. This is not to say that there are no stories that can elicit pride. Sara Ahmed argues in her important analysis of shame and its relation to reconciliation, that the 'pride of some subjects is in a way tautological: *they feel pride at approximating an ideal that has already taken their shape*' (2004, 109; original italics). The attempt to shift shame to pride within a discourse of embracive reconciliation thus already takes the form of pre-emptive coming together articulated within an attitude of *despite*, rather than *with*, differences. Ahmed warns of the danger of repeating the 'passing over' of the 'brutality of this history' by the ideal insistence that the national 'we' move forward into a state of 'pride' (2004, 111).

In terms of the white father, while he can be seen as a common point of reference between white and Aboriginal histories, it is important that this is not translated into a shared history if that also comes to mean a resolution of his meaning(s). The contestations, differences and divergences are vital. I do not see this book, for instance, as one that promotes a shared history, or shared literature or shared cultural study necessarily, because to do so would contradict an important argument about difference. Each chapter of this book shows that what white people were saying, doing and writing, or thought they were saying, doing and writing, was not the same as how they were perceived, experienced and theorised by Aboriginal people. That applies to my own work, which, in maintaining a critical focus on whiteness, engages with both white and Aboriginal scholarship and writings and thereby *produces* shadow lines as well as working with shadow lines. An awareness of shadow lines brings with it a methodology that emphasises an active looking for them, rather than seeking to reconcile the irreconcilable. The shadow lines that Kinnane writes of have a very different shape and form to embracive reconciliation. Shadow lines are always already ahead of, in front of and away from, the national body that might attempt to pass over them with an uplifting pride.

The ramifications of embracive reconciliation reach directly into a crisis of sovereignty. Stuart Bradfield recently asked why 'Australia has never seriously entertained a policy approach which recognises Indigenous Australians as distinct nations or peoples' (2006, 80). One answer to this question would point to the tradition of embracing Aboriginal people as precisely 'not distinct', but envisaged to settlers under the 'nation as family' trope; a trope is, as George Lakoff (2001) describes, 'part of our standard conceptual repertoire' for political organisation. Family and kinship are also tied very closely to racial ideologies (Collins 1998; Bammer 1994; Nash 2003; Williams 1995) and the image of the nation as family takes specific form in colonial societies where the colonised are positioned as children under the coloniser's parental control. Indeed, protection boards in Australia often made reference to their power as *in loco parentis* over Aboriginal people. From the earliest days of white colonisation, Aboriginal children have been targeted by whites as a way of 'attaching them to us', to adapt a phrase used by

Watkin Tench, a phrase that unites the familial with the colonial, naturalising the conditions of colonisation and giving 'state and imperial intervention the alibi of nature' (McClintock 1995, 45).

Anne McClintock contends that the family took on two main roles that were important to the naturalisation of imperialism. One was that it made social hierarchies appear natural. That is, the 'family offered an indispensable figure for sanctioning social hierarchy within a putative organic unity of interests' (45). Secondly, the family made possible a figuration of 'historical time' in which 'historical change (diachronic hierarchy) could be portrayed as natural and inevitable, rather than as historically constructed and therefore subject to change'. Thus, what was 'murderously violent change' under imperialism could be 'legitimised as the progressive unfolding of natural decree' (McClintock 1995, 45). If this resonates today with Australian kin-fused reconciliation, it is because the family is seen not as the place in which murderous violence might be enacted, but as a natural outcome of the presence of settlers and Aboriginal people cohabiting this country.

Familial tropes disguise the conditions under which the 'children' of conquest, the colonised, are made available for attachment and the conditions necessary for surrogacy. 'My native boy' wrote Reverend Marsden in 1799, 'whom I have had now more than four years improves much; he is become useful in the family; can speak the English Language very well; and has begun to read' (quoted in Woolmington 1988, 21). How did Reverend Marsden come to 'have' his 'native boy'? Under what conditions did he make him 'useful in the family'? The taking of Aboriginal children into white homes was seen as an essential part of the work of civilisation, as a letter to the *Sydney Gazette*, dated 11 August 1810 from a 'Friend to civilisation' attests: it argues for 'the necessity of adopting as many of the native children as we can procure, and making them members of our own families', in the event that they will then 'contribute as much as possible to the work of civilisation' (quoted in Woolmington 1988, 58). Shirleene Robinson notes in her study of Aboriginal child slavery in Queensland that white settlers stole, traded and bought over a thousand children to labour for them during the period 1842 to 1945. They focused on procuring children because they were seen as 'more easily controlled than adult Aboriginal workers' and taking them would reduce the threat posed by Indigenous people (2008, 29). Taking the children was like taking the future, 'breaking the circle' (Haebich 2000), disrupting and fragmenting the transmission of cultural memory and attachment to country.

That the 'family' could function biopolitically (and not simply as a form of sentimental inclusion) is not surprising given its proximity to the nation. As Anderson puts it, nationalism is often treated as an ideology but 'it would, I think, make things easier if one treated it as if it belonged with "kinship" and "religion" ' (Anderson 1993, 15). Feminist scholarship on nationalism consistently points out that it 'cannot be understood without a theory of gender power' (McClintock 1995, 355). A number of feminist scholars have noted that while men are enlisted into an 'imagined nation' (Anderson 1993) by the trope of, and political organisation of, fraternity (Pateman 1988; West 1997, xvi), women are more often figured as 'not equal to the nation but symbolic of it' (Sharp 1996, 99), and, importantly, are often mobilised in terms of women's capacity to symbolically as well as literally reproduce the nation and its citizens (Anthias & Yuval-Davis 1989). Alys Eve Weinbaum argues that the 'privileged discursive cluster' of the terms 'reproduction', 'race', 'nation' and 'genealogy' expresses the 'raciological thinking that molded exclusionary forces into their most violent and enduring forms' (Weinbaum 2004, 3). In challenging the 'whitening' of family trees, the concentration of nation in race:reproduction (as Weinbaum puts it) of whiteness, Weinbaum mobilises what she, following Foucault, calls a critical genealogy, a method of analysis that privileges that which does not fit in to exclusionary categories, such as the exalted family trees on which national identities rely. Writing in the context of American histories of racial segregation, Weinbaum highlights how 'wayward reproduction' – a wonderful phrase – threatens the exclusionary categories of nation by the discovery of 'disrupted pedigree', and 'those subjects who threaten to disrupt even the most reputable lineages' (60). In the US, the 'one drop rule' of hypodescent and the ban on marriage between white and African Americans until 1967 make such discoveries of 'disrupted pedigree' pertinent and indeed critical. But in the context of Australia, where we had segregation *and* biological assimilation of Indigenous people (and Margaret D Jacobs points out that Australia's assimilation of Aborigines was more extreme than US assimilation of Native Americans; 2009, 66), then the 'one drop rule' does not have the same intensity, the same revelatory effect of blasting open family secrets. In Australia it is not just or only a question of denial or suppression, though the example of Judith Drake-Brockman's response to Sally Morgan's *My place* is certainly a good example. A critical genealogy of Australia's race:reproduction nexus would also have to highlight the role of the embracing of Aboriginal people, by which I mean incorporated by an entrepreneurial whiteness that is not troubled or disrupted by Aboriginality, but is able to absorb and consume and replace (to go back to Wolfe's point). This is only a fantasy of course, a white fantasy, but it is one that circulates today while perhaps forgetting its own genealogies. This is why I would agree with Moran's concern that, in the absence of binding recognition of Aboriginal people's sovereignty with indigenous rights (see Watson 2005; Brennan, Behrendt, Strelein & Williams 2005), strategies of 'indigenizing settler nationalism' run the risk of appropriation and 'window dressing' (Moran 2002, 1036).

Take, for example, McKenna's work on reconciliation and republicanism, the 'two great symbolic issues of Australian politics in the 1990s' (McKenna, 2004) where the Queen is presented as being *in the way* of the transformation of Australia's national identity while Aboriginal people represent *the way in*. McKenna's framing of Australia highlights some of the ways that gender and race are troped within current discourses of reconciliation and republicanism. The gendering of the struggle for national identity is well documented in Australia (see particularly Lake 1994, 1997 as well as Grimshaw, Lake, McGrath & Quartly 1994), and in McKenna's book it is given stark realisation in the form of Garry Shead's accompanying paintings. McKenna is drawn to Shead's work because 'to remove the Queen from Shead's landscapes and imagine a republic implicitly suggests the assertion of a long-denied indigenous presence, the recognition of Aboriginal culture and Aboriginal ownership of land' (McKenna 2004, 29). The first painting that appears in the book is 'Mounted couple' (1996). It shows a white man and white woman who wears a crown that hovers over her head like a 'queenly' white woman and/or a white woman queen. The two are riding on horseback away from a group of Aboriginal people camped by the side of a road. An Aboriginal woman stands apart from this group with her hands outstretched towards the white couple, leaning towards them while she gazes directly out at us. The white man's eyes are shaded, obscured by his low fitting hat and the white woman gazes off centre, away from the other woman. To me, this painting hints at sexual rivalry on the frontier, where the white man married the white woman, sometimes leaving his Aboriginal partner behind. 'Removing' the queenly white woman from this picture allows not just the recognition of 'long denied indigenous presence', it also places the white man in the potential 'embrace' of the Aboriginal woman. Recalling Xavier Herbert in chapter 2, this image conjures up a symbolic 'naturalizing' (Goldie 1989; Collins 1998; Williams 1995) for the settler (male) who lacks 'indigeneity'. In relation to women particularly, Shead's imagery echoes the way that rivalry over land, belonging and legitimacy is sexualised in Australia as a competition between 'reproducers' of different kinds of nations (Anthias & Yuval-Davis 1989). In Australia, this rivalry has played out in divisions between Aboriginal women and white women from the early decades of the 20th century onwards.

First-wave white feminist campaigners in Australia promoted a sisterhood between Aboriginal and white women on the basis of shared maternity as well as a shared status as British subjects (Lake 1994, 1998b; Paisley 1995, 262; see also Sheridan 1995 and Grimshaw 1996). Myra Tonkinson finds in 'Sisterhood or Aboriginal servitude? Black women and white women on the Australian frontier' that, contrary to 20th-century Australian feminist rhetoric, there is no evidence for a sisterhood based on friendship between Aboriginal and white women. What she finds are 'relationships of mistress and servant, custodian and charge, teacher and pupil, occasionally mentor and protégé, or co-workers' (Tonkinson 1998, 38). Relationships between Aboriginal and white women were 'mediated through [white] men' (1998, 39) which had the effect of producing a veiled sexual rivalry (Tonkinson 1998, 38) and unequal contest for position in relation to white men. Margaret Jolly (1993) and Jenny Sharpe (1993) both make the point that 'colonising women' were often stereotyped or represented as supporting harsh racial segregation to control the sexual habits of their husbands (Jolly 1993; Sharpe 1993). This was not a view promoted only by white men whose interests it might have served. It was something that Aboriginal women also pointed out. Ella Simon suggests that white women were more interested in maintaining the racial hierarchy than white men:

> One thing I have noticed, though, is that men accepted me more than women generally. Somehow the white woman seemed to have a thing about having to show she was better than I was. And make it

obvious, what's more. I don't know why. Could it have been jealousy? If so, jealousy of what, for heaven's sake? (Simon 1978, 172)

Matt Savage argues that the jealousy between Aboriginal and white women was sexually and class based:

> The station wives hated the lubras. I suppose they were jealous. They treated the blacks like animals ... they would arrive in the Kimberleys where they had nothing to do but to queen it over an army of black servants. (Savage quoted in Willey 1971, 84)

Savage depicts the white women as 'queening' it over the blacks, though they were 'slaveys' with the 'same thing' as the Aboriginal women. Matt Savage concludes that 'in my experience every one of these blokes went back to the lubras. And the wives hated them for it' (Savage quoted in Willey 1971, 18).

In her critique of white Australian feminism's blindness to white race privilege, Moreton-Robinson argues that first-wave feminism 'sought to civilise Indigenous women, in particular our sexuality, to minimise racial impurity' (Moreton-Robinson 2000, 123) and that white women sought to maximise their own status within the white nation by reproducing whiteness (O'Shane quoted in Moreton-Robinson 2000, 168; see also Jackie Huggins 1994). National policies regarding the birth rate explicitly sought to (and still do – see Jackson 1999 and Robertson 2005) populate the country with white babies while restricting and fragmenting Aboriginal families (Haebich 2000). Fiona Paisley notes that in the 1930s white women were positioned as (and saw themselves as): 'mothers of *the* race and Aboriginal women as mothers of *race*' (1995, 254; original italics). What about today when national identity is still a source of anxiety, and deemed to be in need of transformation? What roles do women as reproducers of collective identities play? The transformation of settler identity, posed as a choice between women (as political sovereignties) continues this rivalrous reproduction of the nation. And although McKenna represents reconciliation and republicanism as a heterosexual, male choice between women, it is not only men who do the embracing: white women too can make powerful claims for the transformative effects of embracing an Aboriginal presence.

Whereas in colonial mythology the embrace of white women by the colonised justified colonial rule and retaliation against an unruly native populace (see Sharpe 1993; Inglis 1974), in postcolonial mythology such an embrace can mark a naturalisation and indigenisation of the settlers and a rejection of imperial history. In 1995 the painter Arthur Boyd, Australian of the Year, suggested that the Australian flag be redesigned to feature two figures, a white woman and an Aboriginal man in an embrace; a symbol of reconciliation (Morton 1996, 177). Boyd's motif suggests a break with Australia's colonial past in which sexual intimacy between white women and black men was taboo and 'unspeakable' (Haskins & Maynard 2005, 205). But his choice of woman–man union also indicates a continuation of the long-held association of woman with nation. 'Speaking' that relationship and in particular turning it into a discourse on nation and even a postcolonial methodology (as Haskins and Maynard suggest [2005, 191, 195]) does not extend beyond the woman–nation trope, but continues it. The white woman who seeks out 'her own version of integration with Aboriginal society' (Haskins & Maynard 2005, 205), is not necessarily the master of that integration; it may be co-opted by a settler society that delights in her transgression as a welcome transformation of settler identity.

Embracers can be needy. I am reminded of Kinnane's phrase, the 'ability of others to make you inhabit their story of you' (2003, 379), like being stuck in the clutches of an unwanted embrace. If, as I have suggested, the rhetoric of embrace depends on 'making good' on the 'bad blood' and/or unfinished business of white paternity, then how might that embrace take note of the occasional but significant *irrelevance* of white relatives in Aboriginal life histories? That white fathers, white relatives did not matter as much as whites thought and think they do. Melissa Lucashenko points out in the preface to Hilda Jarman Muir's *Very big journey* that 'It mattered little that her father was an unknown white man. This small girl had a name, a loving family, and a secure Aboriginal identity' (2004, ix). Jessie Argyle is quoted in Alice Nannup's *When the pelican laughed* as saying 'My father never claimed me … But I don't care. I remember my mother and I got a life.' (1996, 120). Suzanne Parry argues that 'children born of rape were absorbed into an extended family that did not lack for the absence of the white male' (1995, 143). One testimony from *Bringing them home* evinces abject refusal of her white father, 'I don't want any of his blood in my body' (1997, 240). Life writings are commonly directed at mothers and grandmothers that were left behind, or, in Morgan's case, attempted to pass as white. Doris Pilkington Garimara's *Follow the rabbit-proof fence* is one example of this, although, as Anne Brewster points out, the work constructs a 'counter archive' (2002) which strategically includes the naming of white fathers alongside other disavowed stories. In Donna Meehan's autobiography *It is no secret: the story of a stolen child* (2000), Meehan's father is mentioned only once in the book: 'I was polite when I met him but didn't feel any particular bonding' (198). Aileen Moreton-Robinson notes that in Aboriginal women's autobiographies, 'Indigenous and white men are not mentioned or featured as main characters in the texts; it is Indigenous women's relations with other Indigenous women that are given significance' (2003, 15–16). Also pointedly or strategically irrelevant is Bill Yidumduma Harney's father Bill Harney. Hugh Cairns points out that Yidumduma's 'recollection of W.E. is minimal ... he responded matter-of-factly when mentioning a friend's memory of his father, and quickly moved to a more interesting topic' (xii). Bill Harney did not acknowledge his Aboriginal son and daughter to other whites and, in doing so, it seems that he hoped they would grow up with their own culture and mother, father and extended family, all of whom could provide a far 'more interesting topic' to talk about.

Being strategically irrelevant was a decision that Harney might have made not only to protect himself from prosecution (which is highly probable), but also because it was consistent with his criticism of the child removal policy. It is difficult to reconcile Harney's apparent embrace of his own irrelevance with the politics of embracive reconciliation that circulate today. It might seem strange to end a book about white fathers suggesting that their significance lies close to their irrelevance. But it makes sense given the book's emphasis on figuring out how they were made to matter, biopolitically, in the broad scheme of a troubling hope; to 'make good' the 'bad blood' of settler colonialism, to Indigenise white Australia. Their biopolitical failure to do this is linked to their failure to matter in the same way within Aboriginal life histories and white stories. These differences between and within white and Aboriginal stories are 'difficult to reconcile' (Kinnane 2003) and that is also what matters.

Works cited

Achebe, C (1958). *Things fall apart*. London: Penguin Books.

Ahmed, S (2006). *Queer phenomenology: orientations, objects, others*. Durham and London: Duke University Press.

Ahmed, S (2000). *Strange encounters: embodied others in postcoloniality*. London: Routledge.

Ahmed, S (2004). *The cultural politics of emotion*. Edinburgh: University of Edinburgh Press.

Aldington, R (1932). *Soft answers*. London: Chatto and Windus.

Anderson, B (1993). *Imagined communities*. London: Verso.

Anderson, W (2002). *The cultivation of whiteness: science, health and racial destiny in Australia*. Melbourne: Melbourne University Press.

Ang, I (1995). I'm a feminist but ... : 'other' women and postnational feminism. In B Caine & R Pringle (eds), *Transitions: new Australian feminisms* (pp57–73). London: Allen & Unwin.

Anthias, F (2001). New hybridites, old concepts: the limits of culture. *Ethnic and Racial Studies*, 24(4): 619–41.

Anthias, F & Yuval-Davis, N (1989). *Women–nation–state*. London: Macmillan.

Ashcroft, B, Tiffin, H & Griffiths, G (1989). *The empire strikes back: theory and practice in post-colonial literatures*. London: Routledge.

Astbury, L (1985). *City bushmen: The Heidelberg School and rural mythology*. Melbourne: Oxford University Press.

Attwood, B (1992). Portrait of an Aboriginal as an artist: Sally Morgan and the construction of Aboriginality. *Australian Historical Studies*, 25(99): 302–18.

Austin, T (1997). *Never trust a government man: Northern Territory Aboriginal policy 1911–1939*. Darwin: NTU Press.

Austin, T (1990). Cecil Cook, scientific thought and 'half-castes' in the Northern Territory 1927–1939. *Aboriginal History*, 14(1): 104–22.

Bammer, A (1994). *Displacements: cultural identities in question*. Bloomington, IN: Indiana University Press.

Barrett, JR (2001). Whiteness studies: anything here for historians of the working class? *International Labor and Working-Class History*, 60: 33–42.

Bartlett, F (1999). Clean, white girls: assimilation and women's work. *Hecate*, 25(1): 10–38.

Barwick, DE (1962). Economic absorption without assimilation? The case of some Melbourne part-Aboriginal families. *Oceania*, 33(1): 18–23.

Bashford, A (2004). *Imperial hygiene: a critical history of colonialism, nationalism and public health*. New York: Palgrave Macmillan.

Beckett, J & Lalor, M (2000). *Wherever I go: Myles Lalor's 'oral history'*. Melbourne: Melbourne University Press.

Behrendt, L (2007). The emergency we had to have. In J Altman & M Hinkson (eds), *Coercive reconciliation: stabilise, normalise, exit Aboriginal Australia* (pp15–20). Melbourne: Arena Publications.

Behrendt, L (2000). Consent in a (neo)colonial society: Aboriginal women as sexual and legal 'other'. *Australian Feminist Studies*, 15(33): 353–367.

Behrendt, L (1993). Aboriginal women and the white lies of the feminist movement: implications for rights discourse. *Australian Feminist Law Journal*, 1: 27–44.

Bennett, MM (1934). Submission to the Aborigines Royal Commission (Moseley). NA Moseley 005/2, 213–252.

Bennett, MM (1928). *Christison of Lammermoor*. London: Alston Rivers.

Berlant, L (1998). Poor Eliza. *American Literature*, 70(3): 635–668.

Berlant, L (1997). *The Queen of America goes to Washington City: essays on sex and citizenship*. Durham: Duke University Press.

Birch, T (2004). Responses. In G Greer, *Whitefella jump up: the shortest way to nationhood* (pp171–179). London: Profile Books.

Bird, C (1998). *The stolen children: their stories*. Sydney, Random House.

Blackburn, K (1999). White agitation for an Aboriginal state in Australia (1925–1929). *The Australian Journal of Politics and History*, 45(2): 157.

Blagg, H (1997). A just measure of shame? Aboriginal youth and conferencing in Australia. *British Journal of Criminology*, 37(4): 481–501.

Blair, N (1993). In S Rintoul (ed.), *The wailing: a national black oral history* (pp346–355). Port Melbourne: William Heinemann Ltd.

Bolt, A (2001). Painful and hard truth, *Herald Sun*, 23 February, 21.

Bradfield, S (2006). Separatism or status-quo? Indigenous affairs from the birth of land rights to the death of ATSIC. *Australian Journal of Politics and History*, 52(1): 80–97.

Brennan S, Behrendt L, Strelein L & Williams G (2005). *Treaty*. Sydney: Federation Press

Works cited

Brewster, A (2002). Aboriginal life writing and globalisation: Doris Pilkington Garimara's *Follow the rabbit-proof fence. Australian Humanities Review,* March [Online] Available: www.australianhumanitiesreview.org/archive/Issue-March-2002/brewster.html [Accessed 8 April 2011].

Breytenbach, B (1984). *The true confessions of an albino terrorist.* London: Faber and Faber.

Broadbent, D (1989). The Elsey myth revealed. *The Age,* 12 May.

Brock, P (1996). Aboriginal families and the law in the era of segregation and assimilation, 1890s–1950s. In D Kirkby (ed.), *Sex, power and justice: historical perspectives on law in Australia* (pp133–47). Melbourne: Oxford University Press.

Brown, W (1995). *States of injury: power and freedom in late modernity.* Princeton, NJ: Princeton University Press.

Butler, J (1991). Imitation and gender insubordination. In D Fuss (ed.), *Inside/out: lesbian theories, gay theories* (pp13–31). New York: Routledge, 1991.

Butler, J (2004). *Precarious life: the powers of mourning and violence.* London: Verso.

Butler, J (2010). *Frames of war: when is life grievable?* London: Verso.

Byrne, DR (2003). Nervous landscapes: race and space in Australia. *Journal of Social Archaeology,* 3(2): 169–93.

Cairns, HC & Harney, BY (2003). *Dark sparklers: Yidumduma's Wardaman Aboriginal astronomy.* Cairns: Hugh Campbell.

Chatterjee, P (1993). *The nation and its fragments.* New Jersey, NJ: Princeton University Press.

Chow, R (1999). The politics of admittance: female sexual agency, miscegenation, and the formation of community in Frantz Fanon. In AC Alessandrini (ed.), *Frantz Fanon: critical perspectives* (pp34–56). London: Routledge.

Clark, M (1983) Foreword. In *Bill Harney's war,* Harney B, South Yarra: Currey O'Neil Ross.

Cohen, S (2010). *States of denial: knowing about atrocities and denial.* London: Polity Press.

Cole, T (1992). *Crocodiles and other characters.* Sydney: Pan Macmillan.

Collins, PH (1998). It's all in the family: intersection of gender, race and nation. *Hypatia,* 13(3): 62–83.

Cook, C (1933–1940). Marriage of white men to half caste women. Correspondence file, Class 1. Australian Archives: CRS A659 item 40/1/408.

Cowlishaw, G (1999). *Rednecks, eggheads and blackfellas.* Sydney: Allen & Unwin.

Cowlishaw, G (1988). *Black, white or brindle: race in rural Australia.* Cambridge: Cambridge University Press.

Curthoys, A (2002a). *Freedom Ride: a freedom rider remembers.* Sydney: Allen & Unwin.

Curthoys, A (2002b). The Freedom Ride, it's significance today, Public lecture, National Museum of Australia [Online]. Available: www.kooriweb.org/foley/resources/pdfs/37.pdf [Accessed 23 November 2012].

Curthoys, A (1999). Expulsion, exodus and exile in white Australian historical mythology. *Journal of Australian Studies*, 61: 1–18.

Cuthbert, D (2000). 'The doctor from the university is at the door ... ': Methodological reflections on research with non-Aboriginal adoptive and foster mothers of Aboriginal children. *Resources for Feminist Research*, 28(1/2): 209–221.

Cuthbert, D (1998). Holding the baby: questions arising from research into the experiences of non-Aboriginal adoptive and foster mothers of Aboriginal children (Who will look after the children? Hide away, steal away). *Journal of Australian Studies*, 59: 39–52.

Dalley, H, Drake-Brockman, J & Morgan, S (interview). (2004). Sally Morgan: claims of fabrication. *Sunday*, Channel 9 [Online]. Available: sgp1.paddington.ninemsn.com.au/sunday/cover_stories/transcript_1507.asp [Accessed 8 March 2013].

Dalziell, R (1999). *Shameful autobiographies: shame in contemporary Australian autobiographies and culture.* Melbourne: Melbourne University Press.

Darian-Smith, K (1993). Capturing the white woman of Gippsland: a frontier myth. In K Darian-Smith, R Poignant & K Schaffer (eds), *Captured lives: Australian captivity narratives* (pp14–34). London: University of London, Sir Robert Menzies Centre for Australian Studies.

Darian-Smith, K, Poignant, R & Schaffer, K (eds) (1993). *Captured lives: Australian captivity narratives.* London: University of London, Sir Robert Menzies Centre for Australian Studies.

de Groen, F (1998). *Xavier Herbert: a biography.* St Lucia: University of Queensland Press.

de Groen, F & Hergenhan, L (eds) (2002). *Xavier Herbert: letters.* St. Lucia: University of Queensland Press.

Docker, J (1991). *The nervous nineties: Australian cultural life in the 1890s.* Melbourne: Oxford University Press.

Docker, J (1998). Recasting Sally Morgan's *My place. Humanities Research*: 1: 3–22.

Dodson, M (1996). Power and cultural difference in native title mediation. *Indigenous Law Bulletin*: 3(84): 18–20.

Dodson, M (2000). Dr Mick Dodson address to Corroboree 2000 [Online]. Available: www.austlii.edu.au/au/orgs/car/media/Dr%20Mick%20Dodson.htm [Accessed 11 March 2013].

Douglas, K (2002). The universal autobiographer: the politics of normative readings (framing stories and poetry). *Journal of Australian Studies*, 26: 173–85.

Works cited

Drake-Brockman, J (2001). *Wongi wongi: to speak*. Perth: Hesperian Press.

Dyer, R (1997). *White*. London: Routledge.

Egan, T (1996). *Justice all their own: the Caledon Bay and Woodah Island killings 1932–1933*. Carlton South: Melbourne University Press.

Elder, C (2001). Ambivalent utopias: representing colonisation and assimilation in *Naked under Capricorn*. *Journal of Australian Studies*, 68: 135–43.

Elder, C (1993). 'The question of the unmarried': some meanings of being single in Australia in the 1920s and 1930s. *Australian Feminist Studies*, 18(Summer): 151–73.

Ellinghaus, K (2006). *Taking assimilation to heart: marriages of white women and Indigenous men in Australia and the United States, 1887–1937*. Lincoln: University of Nebraska Press.

Ellinghaus, K (2001). Regulating Koori marriages: the 1886 Victorian Aborigines Protection Act. *Journal of Australian Studies*, 67: 22–29.

Ellinghaus, K (1997). Racism in the never-never: disparate readings of Jeannie Gunn. *Hecate*, 23(2): 76–94.

Eterna, L (2006). Albinism in popular culture [Online]. Available: web.archive.org/web/200101240804/http://www.lunaeterna.net/popcult/ [Accessed 23 November 2012].

Evans, R (1993). 'Keep white the strain': race relations in a colonial setting. In R Evans, K Saunders & K Cronin (eds), *Race relations in colonial Queensland* (pp1–23). St Lucia: University of Queensland Press.

Evans, R (1982). 'Don't you remember Black Alice, Sam Holt?' Aboriginal women in Queensland history. *Hecate*, 8(2): 6–21.

Evans, T (1990). *Arnhem Land: a personal history*. Occasional papers, No 12. Darwin: Northern Territory Library Service.

Fields, BJ (2001). Whiteness: racism and identity. *International Labor and Working-Class History*, 60: 48–56.

Fink, RA (1957). The caste barrier – an obstacle to the assimilation of part-Aborigines in north-west New South Wales. *Oceania*, 28(2): 100–10.

Flick, I & Goodall, H (2004). *Isabel Flick: the many lives of an extraordinary Aboriginal woman*. Crows Nest: Allen & Unwin.

Foucault, M (2003). *'Society must be defended': lectures at the Collège de France, 1975–76*. D Macey (trans.), M Bertani & A Fontana (eds). London: Allen Lane.

Foucault, M (1990–92). *The history of sexuality*. R Hurley (trans.). London: Penguin.

Francis, M (1996). Social Darwinism and the construction of institutionalised racism in Australia. *Journal of Australian Studies*, 50/51: 90–105.

Frankenberg, R (1997). Introduction: local whitenesses, localizing whiteness. In R Frankenberg (ed.), *Displacing whiteness: essays in social and cultural criticism* (pp1–34). Durham: Duke University Press.

Frankenberg, R (1993). *White women, race matters: the social construction of whiteness*. Minneapolis: University of Minnesota Press.

Franklin, S & McKinnon, S (eds) (2001). *Relative values, reconfiguring kinship studies*. Durham: Duke University Press.

Frow, J (1998). The politics of stolen time. *Australian Humanities Review* [Online]. Available: www.australianhumanitiesreview.org/archive/Issue-February-1998/frow1.html [Accessed 11 March 2013].

Garimara, DP (1996). *Follow the rabbit-proof fence.* St Lucia: University of Queensland Press.

Garimara, N & Watson, C (2002). Nugi Garimara (Doris Pilkington) interviewed by Christine Watson. *Hecate*, 28(1): 23–39.

Gibson, R (2002). *Seven versions of an Australian badland.* Brisbane: University of Queensland Press.

Gifford, P (2002). *Black and white and in-between: Arthur Dimer and the Nullarbor.* Carlisle: Hersperion Press.

Gill, N (1997). Pastoralism, a contested domain. In DB Rose & A Clarke (eds), *Tracking knowledge in north Australian landscapes: studies in Indigenous and settler ecological knowledge systems* (pp 50–67). Darwin: North Australia Research Unit.

Gilman, SL (1985). Black bodies, white bodies: toward an iconography of female sexuality in late nineteenth-century art, medicine, and literature. *Critical Inquiry*, 12(1): 204–42.

Goldie, T (1989). *Fear and temptation: the image of the indigene in Canadian, Australian and New Zealand literatures.* Kingston, Montreal & London: McGill-Queen's University Press.

Goodall, H (1992). 'The whole truth and nothing but …': some intersections of Western law, Aboriginal history and community memory. *Journal of Australian Studies*, 35: 104–19.

Gray, G (1996). 'The natives are happy': AP Elkin, AO Neville and anthropological research in northwest Western Australia. *Journal of Australian Studies*, 50/51: 106–17.

Greer, G (2004). *Whitefella jump up.* London: Profile Books.

Grieves, V (2011). The McClymonts of Nabiac: interracial marriage, inheritance and dispossession in C19th New South Wales colonial society. In A Holland and B Brookes (eds), *Rethinking the racial moment: essays on the colonial encounter* (pp125–56). Newcastle Upon Tyne: Cambridge Scholars Publishing.

Works cited

Grimshaw, P (1996). A white woman's suffrage. In H Irving (ed.). *A woman's constitution? Gender and history in the Australian Commonwealth* (pp19–36). Sydney: Hale & Iremonger.

Grimshaw, P, Lake, M, McGrath, A & Quartly, M (1994) (eds), *Creating a nation*. Ringwood: Penguin.

Grimshaw, P & May, A (1994). Inducements to the strong to be cruel to the weak: authoritative white colonial male voices and the construction of gender in Koori society. In N Grieve & A Burns (eds), *Australian women: contemporary feminist thought*. Melbourne: Oxford University Press.

Guillat, R (2002). A whiter shade of black? *The Sydney Morning Herald (Good Weekend Magazine)*, 15 June.

Gunn, A (1937). The little black princess: her life story. *Brisbane Courier-Mail*. 2 February.

Gunn, A (1908). *We of the never never*. London: Hutchinson & Co.

Haebich, A (1998). Murdering stepmothers: the trial and execution of Martha Rendell. *Journal of Australian Studies*, 59: 66–81.

Haebich, A (2000). *Broken circles: fragmenting Indigenous families 1800–2000*. Fremantle: Fremantle Press.

Haebich, A (1999). Irresistible journeys and imaginings: Boyd's *Bride series* revisited. *Journal of Australian Studies*, 61: 117–125.

Haebich, A (2008). *Spinning the dream: assimilation in Australia 1950–1970*. Fremantle: Fremantle Press.

Hage, G (1998). *White nation: fantasies of white supremacy in a multicultural society*. Sydney: Pluto Press.

Haggis, J & Schech, S (2000). Meaning well and global good manners: reflections on white Western feminist cross-cultural praxis. *Australian Feminist Studies*, 15(33): 387–99.

Hardie M (2010). The closet remediated: inside Lindsay Lohan. *Australian Humanities Review* [Online]. Available: www.australianhumanitiesreview.org/archive/Issue-May-2010/hardie.html [Accessed 11 March 2013].

Harney, WE (1969). *To Ayers Rock and beyond*. Adelaide: Rigby.

Harney, WE (1961). *Grief, gaiety and the Aborigines*. London: Robert Hale Ltd.

Harney, WE (1959). *Tales from the Aborigines*. Adelaide: Rigby.

Harney, WE (1958). *Content to lie in the sun*. London: Robert Hale Ltd.

Harney, WE (1957). *Life among the Aborigines*. London: Robert Hale Ltd.

Harney, WE (1947). *Brimming billabongs*. Sydney: Angus and Robertson.

Harney, WE (1946). *North of 23 degrees: ramblings in northern Australia*. Sydney: Australasian Publishing Company.

Harney, WE (1944), Patrol Officer Report, Native Affairs Branch, 6 April. National Archives Australia: F1 1944/275).

Harney, WE (1943). *Taboo*. Sydney: Australasian Publishing.

Harney, WE & Elkin, AP (1968). *Songs of the songmen: Aboriginal myths retold*. Adelaide: Rigby.

Harney, WE & Lockwood, D (1990). *A bushman's life: an autobiography*. R Lockwood (ed.), Melbourne: Penguin.

Harney, WE & Lockwood, D (1972 [1963]). *The shady tree*. Adelaide: Rigby.

Hartly, J & McKee, A (2000). *The Indigenous public sphere: the reporting and recognition of Indigenous issues in the Australian media, 1994–1997*. New York: Oxford University Press.

Haskins, V (2003). 'Could you see to the return of my daughter': fathers and daughters under the New South Wales Aborigines Protection Board child removal policy. *Australian Historical Studies*, 121: 106–21.

Haskins, V & Maynard, J (2005). Sex, race and power: Aboriginal men and white women in Australian history. *Australian Historical Studies*, 126: 191–216.

Hassan, WS (2003). Gender (and) imperialism: structures of masculinity in Tayeb Salih's *Season of migration to the north*. *Men and Masculinities*, 5(3): 309–24.

Herbert, X (1990 [1938]). *Capricornia*. (Introduction by Mudrooroo Nyoongah). Sydney: Angus & Robertson.

Herbert, X (1975). *Poor fellow my country*. Sydney: Collins.

Herbert, X (1937a). Herbert to Elkin, 22 December 1937 in Elkin Archives, University of Sydney, P130 41/628.

Herbert, X (1937b). Herbert to Elkin, 23 January 1937 in Elkin Archives, University of Sydney, P130 41/628.

Herbert, X (1937c). Herbert to Elkin, 21 May 1937 in Elkin Archives, University of Sydney, P130 41/628.

Herbert, X (1937d). Herbert to Elkin, 6 September 1937 Elkin Archives, University of Sydney, P130 41/628.

Hill, B (2002). *Broken song: TGH Strehlow and Aboriginal possession*, Sydney: Random House.

Hill, E (1970). *The territory*. Sydney: Walkabout Pocket Books.

Holt, L (1993). One Aboriginal woman's identity: walking in both worlds. *Australian Feminist Studies*, 18(Summer): 175–79.

Howard, J (1999). Motion for reconciliation. Parliament of Australia Website [Online]. Available: parlinfo.aph.gov.au/parlInfo/search/display/display.w3p;query=(Id:media/pressrel/23e06);rec=0 [Accessed 11 March 2013].

Howard, R (1910). Annual Report for the Protector of Aboriginals for 1910 [Online]. Available: archive.aiatsis.gov.au/removeprotect/63720.pdf [Accessed 23 November 2012].

Howard, R (1906). Annual Report for the Protector of Aboriginals for 1906 [Online]. Available: archive.aiatsis.gov.au/removeprotect/63567.pdf [Accessed 23 November 2012].

Howard, R (1905, 1906, 1910). Annual Report for the Protector of Aboriginals for 1905 [Online]. Available: archive.aiatsis.gov.au/removeprotect/63539.pdf [Accessed 23 November 2012].

Huggins, J (2003). Always was always will be. In M Grossman (ed.), *Blacklines: contemporary critical writing by Indigenous Australians* (pp60–65). Melbourne: Melbourne University Press.

Huggins, J (1998). *Sister girl: the writings of Aboriginal activist and historian Jackie Huggins*. St Lucia: University of Queensland Press.

Huggins, J (1994). A contemporary view of Aboriginal women's relationship to the white women's movement. In N Grieve & A Burns (eds), *Australian women: contemporary feminist thought* (pp70–79). Melbourne: Oxford University Press.

Human Rights and Equal Opportunity Commission (HREOC) (1997). *Bringing them home: Report of the National Inquiry into the Separation of Aboriginal and Torres Strait Islander Children from their Families*. Sydney: HREOC.

Hyam, R (1990). *Empire and sexuality: the British experience*. Manchester: Manchester University Press.

Inglis, A (1974). *Not a white woman safe: sexual anxiety and politics in Port Moresby 1920–1934* Canberra: ANU Press.

Irving, H (1996). Thinking of England: women, politics and the Queen. *Journal of Australian Studies*, 47: 33–41

Jackson, N. (1999). Understanding population ageing: a background. *Australian Social Policy*, 1: 203–24.

Jacobs, M (2009) *White mother to a dark race: settler colonialism, maternalism, and the removal of indigenous children in the American West and Australia, 1880–1940*. Lincoln NE: University of Nebraska Press.

Jebb, MA (2002). *Blood, sweat and welfare: a history of white bosses and Aboriginal pastoral workers*. Perth: University of Western Australia Press.

Jolly, M (1993). Colonizing women: the maternal body and empire. In S Gunew & A Yeatman (eds), *Feminism and the politics of difference*. St Leonards: Allen & Unwin.

Jordan, ME (2005). *Balanda: my year in Arnhem Land*. Sydney: Allen & Unwin.

Jose, N (2002). *Black sheep: journey to Borroloola*. Melbourne: Hardie Grant.

Keeffe, K (2003). *Paddy's road: life stories of Patrick Dodson*. Canberra: Aboriginal Studies Press.

Kenneally, T (1972). *The chant of Jimmie Blacksmith*. Sydney: Angus and Roberston.

Kidd, R (2000). *Black lives, government lies*. Sydney: UNSW Press.

Kidd, R (1997). *The way we civilise: Aboriginal affairs – the untold story*. St Lucia: University of Queensland Press.

Kinnane, S (2003). *Shadow lines*. Fremantle: Fremantle Arts Centre Press.

Kinnane, S (2005). Unpublished interview with Fiona Probyn-Rapsey, Canberra, 29 March.

Kinnane, S & Stasius, G (2010). Keepers of our stories. *Australian Journal of Indigenous Education*, 39(supp.): 87–95.

Kinoshi, S (2011). The four fathers of Australia: Baz Luhrmann's depiction of Aboriginal history and paternity in the Northern Territory. *History Australia*, 8(1): 23–41.

Kirk-Greene, A (1986). Colonial administration and race relations: some research reflections and directions. *Ethnic and Racial Studies*, 9(3): 275–87.

Kunoth-Monks, R (1993). Rosalie Kunoth-Monks. In S Rintoul (ed.), *The wailing: a national black oral history* (pp329–36). Port Melbourne: Heinemann.

Lake, M (2003). On being a white man, Australia, c. 1901. In HM Tao & R White (eds), *Cultural history in Australia* (pp98–112). Sydney: UNSW Press.

Lake, M (2003). Woman, black, indigenous: recognition struggles in dialogue. In B Hobson (ed.), *Recognition struggles and social movements, contested identities, power and agency*. Cambridge University Press: Cambridge.

Lake, M (1998a). Australian frontier feminism and the marauding white man. In C Midgley (ed.), *Gender and imperialism* (pp123–36). Manchester: Manchester University Press.

Lake, M (1998b). Feminism and the gendered politics of antiracism: Australia 1927–1957: from maternal protectionism to leftist assimilationism. *Australian Historical Studies*, 110: 91–108.

Lake, M (1998c). The inviolable woman: feminist conceptions of citizenship in Australia, 1900–1945. In JB Landes (ed.), *Feminism, the public and the private* (pp223–40). Oxford: Oxford University Press.

Lake M (1997). 'Stirring tales': Australian feminism and national identity, 1900–40. In Stokes G (ed.), *The politics of identity in Australia* (pp78–91). Melbourne: Cambridge University Press.

Lake, M (1994). Between old world 'barbarism' and Stone Age 'primitivism'. In N Grieve & A Burns (eds), *The double difference of the white Australian feminist. Australian women: contemporary feminist thought* (pp80–91). Melbourne: Oxford University Press.

Lake, M (1994). Between old worlds and new: feminist citizenship, nation and race, the destabilisation of identity. In C Daley & M Nolan (eds), *Suffrage and beyond: international feminist perspectives* (pp277–94). Auckland: Auckland University Press & Pluto Press.

Lake, M (1986) The politics of respectability: identifying the masculine context. *Australian Historical Studies*, 22(86): 116–36.

Works cited

Lakoff, G (1996). *Moral politics: what conservatives know that liberals don't.* Chicago: Chicago University Press.

Lalor, M (2000). *Wherever I go.* Melbourne: Melbourne University Press.

Landon, C (2006). *Jackson's Track revisited: history, remembrance and reconciliation.* Clayton, Victoria: Monash University ePress.

Langton, M (1993). 'Well I heard it on the radio and I saw it on the television': an essay for the Australian Film Commission on the politics and aesthetics of filmmaking by and about Aboriginal people and things. North Sydney: Australian Film Commission.

Lattas, A (1992). Primitivism, nationalism and individualism in Australian popular culture. *Journal of Australian Studies*, 35, 45–58.

Lattas, A (1989). Colonising the other: dreaming, Aboriginal painting and white man's search for a soul. *Bulletin of the Olive Pink Society*, 1(2): 23–29.

Laurie, V (1999). An interview with Sally Morgan. UnionsVerlag [Online]. Available: www.unionsverlag.com/info/ link.asp?link_id=6000&pers_id=91&pic=../portrait/ MorganSally.jpg&tit=Sally%20Morgan [accessed on 15 January 2013].

Lucashenko, M (1994). No other truth? Aboriginal women and Australian feminism. *Social Alternatives*, 12(2): 21–24.

Luhrmann B (2008) *Australia.* Twentieth Century Fox, US.

Mahood K, (2000). *Craft for a dry lake.* Sydney: Anchor Books.

Manne, R (2001). *In denial: the Stolen Generations and the right.* Melbourne: Black Inc.

Marcus, J (2001). *The indomitable Miss Pink.* Sydney, UNSW Press.

Marcus, J (1987). Olive Pink and the encounter with the Academy. *Mankind*, 17(3): 185–97.

Marr, D (1991). *Patrick White: a life.* Milsons Point: Random House.

Marshall, A (1948). *Ourselves writ strange.* Melbourne: FW Cheshire.

Maynard, M (1999). Staging masculinity: late nineteenth century photographs of Indigenous men. *Journal of Australian Studies*, 66: 129–37.

Mazzei, LA (2003). Inhabiting silences: in pursuit of a muffled subtext. *Qualitative Inquiry.* 9(3): 355–68.

McClintock, A (1995). *Imperial leather.* Routledge: London.

McGrath, A (1994). The state as father, 1910–1960. In P Grimshaw, M Lake, A McGrath & M Quartly (eds), *Creating a nation* (pp269–78), Ringwood, Victoria: Penguin.

McGrath, A (1987). *Born in the cattle: Aborigines in cattle country.* Sydney: Allen & Unwin.

McGregor, R (1997). *Imagined destinies: Aboriginal Australians and the doomed race theory, 1880–1939.* Carlton: Melbourne University Press.

McGregor, R (1996). Intelligent parasitism: AP Elkin and the rhetoric of assimilation. *Journal of Australian Studies*, 50/51: 118–30.

McGregor, R (1994). The clear categories of Olive Pink. *Oceania*, 65(1): 4–13.

McKenna, M (2004). *This country*. Sydney: UNSW Press.

McKenna, M (1997). *The captive republic: a history of republicanism in Australia 1788–1996*. Cambridge: University of Cambridge Press.

McLean, I (1998) *White Aborigines: identity politics in Australian art*, Cambridge: Cambridge University Press.

Meehan, D (2000). *It is no secret: the story of a stolen child*. Sydney: Random House.

Mellor, D & Haebich, A (eds) (2003). *Many voices: reflections on experiences of Indigenous child separation*. Canberra: National Library of Australia.

Merlan, F (1978). 'Making people quiet' in the pastoral north: reminiscences of Elsey Station. *Aboriginal History*, 2(1): 71–106.

Meston A (1903) Correspondence to the Under Secretary, Department of Public Lands, 24 October 1903, QSA, A/58764.

Miller A (2002). *Journey to the stone country*. Sydney: Allen & Unwin.

Miller, DA (1988). *The novel and the police*. California: University of California Press.

Miller, J (1982). *Koori: a will to win*. Sydney: Angus and Robertson.

Moran, A (2002) As Australia decolonizes: Indigenizing settler nationalism and the challenges of settler/Indigenous relations. *Ethnic and Racial Studies*, 25(6) 1013–42.

Moreton-Robinson, A (2003). *Talkin' up to the white woman*. St Lucia: University of Queensland Press.

Moreton-Robinson, A (2003b). I still call Australia home: Aboriginal belonging and place in a white postcolonizing society. In S Ahmed, C Castaneda, AM Fortier & M Sheller (eds), *Uprootings/regroundings: questions of home and migration* (pp23–40). Oxford: Berg.

Moreton-Robinson, A (2000). Troubling business: difference and whiteness within feminism. *Australian Feminist Studies*, 15(33): 343–52.

Morphy, H (1996). Proximity and distance: representations of Aboriginal society in the writings of Bill Harney and Bruce Chatwin. In MacClancy J & McDonagh C, (eds), *Popularising anthropology* (pp157–179). London: Routledge,

Morton, J (1996). Aboriginality. Mabo and the republic: indigenising Australia. In B Attwood (ed.), *The age of Mabo* (pp117–136). St Leonards: Allen & Unwin.

Morgan, S (1988). *My place*. Fremantle: Fremantle Arts Centre Press.

Morris, B (1992). Frontier colonialism as a culture of terror. *Journal of Australian Studies*, 35: 72–87.

Morris, M (2006). *Identity anecdotes*. London: Sage Publications.

Works cited

Morris, M (1988). Panorama: the live, the dead and the living. In P Foss (ed.), *Island in the stream: myths of place in Australian culture* (pp160–87). Sydney: Pluto Press.

Morrison, T (1992). *Playing in the dark: whiteness and the literary imagination.* Cambridge: Harvard University Press.

'Mother all White' (1933). A letter to the editor, *Northern Standard*, 20 June.

Muecke, S (1992). Lonely representations: Aboriginality and cultural studies. *Journal of Australian Studies*, 35: 32–44.

Muir, H (2004). *Very big journey: my life as I remember it.* Canberra: Aboriginal Studies Press.

Mulvaney, D (1989). *Encounters in place: outsiders and Aboriginal Australians, 1606–1985.* St Lucia: University of Queensland Press.

Nash, C (2003). 'They're family!' Cultural geographies of relatedness in popular genealogy. In S Ahmed, C Castaneda, AM Fortier & M Sheller (eds), *Uprootings/regroundings: questions of home and migration* (pp179–203). Oxford: Berg.

Nannup, A, Marsh, L & Kinnane, S (1996). *When the pelican laughed.* Fremantle: Fremantle Arts Centre Press.

Neville, AO (1947). *Australia's coloured minority: its place in our community.* Sydney: Currawong Publishing.

Nicoll, F (2001). *From diggers to drag queens: configurations of Australian national identity.* Sydney: Pluto Press.

Nicoll, F (2000). Indigenous sovereignty and the violence of perspective: a white woman's coming out story. *Australian Feminist Studies*, 15(33): 369–386.

Nicoll, F (2002) De-facing Terra Nullius and facing the public secret of Indigenous sovereignty in Australia. *Borderlands e-journal*, 1(2): 1–13 [Online]. Available: www.borderlands.net.au/vol1no2_2002/nicoll_defacing.html [Accessed 15 January 2013].

NOAH (The National Organization for Albinism and Hypopigmentation) (2006). A call for Hollywood to retire the evil albino character [Online]. Available: www.albinism.org/Events/NOAH%20PRESS%20RELEASE%20030506.pdf [Accessed 15 January 2013].

Nolan, M (2004). In his own sweet time: Carmen's coming out. *Australian Literary Studies*, 16(4): 134–48.

O'Donoghue, L (2001). Media release, 28 February. *Australian Humanities Review* [Online]. Available: www.australianhumanitiesreview.org/archive/ Issue-March-2001/odonoghue.html [Accessed 15 January 2013].

Oliver K (2001). *Witnessing: beyond recognition.* Minneapolis, University of Minnesota Press.

Olubas, B & Greenwell, L (1999). Re-membering and taking up an ethics of listening: a response to loss and the maternal in 'the stolen children'.

Australian Humanities Review. [Online] Available: www.australianhumanitiesreview.org/archive/Issue-July-1999/olubas.html [Accessed 15 January 2013].

Paisley, F (2000). *Loving protection: Australian feminism and Aboriginal women's rights 1919–1939*. Carlton: Melbourne University Press.

Paisley, F (1995). Feminist challenges to white Australia, 1900–1930. In D Kirkby (ed.). *Sex, power and justice: historical perspectives on law in Australia* (pp252–69). Melbourne: Oxford University Press.

Parry, S (1995). Identifying the process: the removal of 'half–caste' children from Aboriginal mothers. *Aboriginal History*, 192: 141–53.

Pascoe, B (2007). *Convincing ground: learning to fall in love with your country*. Canberra: Aboriginal Studies Press.

Pateman, C (1988). *The sexual contract*. California: Stanford University Press.

Perkins, M (2004). 'False whiteness': passing and the Stolen Generations. In Moreton-Robinson A (ed.), *Whitening race: essays in social and cultural criticism* (pp164–75). Canberra: Aboriginal Studies Press.

Perkins, R (producer) (1993). *Blood brothers: freedom ride* [DVD]. Sydney: SBS Independent.

Peters-Little, F (1999). The community game: Aboriginal self–definition at the local level (AIATSIS Discussion Paper No. 10). Canberra: Australian Institute of Aboriginal and Torres Strait Islander Studies.

Pettman, J (1992). Gendered knowledges: Aboriginal women and the politics of feminism. *Journal of Australian Studies*, 35: 120–31.

Pierce, P (1999). *The country of lost children: an Australian anxiety*. Melbourne: Cambridge University Press.

Pink, O (1947). Native Affairs Dept. Inefficient Police. Letters to the editor, *Northern Standard*, 3 April, 6.

Pitt-Rivers GHLF (1927) *The clash of culture and the contact of races* London: Routledge and Sons.

Povinelli, EA (2002a). Notes on gridlock: genealogy, intimacy, sexuality. *Public Culture*, 14(1): 215–38.

Povinelli, EA (2002b). *The cunning of recognition*. Durham and London: Duke University Press.

Prichard, KS (1974). *Brumby Innes*. Sydney: Currency Press.

Prichard, KS (1990 [1929]). *Coonardoo*. Sydney: Angus & Robertson.

Probyn, F (2003). The white father: paternalism, denial and community. *Cultural Studies Review*, 9(1): 60–76.

Probyn, F (2004). Playing chicken at the intersection: the white critic of whiteness. *Borderlands e-journal* 13:2 [Online]. Available: www.borderlands.net.au/vol3no2_2004/probyn_playing.htm [Accessed 23 January 2013].

Probyn-Rapsey, F (2007). Some whites are whiter than others: the whitefella skin politics of Cecil Cook and Xavier Herbert. *JASAL: Journal for the Study of Australian Literature, Special Issue: Spectres, screens, shadows, mirrors*, 7: 157–73.

Pybus, C (1994). Review of *The white woman*: 'searching for the Chimera'. *The Age*, 1 October.

Randall, B (2003). *Songman: the story of an Aboriginal elder of Uluru*. Sydney: ABC Books.

Read, P (1999). Leaving home. *Journal of Australian Studies*, 61: 36–46.

Read, P (1998). The return of the Stolen Generations. *Journal of Australian Studies*, 59: 8–19.

Read, P (1983). 'A rape of the soul so profound': some reflections on the dispersal policy in New South Wales. *Aboriginal History*, 7(1): 23–33.

Reay, M & Sitlington, G (1948). Class and status in a mixed blood community. *Oceania*, 8(3): 179–207.

Reed, AJ (2001). Response to Eric Arnesen. *International Labor and Working-Class History*, 60, 69–80.

Reed, L (2002). White girl 'gone off with the blacks'. *Hecate*, 28(1): 9–23.

Reed, L (1999). 'Part of our own story': representations of Indigenous Australians and Papua New Guineans within 'Australia remembers 1945–1995' – the continuing desire for a homogeneous national identity. *Oceania*, 69(3): 157–70.

Reid, G (1990). *A picnic with the natives: Aboriginal–European relations in the Northern Territory to 1910*. Melbourne: Melbourne University Press.

Reese, V (1996–2011). Skinema [Online]. Available: www.skinema.com/Lobby.html [Accessed 12 April 2011].

Renda, MA (2001). 'Sentiments of a private nature': a comment on Ann Laura Stoler's *Tense and tender ties*. *The Journal of American History*, 88(3): 882–887.

Reynolds, H (2005). *Nowhere people: how international race thinking shaped Australia's identity*. Melbourne: Viking Press.

Reynolds, H (1987). *The law of the land*. Melbourne: Penguin.

Ricoeur, P (1979). The metaphorical process as cognition, imagination, and feeling. In S Sacks (ed.), *On metaphor* (pp141–57). Chicago: University of Chicago Press.

Richards, D (1985). The last words of Xavier Herbert. *National Times*, 18–24 January, pp29–30.

Riddett, L, (1993). Watch the white women fade: Aboriginal and white women in the Northern Territory 1870–1940. *Hecate*, 1(19): 73–93.

Rintoul, S (2003). The Dodson's white songline [Online]. Available: kooriweb.org/foley/news/dodson1.html [Accessed 12 April 2011].

Robert, H (2001). Disciplining the female Aboriginal body: interracial sex and the pretence of separation. *Australian Feminist Studies*, 16(34): 69–81.

Robertson, H (2005). 'One for the father, one for the mother, and one for the country': case studies in contemporary Australian motherhood. Unpublished honours thesis, Department of Gender and Cultural Studies, University of Sydney.

Robinson, S (2002). The unregulated employment of Aboriginal children in Queensland, 1842–1902. *Labour History* 82: 2–15.

Robinson, S (2008) *Something like slavery? Queensland's Aboriginal child workers, 1842–1945*. Melbourne: Australian Scholarly Publishing.

Rose, DB (2004). *Reports from a wild country: ethics for decolonisation*. Sydney: UNSW Press.

Rose, DB (1997a). Dark times and excluded bodies in the colonisation of Australia. In G Gray & C Winter (eds), *The resurgence of racism: Howard, Hanson and the race debate* (pp97–116). Melbourne: Monash Publications in History.

Rose, DB (1997b). The year zero and the north Australian frontier. In DB Rose & A Clarke (eds), *Tracking knowledge in north Australian landscapes: studies in Indigenous and settler ecological knowledge systems* (pp19–36). Darwin, North Australia Research Unit.

Rose, DB (1996). Land rights and deep colonising: the erasure of women. *Indigenous Law Bulletin*, 3(85): 6–13.

Rose, DB (1991). *Hidden histories: black stories from Victoria River Downs, Humbert River and Wave Hill Stations*. Canberra: Aboriginal Studies Press.

Rose, F (1965). *The winds of changes in central Australia: the Aborigines at Angas Downs 1962*. Berlin: Akademie-Verlag.

Roth, WE (1904). Annual Report of the Northern Protector of Aboriginal for 1903, Queensland State Archives.

Roth, WE (1901). Aboriginal Protection and Restriction of Sale of Opium Bill, 1897. Parliamentary Council Debates, QSA.

Roth, WE (1906). Correspondence to Protector Driscoll, Maryborough, Queensland State Archives, A/58749 and A/58750.

Rowley, S (1989). Inside the deserted hut: the representation of motherhood in bush mythology. *Westerly* 34: 76-96.

Rowntree, L (1997). The landscape: a view from geography. In DB Rose & A Clarke (eds), *Tracking knowledge in northern Australian landscapes: studies in Indigenous and settler ecological knowledge systems* (pp1–18). Darwin: North Australia Research Unit.

Rowse, T (1987). 'Were you ever savages?' Aboriginal insiders and pastoralists' patronage. *Oceania*, 58(2): 81–99.

Rowse, T (1988). Tolerance, fortitude and patience: frontier pasts to live with? *Meanjin*, 47(1): 21–29.

Rowse, T (2007). Cook, Cecil Evelyn Aufrere (Mick) (1897–1985), *Australian dictionary of biography*, National Centre of Biography, Australian National University [Online]. Available: adb.anu.edu.au/biography/cook-cecil-evelyn-aufrere-mick-12343/text22175 [Accessed 23 January 2013].

Russell, L (2002). *A little bird told me: a memoir*. St Leonards: Allen & Unwin.

Ryan, J (1999). 'She lives with a Chinaman': orient-ing 'white' women in the courts of law. *Journal of Australian Studies*, 60: 149–59.

Sabbioni, J (1993). 'I hate working for white people' (Investigation of the effects of White Australia Policy 1901 on Aboriginal women). *Hecate*, 2(19): 7–23.

Said, E (1989). Representing the colonized: anthropology's interlocutors. *Critical Inquiry*, 15: 205–25.

Sansom, B (2006). Looter of the Dreamings: Xavier Herbert and the taking of Kaijek's newsong story. *Oceania*, 76(1): 83–105.

Saunders, S (1990). Another dimension: Xavier Herbert in the Northern Territory. *Journal of Australian Studies*, 26: 52–66.

Sawtell, M (1940). The Aborigines. *Northern Standard*, 31 May, 3.

Schaffer, K (2001). Manne's generation: white nation responses to the *Stolen Generation Report*. *Australian Humanities Review* [Online]. Available: www.australianhumanitiesreview.org/archive/Issue-June-2001/schaffer.html [Accessed 11 March 2013].

Schaffer, K (1996). *In the wake of first contact: the Eliza Fraser stories*. Cambridge: Cambridge University Press.

Scott, J & Evans, R (1996). The moulding of menials: the making of the Aboriginal female domestic servant in early twentieth century Queensland. *Hecate*, 22(1): 140–57.

Scott, K (1999). *Benang: from the heart*. Fremantle: Fremantle Arts Centre Press.

Scott, K & Brown, H (2005). *Kayang and me*. Perth: Fremantle Arts Centre Press.

Secomb, L (2000). Fractured community. *Hypatia*, 15(2): 133–50.

Sedgwick, EK (1990). *Epistemology of the closet*. California: University of California Press.

Sedgwick, EK (1985). *Between men: English literature and male homosexual desire*. New York: Columbia University Press.

Sharp, JP (1996). Gendering nationhood: a feminist engagement with national identity. In N Duncan (ed.), *BodySpace: destabilizing geographies of gender and sexuality* (pp97–108), London: Routledge.

Sharpe, J (1993). *Allegories of empire: the figure of woman in the colonial text*. Minnesota: University of Minnesota Press.

Sheridan, S (1995). *Along the faultlines: sex, race and nation in Australian women's writing 1880s–1930s.* St Leonards: Allen & Unwin.

Simon, E (1978). *Through my eyes.* Adelaide: Rigby Ltd.

Slemon, S (1990). Unsettling the empire: resistance theory for the second world. *World Literature Written in English*, 30(2): 30–41.

Smyth, R (1995). 'White Australia has a black past': promoting Aboriginal and Torres Strait Islander land rights on television and video. *Historical Journal of Film, Radio and Television*, 15(1): 105–24.

Spigelman, J (2005). Dr Charles Perkins AO Annual Memorial Oration 2005 [Online]. Available: sydney.edu.au/koori/news/2005_Spigelman.pdf [Accessed 23 January 2013].

Stanner, WEH (2009). *The dreaming and other essays.* Melbourne: Black Inc.

Stein, J (2001). Whiteness and United States history: an assessment. *International Labor and Working-Class History*, 60: 1–2.

Stevens, J (1999). *Reproducing the state.* Princeton, NJ: Princeton University Press.

Stiehm, J (1989). *Arms and the enlisted women.* Philadelphia: Temple University Press.

Stiehm, J (1983). *Women and men's wars.* New York: Pergamom Press.

Stoler, AL (1989). Rethinking colonial categories, European communities and the boundaries of rule. *Comparative Studies in Society and History*, 31: 134–61.

Stoler, AL (2002). *Carnal knowledge and imperial power: race and the intimate in colonial rule.* Berkeley: University of California Press

Strang, V (2001). Of human bondage: the breaking in of stockmen in Northern Australia. *Oceania*, 72: 53–78.

Stratton, J (1996). The colour of Jews: Jews, race and the White Australia Policy. *Journal of Australian Studies*, 50/51: 51–65.

Sweeney, G (1947). Patrol of stations in Timber Creek and Wave Hill Districts 1947, National Archives of Australia, Darwin Office, CRS F315/0, Item 1949/393A Part 1.

Taussig, M (1999). *Defacement: public secrecy and the labor of the negative.* California: Stanford University Press.

Taylor, C (2003). Constructing Aboriginality: Archibald Meston's literary journalism, 1870–1924. *JASAL*, 2: 121–39

Thompson, J (2002). *Taking responsibility for the past: reparation and historical injustice.* Cambridge: Polity Press.

Tiffin, S (1982). In pursuit of reluctant parents: desertion and non-support legislation in Australian and the United States 1890–1920. In Sydney Labour Group (eds), *What rough beast? The state and social order in Australian history* (pp130–50). Sydney: Allen & Unwin.

Tindale, NB (1953). Growth of a people: formation and development of a hybrid Aboriginal and white stock on the islands of Bass Strait, Tasmania,

1815–1949. *Records of the Queen Victoria Museum, Launceston, New Series*, 2: 1–63.

Tindale, NB (1941). Survey of the half-caste problem in South Australia. *Proceedings of The Royal Geographical Society of South Australia*, 42: 66–161.

Tonkin, D & Landon, C (1999). *Jackson's Track: memoir of a Dreamtime place*. Ringwood: Viking.

Tonkinson, M (1988). Sisterhood or Aboriginal servitude? Black women and white women on the Australian frontier. *Aboriginal History*, 12(1): 27–39.

TuSmith, B (1993). The 'inscrutable albino' in contemporary ethnic literature. *Amerasia Journal*, 19(3): 85–103.

Turner, G (1986) *National Fictions: Literature, film and the construction of Australian Narrative*. Sydney, Allen and Unwin.

van Krieken, R (2001). Is assimilation justiciable? *Lorna Cubillo and Peter Gunner v. Commonwealth. The Sydney Law Review*, 23(2): 239–60.

Walden, I (1995). 'To send her to service': Aboriginal domestic servants. *Indigenous Law Bulletin*, 3(76): 12–14.

Walker, CE (2010). *Mongrel nation: the America begotten by Thomas Jefferson and Sally Hemings*. Virginia: University of Virginia Press.

Walsh, M (1997). The land still speaks? In DB Rose & A Clarke (eds), *Tracking knowledge in North Australian landscapes: studies in Indigenous and settler ecological knowledge systems* (pp105–19). Darwin: North Australia Research Unit.

Ward, G (1988). *Wandering girl*. London: Virago.

Ward, R (1958). *The Australian legend*. Melbourne: Oxford University Press.

Ware, V (1992). *Beyond the pale: white women, history and racism*. London: Verso.

Watson, I (2005). Settled and unsettled spaces: are we free to roam? *Australian Critical Race and Whiteness Studies Association (ACRAWSA) Journal*, 1, 40-52.

Watson, P (1998). *Frontier lands and pioneer legends: how pastoralists gained Karuwali land*. Sydney: Allen & Unwin.

Weinbaum, A E (2004) *Wayward reproductions: genealogies of race and nation in transatlantic modern thought*, Durham: Duke University Press

Welsing, FC (1991). *The Isis Papers: keys to the colors*. Chicago: Third World Press.

West, L (1997). *Feminist nationalism*. London: Routledge.

Whitlock, G (2001). In the second person: narrative transactions in Stolen Generations testimony. *Biography*, 24(1): 197–214.

Whitlock, G (2000).*The intimate empire: reading women's autobiography* . London: Carsell.

Wilde, WH, Hooton, J & Andrews, B (eds) (1994). *Oxford companion to Australian literature*. 2nd edn. Oxford: Oxford University Press.

Willey, K (1971). *Boss drover*. Adelaide: Rigby.

Winnicott DW (2009). Transitional objects and transitional phenomena. In F Candlin & R Guins (eds), *The object reader*, London: Routledge.

Williams, BF (1995). Classification systems revisited: kinship, caste, race, and nationality as the flow of blood and the spread of rights. In S Yanagisako & C Delaney (eds), *Naturalizing power: essays in feminist cultural analysis* (pp201–38). New York, Routledge.

Willshire, WH (1896). *Land of the dawning: being facts gleaned from cannibals in the Australian Stone Age*. Adelaide: WK Thomas & Co.

Wilson, SR (1994). Foreword. In D Graham (ed.). *Being whitefella* (pp11–15). Fremantle: Fremantle Arts Centre Press.

Wilson, B & O'Brien, J (2003). 'To infuse a universal terror': the Coniston killings of 1928. *Aboriginal History*, 27: 59–78 [Online]. Available: epress.anu.edu.au/wp-content/uploads/2011/05/ch0452.pdf [Accessed November 2012].

Wilson, T J & Link-Up (NSW) (1997). *In the best interests of the child? Stolen children: Aboriginal pain/white shame*. Canberra: Aboriginal History Inc.

Wise, T (1985). *The self-made anthropologist: a life of AP Elkin*. Sydney: Allen & Unwin.

Wolfe, P (1994). Nation and miscegenation. *Social Analysis*, 36: 93–153.

Wolfe, P (2001). Land, labor, and difference: elementary structures of race. *The American Historical Review*, 106(3): 1–60.

Wolfe, P (2006). Settler colonialism and the elimination of the native. *Journal of Genocide Research*, 8(4): 387–409.

Woollacott, A (1999). White colonialism and sexual modernity. In AM Burton (ed.), *Gender, sexuality and colonial modernities* (pp49–62). London: Routledge.

Woolmington, J (1988). *Aborigines in colonial society, 1788–1850: from 'noble savage' to 'rural pest'*. Armidale: University of New England Press.

Wositzky J (2011). Bilarni, *Hindsight*, ABC Radio National, 26 January [Online]. Available: www.abc.net.au/rn/hindsight/stories/2011/3120512.htm [Accessed 23 January 2013].

Wositzky J, Egan T, Jose N & Forrest P (2002). The ants that ate Plutarch, *Books and writing*, Radio National, 15 June. Available at: www.abc.net.au/rn/arts/bwriting/stories/s576485.htm [Accessed 1 March 2013].

Wositzky J & Harney Yidumduma B (1996). *Born under the paperbark tree*. Sydney: JB Books.

Wright, J (1994). Being white woman. In D Graham (ed.), *Being whitefella* (pp177–81). Fremantle: Fremantle Arts Centre Press.

Yanagisako, S (1995). Transforming Orientalism: gender, nationality, and class in Asian American studies. In S Yanagisako & C Delaney (eds), *Naturalizing power: essays in feminist cultural analysis* (pp275–98). New York: Routledge.

Works cited

Yanagisako, S & Delaney, C (1995). Naturalizing power. In S Yanagisako & C Delaney (eds), *Naturalizing power: essays in feminist cultural analysis* (pp1–24). New York, Routledge.

Young, IM (2003). The logic of masculinist protection: reflections on the current security state. *Signs: Journal of Women in Culture and Society*, 29(1): 1–12.

Index

Index

Index

Index

www.ingramcontent.com/pod-product-compliance
Lightning Source LLC
Chambersburg PA
CBHW072002090426
42740CB00011B/2045